U.S. Diplomats in Europe, 1919–1941

U.S. Diplomats in Europe, 1919–1941

Reprint Edition
with new introduction by the editor

Edited by
Kenneth Paul Jones

Foreword by
Alexander DeConde

ABC–Clio

Santa Barbara, California

Oxford, England

Reprint edition with new
introduction by Kenneth Paul Jones

Library of Congress Cataloging in Publication Data

Main entry under title:

U.S. Diplomats in Europe, 1919–1941.

    Bibliography: p. 225
    Includes index.
    1. Europe–Foreign relations–United States–
Addresses, essays, lectures. 2. United States–
Foreign relations–Europe–Addresses, essays,
lectures. 3. United States–Foreign relations–
20th century–Addresses, essays, lectures.
4. Diplomats–United States–Biography–Addresses,
essays, lectures. I. Jones, Kenneth Paul.
II. Title: US diplomats in Europe, 1919–1941.
D34.U5U18   1983   327.7304   82-24402
ISBN 0-87436-349-7
ISBN 0-87436-351-9 (pbk)

Photo credits: *Thomas W. Lamont,* courtesy of the Baker Library, Harvard University
Graduate School Business Administration; *Alanson B. Houghton,* courtesy of the Honor-
able Amory Houghton and the Corning Glass Works Archives; *Owen D. Young,* National
Archives 306–NT–8063; *John B. Stetson,* National Archives 306–NT–15910; *Hugh
Gibson,* National Archives 306–NT–156333c; *Prentiss B. Gilbert,* courtesy of P.B.
Gilbert; *George S. Messersmith,* National Archives 208–N–10402; *Claude Bowers,*
National Archives 306–NT–107.895c; *Loy W. Henderson,* courtesy of L. W. Henderson;
Joseph P. Kennedy, John F. Kennedy Library.

ABC-Clio, Inc.
Riviera Campus
2040 Alameda Padre Serra, Box 4397
Santa Barbara, California 93103

Clio Press Ltd.
55 St. Thomas Street
Oxford, OX1 1JG, England

Manufactured in the United States of America

To Julie, Elizabeth, and Craig

Contents

Contents

Preface

The last decade has witnessed revived interest in the biographical approach to American foreign policy during the interwar years. Understandably, most of the growing literature has focused upon the presidents and cabinet officials who played key roles in the decision-making process. This book emerged out of the belief that the second-echelon diplomats who served abroad also deserve our attention. Although it is concerned solely with American diplomats, the book was conceived as a companion to *Diplomats in Crisis: United States–Chinese–Japanese Relations, 1919–1941*, edited by Richard Dean Burns and Edward M. Bennett (ABC-Clio, 1974). To paraphrase the preface to that volume, these essays offer the reader a sampling of the personalities involved in the frustrating and ultimately futile efforts to resolve the tension and turmoil engendered by World War I. Like the much earlier monumental study of *The Diplomats* edited by Gordon A. Craig and Felix Gilbert, it focuses upon the actions and attitudes of the diplomats in Europe. Interwar events are treated from their points of view rather than that of the decision makers in Washington. While they shared with Washington an equal commitment to the search for peace in Europe, they demonstrated the diversity of methods attempted and suggested for achieving this goal. They frequently experienced frustration as they attempted to implement and/or influence their country's foreign policy. Although their influence was limited and ultimately futile, this study hopefully offers additional insight for those attempting to assess America's European diplomacy: its options, its goals, and its actions or inaction.

Several criteria influenced the selection of diplomats for this volume. An attempt was made to provide a cross section of those who served abroad. There are representatives to lesser powers as well as to major powers, diplomats below as well as at the ambassadorial rank, and delegates to special international organizations or conferences as well as to specific countries. The variety of individuals who served abroad is also conveyed by including unofficial and semiofficial diplomats, and by including political appointees and products of the consular service as well as the career foreign service diplomats. Some "obvious" choices have been excluded in order to offer original essays concerning individuals who have received little attention in the past, or in a few instances, those who deserve a new look based upon the documentary evidence now available, especially the subjects' own papers.

This book is the joint effort of the contributors whose prompt responses to my various requests are duly acknowledged and appreciated. I particularly thank Professor John M. Carroll for his assistance and advice. My efforts to provide some regularity to the text and notes of this multiauthored book have been greatly facilitated by Elizabeth McNamara and the other members of the editorial staff at Clio Books. Finally, I am indebted to Ms. Kitty Cashion for her research assistance, to the Department of History and Political Science at the University of Tennessee at Martin for its encouragement and support of this project, and to Mrs. Patricia Harrell for her patient and even enthusiastic contribution to the preparation of the manuscript.

The contributors wish to express their appreciation to the libraries and institutions which gave them permission to use the personal papers of the following:

Library of Congress for the papers of Chandler P. Anderson, Leonard P. Ayres, Calvin Coolidge, Stuart M. Crocker, Josephus Daniels, Joseph E. Davies, William E. Dodd, Henry P. Fletcher, Felix Frankfurter, Charles E. Hughes, Cordell Hull, James M. Landis, Russell C. Leffingwell, Elihu Root, Laurence A. Steinhardt, Arthur Sweetser, and Woodrow Wilson.

Herbert Hoover Presidential Library for the papers of William R. Castle, Jr., Herbert Hoover, Irwin B. Laughlin, and Vance McCormick.

Franklin D. Roosevelt Library for the papers of R. Walton Moore, Henry M. Morgenthau, Jr., Franklin D. Roosevelt, and John C. Wiley.

Yale University's Sterling Library for the papers of Arthur Bliss Lane, John Flournoy Montgomery, and Henry L. Stimson.

Hoover Institution on War, Revolution, and Peace for the papers of Hugh Gibson, Loy W. Henderson, and Arthur N. Young.

Harvard University's Houghton Library for the papers of Ellis Loring Dresel, Joseph C. Grew, Jay Pierrepont Moffat, William Phillips, and Oswald Garrison Villard. Harvard University's Baker Library for the papers of Thomas W. Lamont.

Archives Generale du Royaume for the papers of Henri Jaspar; Federal Reserve Bank of New York for the papers of Benjamin Strong; Indiana University's Lilly Library for the papers of Claude Bowers; Minnesota Historical Society for the papers of Frank B. Kellogg; Ohio Historical Society for the papers of Warren G.

Harding; Stanford University Library for the papers of Stanley K. Hornbeck; University of Chicago for the papers of Samuel Harper; and University of Delaware for the papers of George S. Messersmith.

Finally, special thanks are offered for the permission given and assistance provided by Mr. and Mrs. S. Everett Case for use of the Owen D. Young Papers, the Honorable Loy W. Henderson for use of his "Memoirs," the Honorable Amory Houghton, Sr. for use of the papers of Alanson B. Houghton, and Emery Kelen for use of his papers.

Foreword

Most studies in the history of American foreign relations focus on the people in Washington who comprise the elite within government which decides what will or will not be done in vital matters concerning war and peace. Scholars often refer to these men—the presidents, the secretaries of state and defense, and others—as policymakers. Sometimes diplomatic historians and social scientists go beyond the study of these elite policymakers and investigate the activities and ideas of people who as individuals or as members of groups are concerned about foreign policy and try to influence it, but who have only minor official status or none at all. This kind of scholarship often concentrates on the activities of secondary personalities in government or attempts to ascertain the importance of public opinion, the influence of politically powerful private individuals, and the role of special interest groups on the shaping of policy in particular instances.

This book of ten original essays fits into the second category of scholarship. The ten authors explore the diplomatic activities, attitudes, small successes, and failures of individuals who were never part of the group which shaped foreign policy from the top. The subjects of the essays are men who were, in one way or another, involved in the machinery of American diplomacy in Europe in the era between the two world wars. The personalities scrutinized in this book comprise a select, perhaps representative, group of diplomats who observe developments abroad or who carry out policy rather than initiate it. They are career officers, political appointees, businessmen, experts on financial diplomacy, and unofficial advisers to the policymakers. Several of the diplomats were important men in their own right, heads of corporations or Wall Street financiers; one or two were essentially minor functionaries within the American diplomatic establishment; and several had direct access to the pinnacle of power in the shaping of foreign policy. Regardless of how close or far each diplomat stood from the source of power, all were, as the authors explain, practitioners in international politics planted in the second echelon of the foreign policy establishment.

These then are men who served on the periphery of power. They were lower-level servants of government now known mainly to scholars specializing in the study of the history of American diplomacy. The concerns of these diplomats over such matters as reparations payments, control of armaments, and the rise of Nazi Germany also may seem peripheral, for, as these pages reveal, what these men thought and did seldom influenced the unfolding of policy even in their own areas of concern. Perhaps, as servants of a democratic society, they functioned as they should; for they did not hold elective office nor occupy positions of sufficient responsibility or power to enable them to transfer their ideas into policy. Yet all desired in some way to influence the course of international affairs, and several thought that they did. Perhaps their failure, in terms of power, demonstrates one of the realities of modern diplomacy. In their time, and more so since, the technology of rapid communication over great distances has doomed old-fashioned diplomatic negotiation where ministers or ambassadors abroad had important powers of decision.

Despite their lack of substantive power, the men depicted in these pages are worth knowing. They represent a special breed, a unique class within the American foreign policy establishment. They not only observed great events but also were part of them; several reported astutely on what they saw and experienced, and others offered to their superiors analyses of developments in Europe that merited more attention than they received. Perhaps most of the thinking of these men is ordinary, but some of their ideas were worthy of forming the basis for policy decisions. Some of these ideas, either because of the domestic political connections of the diplomat who generated them or because of his professional competence, may have influenced the course of policy. On the whole, however, the influence of the men herein studied on the shaping of policy was small not because their ideas lacked substance, but because they failed to reach the top. Essentially, therefore, these essays document failure. They demonstrate that modern diplomats, no matter how intelligent or resourceful, can seldom have an impact on the making of policy unless they have direct access, in their own right, to the nation's leaders in Washington. Even if diplomats in the field have such access, their ideas must, as more than one of the authors suggest, coincide with those of the leaders, or must at least be congenial to the prevailing wisdom of the governing elite.

If the men portrayed in this book failed to influence policy or the policymakers at the top, why study them? The direct answer is simple. We cannot understand success without knowing something about failure. In a democracy, moreover, while foreign policy most often emanates from an elite, it is not always and solely the product of policymaking elitists. Occasionally, and perhaps even frequently, policy develops out of a pattern of ideas and attitudes, out of observations and responses that at times come from people in private life, from second-level bureaucrats, and from the men and women in the field. In the process of carrying out someone else's views, these people may modify them and may as a consequence in some instances re-direct policy in a small way.

These essays explain how and why diplomats attempt to modify policy and reveal much about the functioning of the bureaucracy in foreign relations. These scholarly investigations, therefore, enrich our understanding of how diplomats in the field may or may not add something to the broad pattern of foreign policy. The contribution these essays make to knowledge is solid, for all rest on foundations built from archival materials and from the important secondary literature. The authors, moreover, do not uncritically absorb and merely rearrange conventional wisdom. They evaluate anew on the basis of their own research. The result is a series of penetrating sketches of personalities integrated skillfully into provocative interpretations of the larger issues of foreign policy. Each sketch, moreover, is interesting, and all fit well together to form a cohesive book. In summary, from the perspective of ten second-level diplomats the authors tell us a great deal about the foreign policy establishment of the 1920s and 1930s. In addition, they direct more light on the reasons why peace failed and war erupted in Europe in 1939, and why two years later it engulfed the United States in worldwide violence.

Alexander DeConde
University of California
Santa Barbara

Introduction

Although each of the chapters in this book may be read independently, as a group they introduce the reader to several themes in America's interwar European diplomacy. They reveal the elements of continuity and change in American foreign policy both during the years of Republican ascendancy in the 1920s and during Franklin D. Roosevelt's presidencies in the 1930s. They show the continuing concern for European economic recovery from war and then depression, and the continuing faith in free trade as the pathway to peace. Another theme running through these biographical sketches is the preoccupation with Bolshevik Russia. The containment of bolshevism was a constant in American diplomacy which intertwined with a third theme, America's response to the "German problem." As the chapters in this book will show, American diplomats struggled throughout the interwar years to answer the question, How much should Germany be appeased? The response of different diplomats depended upon the importance they attached to the other themes. The result was a pro-German consensus in the 1920s which lingered on into the 1930s.

The essays concerning the 1920s delineate the nature and extent of American involvement in European affairs under the Republicans. They reveal a professional State Department which shared with its executive leadership and most private bankers and businessmen a common set of assumptions concerning the inseparability of American economic progress, world peace, and European economic and political stability. These groups also shared a common outlook concerning the active role America must play, within certain constraints, to stimulate peace and prosperity.

The constraints to American engagement in European affairs were largely self-imposed. Congress had imposed certain limits by forbidding official membership in the League of Nations and official participation on the various inter-Allied bodies created to implement the World War I peace settlement. These limitations, however, never prevented the State Department from sending observers who could keep Washington informed and negotiate behind the scenes whenever necessary. The Republican leadership was constrained more by its own domestic political considerations—the desire to reduce taxes, combat inflation, protect American industry and agriculture, and thereby win elections. These considerations constrained Republican secretaries of state from offering to cancel war debts, or lower tariffs, in spite of their value as diplomatic bargaining chips.

Another constraint was the fear of entangling political commitments. Secretary of State Charles Evans Hughes and his successors actually welcomed America's observer status on the various European councils such as the Reparation Commission. It allowed the United States to stay clear of possible manipulation by the French who seemed determined to embroil Washington in their schemes to impede German revival. Furthermore, the Republicans realistically recognized that the primary responsibility for resolving Europe's problems belonged to the Europeans. The role officials in Washington chose to play was that of the mediator who works behind the scenes to help the interested parties reconcile their differences. In moving the conflicting parties toward economic moderation and peaceful treaty revision, it would of course be legitimate to use America's economic power as a carrot and a stick. This meant that American intervention in European affairs would follow largely an unofficial, economic approach, instigated with the cooperation of private business and banking groups.

Michael J. Hogan, in the opening essay on Thomas W. Lamont of J. P. Morgan and Company, introduces the reader to this set of assumptions and constraints which guided and controlled American involvement in European affairs during the 1920s. Hogan's special contribution is his emphasis on the "corporatist" nature of Republican policy toward postwar European reconstruction. As Hogan explains, "it meant putting private power in the service of public policy." It involved a voluntary partnership between government officials and private groups for the effective management of the international economy. Private experts would serve as quasi-official statesmen who worked with their counterparts in Europe to "depoliticize" the divisive issues which hindered an efficient and peaceful management of European recovery.

The most divisive and decisive issue in postwar Europe was the question of Germany's reparations obligations under the Treaty of Versailles. The dispute over how much Germany could pay first arose at the Paris Peace Conference and continued to plague the nations of Europe during the postwar decade. Until it was resolved, Germany's economic recovery seemed impossible to America's leadership. Germany's recovery was important to the Republican leadership for two reasons. First, they perceived a direct link between Germany's recovery, Europe's recovery, and America's economic growth. Second, a revitalized Germany would be a bulwark against Bolshevik Russsia rather than a breeding ground for bolshevism. The "coporatist" solution, therefore, was to delegate to the appropriate "experts" (i.e, private bankers and manufacturers) the task of determining what Germany should pay. Freed from the political pressures which plagued governments, they could quickly provide a "business-like" solution.

These characteristics of the American corporatist approach are reinforced in the succeeding biographical sketches of Alanson B. Houghton and Owen D. Young by Kenneth Paul Jones and John M. Carroll. The acitvities of Lamont, Houghton, and Young during the reparations negotiations which led to the Dawes Plan (1924) and the later Young Plan (1929) demonstrate the significant role America played in postwar European affairs. By working through quasi-official negotiators such as Young amd Lamont, Washington short-circuited French efforts to consolidate the status quo while at the same time maximizing American financial leverage. Lamont, Houhgton, and Young used the European dependence on American capital as a lever to move Germany and France into agreement on a multinational reparations settlement in accord with American moral principles and economic self-interest.

Frank Costigliola's essay on John B. Stetson as minister to Poland traverses much of the same ground but highlights the nature and implications of America's moderate revisionism. Stetson challenged the pro-German stance advocated by Houghton and endorsed in Washington. He showed that the prevailing policy not only entailed economic appeasement of Germany, it also implied territorial revision. He raised questions that others ignored. How could Germany be used to contain Bolshevik Russia without endangering the survival of Poland? How could Germany be revitalized without encouraging the expansion of German power into southeastern Europe? Stetson therefore cautioned against the appeasement of Germany. He offered instead a program of direct American financial and commercial penetration of East Europe which would supplant both German and West European influence and simultaneously deter bolshevism.

In an age of economic progress and diplomatic rapproachment, Stetson was a prophet scorned. Germany and its former enemies had come together at the resort of Locarno in 1925 to renounce the use of force in the settlement of their remaining differences. The Dawes Plan seemed to bring economic and political stability to Germany and the rest of Europe. Confronted by a largely cooperative Weimar Republic, it made no sense to question America's appeasement of Germany.

America's intervention in European affairs was not limited to economic issues such as German reparations. Washington was also actively involved in the interwar disarmament negotiations. The nature and extent of American participation is illuminated in Ronald E. Swerczek's study of Hugh Gibson, America's principal delegate in the disarmament negotiations of the late 1920s and early 1930s. Disarmament appealed to all three Republican administrations. They looked upon heavy expenditures for armaments as a destabilizing factor, economically as well as politically. Arms reduction was a corollary of their economic principles. It deserved their support not only because it increased the chances for lasting peace, but also because it would ease the task of balancing the budget and thereby speed up economic recovery. Given these assumptions, the French arms buildup reinforced their suspicions of French motives and strengthened their conviction to use America's financial leverage to influence European attitudes.

As Swerczek explains, the widespread acceptance of these assumptions allowed the State Department to participate in a number of disarmament sessions without fear of recrimination. Gibson was allowed to represent the United States at a series of League-sponsored disarmament sessions between 1926 and 1932. More significantly, the Republicans played a leading role in the sequence of naval conferences held in Washington (1921-22), Geneva (1927), and London (1930).

Still, the history of America's disarmament negotiations is a story of hopes raised at the Washington Naval Conference but largely unfulfilled during the next decade. Unlike the reparations issue, America's financial power provided only limited leverage for Gibson as he attempted to mediate the competing interests of the major participants. American disarmament policy also suffered from its self-imposed constraints. Gibson's career demonstrates that the United States was never ready to lower significantly its own armaments level in spite of its frequent criticisms of French recalcitrance. The United States carefully distinguished between the specific, self-serving limitations agreed upon at the Washington and London Naval Conferences and the more significant proposals under discussion in the General Disarmament Conference. Furthermore, the State Department characterized the latter negotiations as a non-American problem. Whereas the European powers welcomed Gibson's participation and possible mediation, the State Department tried to restrain him. It was a European peace conference; he was supposedly there only to observe.

The role of observer, which frustrated so many interwar diplomats, is even more strikingly depicted by J. B. Donnelly in his sketch of Prentiss Bailey Gilbert who served as consul (1930-37) at Geneva, the home of the League of Nations. Even more than Gibson, Gilbert had to keep out of the limelight. He could act as the eyes and ears of his government but he could not open his mouth. The one notable exception occurred in October 1931 when he was allowed to sit at the League Council's table and protest the Japanese military incursion into Manchuria.

This episode demonstrates the effective use which could be made of the Kellogg-Briand Pact of 1928. That pact, with its mutual renunciation of war, has been too often belittled. Under Herbert Hoover, it served as an effective instrument for justifying American participation in European affairs.

In sharp constrast is Donnelly's description of the State Department's attitude during the 1935 League crisis over the Italian invasion of Ethiopia. "In fact, the department strenuously avoided invitations to invoke the Kellogg-Briand Pact, or otherwise to repeat the initiatives of the Gilbert mission of 1931." Forced once again to play the role of an almost powerless observer of the League's decline, Gilbert welcomed his transfer to Berlin in 1937. Still, nothing changed; he experienced continued frustration over the paralysis which seemingly gripped the United States and the other Western powers in the face of Nazi terrorism.

The next two chapters, concerning George S. Messersmith's years in Germany and Austria and Claude Bowers's mission to Spain, represent even more clearly the growing frustration of American diplomats in the 1930s and the impotence of their superiors who seemed unable to understand or respond to the diplomatic implications of the Nazi triumph in Germany.

Appeasement of Germany made sense in the 1920s. An economically and politically revitalized Weimar Germany was the pathway to peace, to American economic expansion, and to the containment of communism. Appeasement no longer made sense after 1933. But what could the United States do? Part of the problem was that Franklin Roosevelt felt compelled to appease the isolationists. Still, the isolationist sentiment of the 1930s inadequately explains the creeping paralysis of American diplomacy under Roosevelt. In the 1920s, the Republicans had successfully maximized their financial leverage to offset similar fears of diplomatic entanglement. In the 1930s, the United States could not adjust to the changed economic and diplomatic circumstances.

To someone like Messersmith, who had risen through the ranks of the consular service, it made sense to use governmental regulation of trade as the appropriate economic lever to influence Nazi Germany and contain its expansion into depression-ridden southeastern Europe. He advocated a direct challenge to Germany comparable to what Stetson had proposed in the 1920s. His approach required, however, more flexibility than the tradition-bound professionals in the State Department could muster. Furthermore, it would have required the subordination of short-term domestic economic needs in the interest of the state; even Messersmith was reluctant to advocate this.

America's commercial policy was also the stumbling block in the efforts of Ambassador Bowers to shore up the leftist Republican forces in Spain. Douglas Little traces the optimism with which Bowers, a Jeffersonian Democrat personally chosen by the president, began his appointment and the increasing frustration he experienced as he failed to overcome the sentiments of Secretary of State Cordell Hull and the State Department professionals. Hull held firmly to his belief in reciprocal trade agreements as the path to world prosperity and peace. He rejected Bowers's requests for trade concessions to shore up the new Republican government and use it as a bulwark against the rising threat from the radical Right.

The pro-monarchist State Department professionals reinforced Hull's reluctance to abridge his reciprocal trade principles. As Douglas Little notes, where

Bowers saw "New Deal Liberals" they saw "newsreel Leninists." They viewed the Republic as a breeding ground for bolshevism and repeatedly argued against any concessions. As a result, the ambassador's ties to the president were no more effective than those of another political appointee, William Dodd. As ambassador to Germany, he also struggled to awaken the State Department to the danger of Nazism.

American foreign policy in the 1930s was increasingly shaped not only by an isolationist Congress, but also by a conservative staff of professionals in the State Department who found it hard to accept the implications of opposing rather than appeasing Hitler and Mussolini.

The increasing professionalism of the State Department and the inhibiting impact of its preoccupation with the Soviet Union are further demonstrated in Thomas R. Maddux's study of the professional foreign service officer, Loy Henderson. Henderson was part of the elite group of junior officers who were selected in the 1920s for special training to prepare them for the day when diplomatic relations with Russia would be restored. That day came in 1933. Henderson arrived in Moscow in 1934, steeped in a set of "Riga axioms" concerning the Marxist-Leninist foundations of Stalinist Russia's foreign policy, particularly its commitment to world revolution. Henderson's experience in Moscow altered his outlook somewhat; he began to give some attention to the role that traditional concepts of national interest and security played in Stalin's actions. Nonetheless, neither he nor his colleagues could overcome their distrust of the Soviet Union. They looked upon the Popular Front policy of the Comintern and Soviet entry into the League of Nations as a ruse. Moscow was simply unreliable as a partner in any grand alliance against Nazi Germany. The State Department never wavered from this conviction "until Hitler's shadow stretched from the streets of Madrid to the gates of Moscow."

Finally, Jane Karoline Vieth's description of Joseph P. Kennedy's tenure as ambassador to the Court of St. James's (1938-40), demonstrates the paradox in American thought and deed on the eve of war. Kennedy personified in so many ways the set of assumptions and constraints which determined both the active nature of American diplomacy during the decade of Republican ascendancy and the increasing paralysis and isolation of the Roosevelt years. He shared with the diplomats of the 1920s same assumption concerning the interrelationship between peace, prosperity, capitalism, and democracy. Like them, he abhorred the consequences of the Great War which had strengthened the powers of central governments and created a breeding ground of bolshevism. He too believed the United States must assume the leadership of the West, use its economic influence to remedy political problems, but remain aloof from entanglement in strategic commitments.

As depicted in the biographical sketches for the 1920s, this approach implied Anglo-American cooperation in the appeasement of Germany as a bulwark against communism. Unfortunately, the emergence of Nazi Germany and international fascism in the 1930s required an unhappy choice between further appeasement of Germany or cooperation with communist Russia. "In many ways," as Vieth explains, "Kennedy's perception of the practicality of appeasement throughout 1938 and of the realities of Anglo-American relations were accurate and sound." Given the perceived unreliability of the Soviet Union and the reluctance to use trade as a diplomatic weapon against Germany, Kennedy's arguments for appeasement made sense. Paradoxically, both Roosevelt and the State Department officials considered him an embarrassment. By the eve of war in 1939, he definitely was an embarrassment as he continued to argue for appeasement when even the British government had rejected it. Still, his failure testifies not so much to his limitations as a diplomat, but rather is "a reflection of the indifferently formulated, vague, confused state of American foreign policy in the 1930s." There is little consolation in noting that the other Western powers could do no better.

Kenneth Paul Jones
University of Tennessee at Martin

Selected Chronology

1919	18 January	Paris Peace Conference begins
	14 February	President Wilson presents draft covenant of the League of Nations
	28 June	Treaty of Versailles signed
	10 July	Versailles treaty submitted to U.S. Senate
	29 July	Tripartite Treaty of Guarantee for France submitted to Senate
	4–25 September	Wilson tours the nation
	19 November	Treaty of Versailles fails to receive two-thirds majority in Senate
1920	19 March	Final Senate defeat of Versailles treaty
	27 May	Wilson vetoes joint resolution of Congress declaring end of war with Germany
	2 November	Warren G. Harding elected
1921	11 May	German reparations bill fixed at 132 billion gold marks
	18 October	Senate ratifies separate peace treaties with Germany, Austria, and Hungary
	12 November	Washington Naval Conference opens
1922	6 February	Washington Conference concludes with Five Power Treaty on Naval Limitations, Nine Power Treaty on China, and Four Power Treaty on Pacific Islands
	9 February	Congress authorizes World War Foreign Debt Commission

	10 April– 19 May	Genoa Conference on European economic recovery
	16 April	Treaty of Rapallo restores diplomatic relations between Germany and Soviet Russia
	19 September	Fordney-McCumber Tariff Act raises import duties to record level
	31 October	Benito Mussolini appointed Italian premier
	20 November	Lausanne Conference for peace settlement with Turkey opens with U.S. observers present
1923	10 January	Franco-Belgian Ruhr occupation announced; American Army of Occupation on the Rhine ordered home
	28 February	British Debt Refunding Act signed
	2–3 August	Calvin Coolidge assumes presidency after death of Harding
	31 August	Italy occupies Corfu
	17 September	Italy seizes Fiume
	18 December	Secretary of State Hughes rejects Soviet Russia's plea for diplomatic recognition
1924	9 April	Experts committee chaired by Charles G. Dawes issues German reparations plan
	24 May	Foreign Service Act (Rogers Act) reorganizes and consolidates diplomatic and consular services
	16 July– 16 August	London Conference approves Dawes Plan and ends Ruhr occupation
	30 October	S. Parker Gilbert becomes agent general for German reparations
	4 November	Coolidge elected president
1925	16 October	Locarno Conference concludes with multiple agreements concerning Germany's frontiers
1926	31 January	First Rhineland zone evacuated
	24 April	Russo-German Treaty of Berlin
	29 April	Debt Funding Agreement signed with France
	18 May	Preparatory Commission for General Disarmament Conference (League of Nations) opens with

		U.S. official participation
1927	31 January	Allied Military Control Commission withdraws from Germany
	6 April	French Foreign Minister Aristide Briand proposes agreement with U.S. for outlawing of war
	5 May	International Economic Conference of League of Nations opens at Geneva with U.S. represented
	20 June– 4 August	Geneva Naval Conference ends in stalemate
1928	27 August	Paris Peace (Kellogg-Briand) Pact signed by the United States, France, and twelve other nations
	6 November	Herbert Hoover elected president
1929	11 February– 7 June	Owen D. Young serves as chairman of committee which issues Young Plan for final settlement of German reparations
	22 April	Hugh Gibson presents "Yardstick" Proposal for naval arms limitation to sixth session of Preparatory Commission
	21 July	French Chamber of Deputies ratifies debt settlement with the U.S.
	29 October	New York Stock Exchange crash
	30 November	Second Rhineland zone evacuated
1930	21 January– 22 April	London Naval Conference concludes with British, Italian, and American agreement on cruiser limitation
	17 June	Hawley-Smoot Tariff Bill signed by President Hoover
	30 June	Last Rhineland zone evacuated
1931	6 July	Hoover moratorium provides one-year halt on interallied debts and reparations
	18 September	Japan invades Manchuria
	16 October	Prentiss B. Gilbert, consul at Geneva, participates in League of Nations discussion of Manchurian crisis
1932	7 January	Secretary Stimson enunciates Stimson Doctrine against Japanese attacks upon China

	2 February	General Disarmament Conference begins in Geneva with U.S. participation
	16 June– 9 July	Lausanne Conference ends German reparations
	4 October	Lytton Commission issues report condemning Japanese move into Manchuria
	8 November	Franklin D. Roosevelt defeats Hoover for presidency
	15 December	France and four other nations default on payments to U.S.
1933	30 January	Adolf Hitler appointed Chancellor of Germany
	27 March	Japan withdraws from League of Nations
	19 April	U.S. abandons the gold standard
	12 June– 27 July	London Economic Conference fails
	14 October	Germany withdraws from League of Nations and Disarmament Conference
	16 November	U.S. recognizes the U.S.S.R.
1934	12 February	Export-Import Bank established
	12 April	Senate initiates Nye Committee investigations into profits by American financiers and armament makers during World War I
	13 April	Johnson Debt Default Act prohibits loans to any foreign government in default to the U.S.
	18 September	The U.S.S.R. joins the League of Nations
	29 December	Japan denounces Washington Naval Treaty of 1922
1935	2 May	France and the Soviet Union sign a mutual assistance pact
	31 August	Roosevelt signs first of Neutrality Acts controlling trade with belligerents
	3 October	Italy attacks Ethiopia
	9 December	Second London Naval Conference opens with U.S. participation
1936	7 March	Hitler sends troops into Germany's demilitarized Rhineland
	25 March	New London Naval Treaty signed by

		France, Great Britain, and U.S.
	18 July	Spanish Civil War begins
	3 November	Roosevelt wins reelection
1937	1 March	Reciprocal Trade Agreements Act
	7 July	Sino-Japanese war begins
	5 October	Roosevelt delivers Quarantine speech in Chicago urging U.S. stand against Axis powers
	12 December	Panay Incident: Japanese planes bomb U.S. river gunboat
1938	11 January	Roosevelt proposes a world conference to reduce armaments
	12 March	German army marches into Austria
	27 September	Roosevelt appeals to Hitler and Mussolini for peaceful solution of all issues
	29–30 September	Munich Conference concedes Czechoslovakia's Sudetenland to Germany
	14 November	Ambassador Hugh R. Wilson recalled from Germany "for report and consultation"
1939	15 March	Nazi Germany establishes protectorate over Bohemia-Moravia
	31 March	Prime Minister Chamberlain announces Anglo-French guarantee to Poland
	1 April	U.S. recognizes Franco Spain
	7 April	Italy seizes Albania
	15 April	Roosevelt calls upon Hitler and Mussolini to guarantee non-aggression policy toward neighboring states
	22 May	Germany and Italy sign "Pact of Steel"
	23 August	Nazi-Soviet Pact against Poland signed in Moscow
	1 September	Germany attacks Poland
	5 September	U.S. declares its neutrality
	4 November	Neutrality Act permits "cash and carry" export of arms and munitions to belligerents
	30 November–21 March	Russo-Finnish war
1940	9 February–28 March	Welles mission: Under Secretary of

	State Summer Welles travels to Europe to search for compromise end of war
9 April–11 June	German invasion of Denmark and Norway
10 May–4 June	German invasion of the Netherlands, Belgium, and Luxembourg
11 May	Winston Churchill becomes prime minister of Great Britain
5–22 June	Fall of France
17 June–25 August	Soviet forces occupy and annex Lithuania, Latvia, and Estonia
20 July	Two-ocean navy bill signed by Roosevelt
13 August–17 September	Battle of Britain
3 September	Destroyer-Bases agreement provides for transfer of fifty U.S. destroyers to Britain for lease of bases
16 September	Selective Training and Service Act approved
22 September	Japan takes over air bases in French Indochina
26 September	Roosevelt proclaims an embargo on scrap iron and steel
27 September	Germany, Japan, and Italy sign Tripartite Pact
5 November	Roosevelt wins third term as president
29 December	Roosevelt fireside chat emphasizes U.S. as "the great arsenal for democracy"
1941 11 March	Lend-Lease Act signed by Roosevelt to finance British purchase of war supplies
6 April–1 June	Germany invades Yugoslavia, Greece, and Crete
9 April	U.S. and Denmark reach agreement for American defense of Greenland
22 June	Germany invades the Soviet Union
24 June	President Roosevelt promises U.S. aid to U.S.S.R.
7 July	U.S. forces occupy Iceland
24 July	Japan occupies French Indochina

26 July	U.S. freezes all Japanese credits in U.S.
14 August	Atlantic Charter — joint statement of principles issued by Roosevelt and Churchill
11 September	Roosevelt announces "shoot-on-sight" order for U.S. naval forces against German-Italian vessels in waters west of Iceland
17 November	U.S. merchant marine vessels armed
7 December	Pearl Harbor attacked
8 December	U.S. Congress declares war on Japan
11 December	Germany and Italy declare war on the U.S.

PART I

From Wilson to Roosevelt, 1919—1933

Norway

Sweden

Finland

Estonia

Latvia

Denmark

North Schleswig

Memel

Lithuania

Danzig

East
Prussia

Vilna

Soviet
Russia

Pomorze & Poznan

Netherlands   Germany

Poland

Poland's Eastern Border
drawn by Peace Conference

Eupen-Malmedy

Belgium

Upper Silesia

France

Saar

Czechoslovakia

Alsace-Lorraine

Austria

Hungary

Bessarabia

Switzerland

South Tyrol

Trieste

Romania

Fiume

Italy

Yugoslavia

Montenegro   Serbia

Bulgaria

Albania

Greece

Turkey

Shading shows areas as of 1914
German
Bulgaria

Austria-Hungary
Russia
Turkey

Europe in 1923

Thomas W. Lamont

Thomas W. Lamont

1870	Born 30 September in Claverack, New York
1892	Graduated from Harvard College
1911	Became a partner in J. P. Morgan and Company
1917	Unofficial financial adviser for a United States mission to negotiate the terms of the new alliance with the Allied governments in London and Paris
1919	Representative of the United States Treasury Department on the American Commission to Negotiate Peace, Paris Peace Conference
1919–20	Organized the Second China Financial Consortium
1921	Led a commission to negotiate a settlement of Mexico's foreign indebtedness
1923–25	Helped to negotiate stabilization loans for the Austrian, French, and Italian governments
1924	Represented J. P. Morgan and Company at the London Conference and played a leading role in setting terms for the Dawes loan to Germany
1929	Alternate United States delegate on the Young Committee
1931	Helped to organize the Bank for International Settlements
1933	Delegate to the World Economic Conference in London
1940	Helped to organize the Committee to Defend America by Aiding the Allies
1943	Elected chairman of the board, J. P. Morgan and Company
1948	Died 2 February in Boca Grande, Florida

Chapter 1

Thomas W. Lamont and European Recovery: The Diplomacy of Privatism in a Corporatist Age

Michael J. Hogan

In 1911, when Thomas W. Lamont became a partner in the famed Wall Street firm of J. P. Morgan and Company, America's leading investment houses were being roundly denounced by some progressive critics as the "Money Trust." This ignominious appellation implied that a handful of private banks monopolized the nation's banking system and used this monopoly to advance its own interests at the public's expense. For these critics, it followed that concentrations of private power should be "busted," and such old verities as competition, individual initiative, and natural market forces should be reenthroned as the arbiters of economic and social justice. Yet there were also progressives who thought of blending past ideals with modern realities to forge a new economic system. Under this system, responsible private combinations could remain, but new, man-made forms of collective control, administered by a corps of specially trained experts, would replace the automatic, self-regulating mechanisms of the marketplace as the guarantors of order, progress, and equity.

This emphasis on managerial control led to a larger role for the state in regulating economic activity. Nevertheless, the triumph of statism was incomplete. The tradition of privatism exerted a continuing influence within the new system of bureaucratic regulation that took shape after the turn of the century. Much of the state's authority was apportioned among private and cooperative functional groups, each working in voluntary partnership with the government, and each regulating its own affairs. Advocates of this "corporatist" system justified the emphasis on self-regulation by claiming that thoroughgoing government control was rigid, arbitrary, paternalistic, and wasteful. It represented a type of creeping "Germanism" which could destroy the country's democratic institutions. Industrial self-regulation, on the other hand, seemed more efficient and democratic in its decentralization, its reliance on voluntarism and private experts, its respect for private property, and its opposition to both destructive individualistic competition and oppressive government bureaucracies.

Clearly the corporatist vision made private institutions partners with the state, and transformed private "experts" into quasi-official "statesmen" cloaked in a mantle of public authority. By the time Lamont became a Morgan partner the application of collective intelligence and self-regulation through trade associations, farm cooperatives, and other private groups had become for many the third alternative, the middle-way between statism and the old laissez-faire. As for the new breed of private experts, their professed desire for maximum efficiency, supposed commitment to professional ethics, and alleged ability to transcend parochial interests seemed to merit them the portentous status of public ministers without portfolio.[1]

The success of economic mobilization during the First World War appeared to vindicate this infatuation with collectivist prescriptions for the American economy. For the first time it also became acceptable to consider private bankers and businessmen as part of the new coterie of disinterested economic experts. It was this metamorphosis, from "money truster" to sublime specialist, that permitted Thomas Lamont, Dwight Morrow, Bernard Baruch, Herbert Hoover, and countless other dollar-a-year men to move back and forth between their roles as functional elites and quasi-public statesmen during and after the war.[2]

The Wilson Administration did not establish a "War Banking Board" in 1917, but following the outbreak of hostilities in Europe the Treasury Department organized informal liaisons with the banking community; and the bankers, experimenting with new forms of voluntary cooperation and self-regulation, compiled a credible record of public spiritedness. They supervised their own affairs on the stock exchange, helped to avert a financial crisis in New York City, collaborated with the Treasury Department in drawing up plans for underwriting the cotton trade, and helped the government establish a gold pool which could stabilize dollar exchange and facilitate foreign commerce. After the United States entered the war, the leading investment houses stepped up their efforts to float loans and market securities for the Allied governments. The Investment Bankers Association (IBA) formed a special Foreign Securities Committee to serve as liaison between similar foreign agencies, the Allied governments, and the Treasury Department in Washington. Representatives of the banking community volunteered for duty in one or more of the Treasury Department's wartime organizations. Officials in the department regularly sought the bankers' advice when marketing Liberty Loans, and lenders from both sectors collaborated to manage the flow of private capital in ways that would maximize the war effort.[3]

In all of these activities, especially Allied financing, J. P. Morgan and Company played the central role. Through its affiliates, Morgan, Grenfell and Company of London, and Morgan, Harjes and Company of Paris, the House of Morgan had strong, historic ties with the British and French governments, and all of its partners were frankly pro-Allied. Not surprisingly, the firm served as American purchasing agent for the British and French governments prior to

April 1917, and also managed the marketing of virtually all Allied loans in the United States.[4] These international operations enhanced Morgan's influence at home and led to a growing interpenetration between the firm and the government. Seven Morgan partners served in some official or semi-official capacity during and after the war, or entered the firm following government service.[5] Lamont was the most important of these. Indeed, during the 1920s he acted as Washington's and Wall Street's unofficial ambassador of finance to governments around the world.

The son of a Methodist minister, Lamont was born in upstate New York on 30 September 1870. He spent the better part of his youth in small-town parsonages throughout the Hudson River Valley before attending Phillips Exeter Academy and Harvard College. Following graduation from Harvard in 1892 and a brief career in journalism, he entered the world of business and finance, ultimately becoming a partner in J. P. Morgan and Company just as that firm was about to embark upon its brilliant career as the international leader of private finance. Poised and urbane, an amiable soul to all who knew him, Lamont soon became the front man for Morgan and Company, and especially for the sometimes acerbic J. P. Morgan himself. Like Henry P. Davison, his mentor at Morgan and Company, Lamont seemed to possess those qualities, especially a keen sense of social duty, which fit the public image the firm wanted to project in the years succeeding the Pujo investigations of the banking community.

During the war years Lamont participated in the efforts of the banking community to regulate its own affairs, contribute to the war effort, and promote the Allied cause. He was a member of the IBA's Foreign Securities Committee, joined J. P. Morgan on several Liberty Loan committees, did a "considerable amount of public speaking," and shared responsibility for marketing Allied loans. In the autumn of 1917, President Woodrow Wilson enlisted him as an unofficial financial adviser for an American mission which negotiated the military and economic details of the new coalition with the Allied governments.[6]

Yet Lamont's major contribution would not come until after the war, when he would help shape American policy toward European reconstruction. In framing that policy, he and other Americans for the first time would apply corporatist formulas, especially the emphasis on private leadership and expertise, cooperation among functional groups, and voluntary public-private power-sharing, to the management of the international economy. For private bankers, particularly Lamont and his partners at J. P. Morgan and Company, such a policy meant a partnership with the government. For government officials, especially during the Republican ascendancy of the 1920s, it meant putting private power in the service of public policy. As they saw it, this new version of dollar diplomacy conformed with the private character of the American political economy, avoided wasteful and undemocratic state capitalism, and guaranteed a more efficient and peaceful management of world affairs.

Following the armistice, the Treasury Department appointed Lamont and Norman H. Davis as its representatives on the American Commission to Negotiate Peace at the Paris Peace Conference. When the Conference opened, President Wilson assigned Lamont to Subcommittee No. 2, which was to determine Germany's capacity to pay reparations. During these months Lamont formed the views that would influence his thinking on European recovery throughout the postwar years. Like other economic experts on the American delegation, he believed that without a revitalized Germany, Europe could not be reconstructed; and without the rehabilitation of Europe, world trade and peace, including America's export trade and domestic tranquility, could not be assured. Lamont accordingly called for a definite and moderate reparations figure that was within Germany's capacity to pay and that would leave the Germans with sufficient liquid capital to begin their own recovery. For the French, however, an economically resurgent Germany posed a threat to security. With support from the British they therefore demanded a reparations figure substantially larger than Lamont considered desirable, and they refused to reconsider unless the United States agreed to reduce the war debts owed it by the Allied governments.[7]

Lamont repeatedly explained that the Wilson administration did not possess legislative authority to link reparations and war debts in a mutual reduction. Together with his colleagues on the American Commission, he protested that an excessive reparations bill would weaken Germany as a barrier against Bolshevik radicalism and as a market for foreign exports. He warned that in order to earn the foreign exchange needed to pay reparations, Germany would have to dominate world export markets at the expense of British and French producers. Even with a moderate reparations settlement, Lamont and his American associates insisted, Allied trade discriminations against Germany must end. In fact, all unnecessary government interference with world commerce should cease. Over the course of the war, they lamented, the Allies had become regrettably addicted to statist controls. Now it was time to "cut out" this government "paternalism," restore private initiative, and guarantee equal economic opportunity so that unfettered private interests might get on with the job of revitalizing Europe.[8]

Lamont's position thoroughly mirrored official policy. Both the Treasury Department and President Wilson vetoed several Allied schemes that underwrote European reconstruction at the expense of German recovery and the American taxpayer, or that called for new government loans and debt cancellation, preferential pooling arrangements among the victors, and the perpetuation of wartime government controls over the domestic and international economies. Most importantly, they agreed with Lamont that the British reconstruction proposal drafted by John Maynard Keynes was "impractical." The American delegation had three major objections to the Keynes Plan. It would make the United States responsible for collecting German reparations. If Germany defaulted, it would saddle the American treasury with the bulk of

European indebtedness. Lastly, it would indirectly trap the United States into replenishing the liquid capital siphoned out of Germany in the form of excessive reparations to the Allies.[9]

Initially at least, Wilson and Lamont also agreed on the need for a fixed and reasonable reparations figure. Thus fortified, Lamont, after weeks of acrimonious wrangling with his British and French colleagues on Subcommittee No. 2, drafted a formula regarding Germany's capacity to pay. It called for a reasonable liability fixed at between thirty and forty billion dollars, with half payable in marks and half in currencies selected by the victors. The British and French rejected the proposal as too lenient; and when Lamont asked Wilson to stand behind the formula, the president declined to do so. To Lamont's consternation, Wilson was ready to include the cost of pensions for Allied veterans in the final reparations tab and to leave the total sum for future determination by a new reparation commission. Then and later, Lamont considered the failure to fix a reasonable reparations figure to be the most egregious of several damaging compromises which Allied pressures and Wilson's own befuddled idealism forced upon the president at the peace conference. It wrecked Germany's credit, made it impossible to attract long-term reconstruction loans, and thus retarded European recovery generally. It angered the Germans, encouraged them to evade their treaty obligations, and thereby perpetuated the bitterness growing out of the war. In short, it "led largely to the negation of the peace."[10]

Yet, Wilson's temporizing notwithstanding, Lamont still believed that the United States could make a major contribution to world peace and recovery. At the governmental level, he wanted the Treasury Department to open funding discussions with its European debtors immediately, and to negotiate agreements with an eye to the interests of the debtor countries. Otherwise, he warned, the Allied governments would refuse to fund their debts to each other, industry and finance would remain paralyzed, and Europe would continue in "chaos," with results almost as pernicious "for America as for the rest of the world."[11] At the private level, he wanted American bankers and industrialists to collaborate with each other, informally with the Treasury Department in Washington, and with their counterparts abroad to manage the flow of private capital needed to revitalize European industry and commerce. Lamont, together with Norman Davis, outlined the method of regulation and the terms on which American aid should be dispensed in a major memorandum requested by President Wilson shortly after he rejected the Keynes Plan in April 1919.[12]

The Lamont-Davis memorandum incorporated what became the quintessential themes in American reconstruction policy over the next decade. Unless European economic conditions improved, its authors asserted, "industrial and political revolutions will continue, with disastrous results for Europe and for the world." Indeed, given the interrelatedness of the modern world economy, specifically the dependence of American industries on European export markets, economic chaos in Europe would produce "serious business and industrial depression" in the United States. Self-interest therefore demanded that the

United States assist in Europe's reconstruction. The memorandum outlined several principles that should govern such aid. Limited government loans might be required temporarily, but "so far as possible" long term credits should be "extended through the normal channels of private enterprise." In order to attract private capital and maximize its impact on European conditions, the Allied governments should guarantee all credits extended, adopt orthodox fiscal and monetary policies, eliminate all "tariffs or secret trade understandings" which discriminated against American interests, use the proceeds of American loans only for reproductive commercial and industrial enterprises, and reduce their reparations demands on Germany. Great Britain and the United States, the major creditor powers, should immediately negotiate funding agreements with their debtors. The United States, in particular, should forgive interest payments on all Allied obligations for a three-year period.

Finally, to regulate the extension of American credits, the Lamont-Davis memorandum suggested the formation of two wholly non-governmental committees. An all-European committee organized by the British and French governments, composed of private financial and business leaders, would draft a "general scheme" for the extension of credits "through banking and commercial channels." This European committee would coordinate its activities with a similar syndicate in the United States. Under the "general approval" of the Treasury Department, this syndicate would hammer out the details of the reconstruction scheme and mobilize private American capital in its support. In theory, this kind of organization would guarantee success by substituting a comprehensive and regulated approach to recovery for the vagaries of the marketplace, eliminating artificial and discriminatory restraints on private initiative, reducing the responsibility of the government, and relying on the judgment of cooperating multinational business and financial experts.[13]

Not surprisingly, with Lamont's encouragement, Morgan and Company began taking the steps outlined in the Lamont-Davis memorandum. After consulting with Lamont in Paris, Henry P. Davison, a Morgan partner who was serving as chairman of the Red Cross War Council, returned to New York late in May impressed with the need for prompt action on the European situation. Davison, J. P. Morgan, and representatives of twenty other New York investment houses formed a committee, appointed Morgan as chairman, and laid plans to mobilize investment capital across the country behind some plan for underwriting European recovery. Specifically, they decided to launch a large investment corporation with stock, valued at $100 million, owned jointly by the nation's great banks and export interests. This corporation would cooperate with similar European combines in drafting a plan for financing American capital equipment needed for European reconstruction. Such a program, Lamont explained, would make it possible "to get away from Governmental loans" and return international trade and finance to private control.[14]

As for officials in the Treasury Department, no one doubted their desire to expedite American assistance in European stabilization, provided this aid did not result in further governmental intrusions, debt cancellation, or new government loans that might cause inflation and higher taxes.[15] Yet it was to avoid just these liabilities that the Treasury Department refused to accept responsibility for the Davison scheme, or even for a share of the debentures to be issued by the proposed combine. Opposition to state financing, however, did not prohibit the Department from backing congressional passage of the Edge Act in 1919.[16] This act provided a legal framework for cooperation between American bankers and manufacturers in arranging long-term investment credits. It cleared the way for the formation of a wholly private investment trust, modeled on the Davison scheme, but without government responsibility and underwriting. Accordingly, in 1920, a congeries of business and banking groups joined forces to sponsor the Foreign Trade Financing Corporation (FTFC), an Edge corporation with an authorized capital of $100 million. Despite auspicious beginnings, this initial venture in private and cooperative financing folded when the bankers and manufacturers involved could not agree on the kind of investment program the new combine should launch.[17]

Although it seemed that bankers and manufacturers were failing to exercise the sort of responsible private leadership envisioned in the Lamont-Davis memorandum, Lamont clung resolutely to that recipe for reconstruction. Europeans, he reiterated, had to help themselves by stabilizing their currencies, adopting a "courageous" approach toward debt funding negotiations, and substituting private initiative and ownership for government controls and socialization. The United States, too, had to demonstrate "enlightened self-interest." As a creditor nation with a vital stake in international economic stability and world export markets, it had to adopt a low tariff policy, champion the cause of equal commercial opportunity, continue the campaign for a fixed and reasonable reparations settlement, and deal generously with its debtors.

Lamont excoriated Congress for foisting the World War Foreign Debt Commission on the Harding Administration and then compelling the commission to conclude debt settlements which fixed interest rates at a 4.25 percent minimum and the time for repayment of all principal and interest at a twenty-five-year maximum. These restrictions deprived the administration of any freedom of action on the debt question and discouraged European debtors from negotiating funding agreements. At the very least the commission should thoroughly investigate each debtor's capacity to pay; if the results revealed that total repayment would diminish the capital reserves needed by the debtor to finance reconstruction or purchase American exports, the commission should seek a revision of its congressional instructions. Lamont never advocated wholesale cancellation of the Allied war debts. He believed that outright cancellation might encourage "slackness and extravagance" in Europe. He favored adjusting repayment to the debtor's capacity to pay only if the Allies reciprocated by reducing their reparations demands on Germany. But he did not expect such adjustments to take place until the American people, especially

American farmers, understood "that their prosperity [was] wrapped up in the rehabilitation of Europe."[18]

As this suggests, Lamont did not believe that Americans could exercise their international responsibilities if they remained aloof from world affairs. He had no sympathy for hidebound isolationists who failed to appreciate how the communications and transportation revolution had created an economically interdependent world in which "London and Berlin are much nearer New York to-day than was Buffalo a hundred years ago." He was disconsolate when the Senate rejected the Treaty of Versailles, and so disappointed when Warren G. Harding failed to campaign aggressively for American membership in the League of Nations that he broke a lifelong association with the Republican Party and cast his ballot for the Democrats in 1920. He lamented Washington's refusal to sanction official participation in the first postwar international economic conference at Brussels. He also complained that its absence from the League of Nations deprived the United States of opportunities to collaborate officially with the Reparation Commission and the financial section of the League. These new organizations, he believed, provided ready-made structures for exercising American influence and working out cooperative solutions to such pressing economic problems as war debts, reparations, and tariff barriers.[19]

But if formal participation by the American government was out of the question, there was still room for informal collaboration at the private level. Undeterred by the failure of exporters and bankers to harmonize their interests in the FTFC, Lamont continued to assume that private functional groups could cooperate voluntarily and informally with each other and with the government to manage economic affairs in a fashion conducive to peace and prosperity for all. This was the kind of cooperative control which he had advocated in 1919 and which he and his firm did so much to further in the postwar period. In 1922, for example, Morgan and Company, along with other large banking houses, volunteered to submit proposed foreign loan transactions for government supervision and to accept the responsibility for rejecting any loans that did not conform with public policy. Lamont fully supported the new system of loan control so long as it left primary responsibility in the hands of private lenders. Any attempt at greater, more formal state regulation, he warned, would put the American government in a "bureaucratic position" that was incompatible with private enterprise capitalism.[20]

In effect, the loan control procedure entrusted private lenders with the administration of public policy. It established a mechanism of control by cooperative private officials similar to the one envisaged in the Lamont-Davis memorandum and the Davison scheme. Once more, Lamont assumed that this system of cooperative control could be broadened to include private interests overseas. While Davison's supporters labored vainly to keep the $100 million FTFC above water, Lamont was successfully organizing a multinational financial consortium to manage all foreign loans to the Chinese government. Composed of cooperating American, British, French, and Japanese banking groups, each endowed with government authority, the consortium was to provide a multinational system of public-private collaboration in regulating the flow of foreign capital to China. In this way, so Lamont hoped, the old system of imperialistic competition and spheres of influence would give way to a new order based on international cooperation, the Open Door, and reproductive, rather than political, investment. For China, the result would be greater political stability and more rapid economic modernization. For the great powers it would mean an expansive China market and a new era of peace in the Pacific.[21]

As Lamont saw it, the China consortium proved that the great powers could work together harmoniously, that Americans could participate in world affairs if only at the private level, and that multinational cooperation among responsible private groups could help to eliminate economic problems and organize the international economy in the interest of peace and prosperity for all. The same approach, he insisted, could be used to resolve the great problems of European reconstruction. In other words, private business experts rather than politicians could collaborate in drafting "scientific" stabilization schemes which would be financed by cooperating commercial banking institutions rather than government treasuries. The result would be programs founded on business and economic principles and free of the waste, inefficiency, and potential for conflict that supposedly inhered in government planning. It was this approach that Lamont and others would ultimately apply to Germany, but only after testing it first in the Austrian rehabilitation scheme of 1923.

By 1922, several Austrian reconstruction proposals had folded because political interference from the French and Italian governments and unstable conditions in Vienna discouraged private investors. The League of Nations therefore formed a special committee to draft a stabilization scheme that would appeal to conservative bankers. The members of this committee, according to Lamont, were "highly intelligent and experienced civil servants" and "experts." The plan they drafted called upon Austria to provide adequate security for any reconstruction loan, reduce inflation, and stabilize its currency. To achieve the latter two goals, the Austrian government was to balance its budget, curtail the number of state workers, create a new bank of issue, and raise additional taxes. The plan also demanded that the Allied governments postpone their reparations claims against Austria and guarantee any private loan to the government in Vienna. In order to prevent political interference with the reconstruction scheme, the plan required the Austrian government to transfer state-owned industrial enterprises to private management and bound the Allies to sign a protocol pledging their respect for Austria's political and territorial integrity and their readiness to accept administration of the scheme by an independent, nonpolitical commissioner, preferably a banker.

These conditions appealed to Lamont and his partners at Broad and Wall streets. Accordingly, after the governments concerned accepted the plan, a group of bankers met in London and agreed to float a $130 million Austrian reconstruction loan. Morgan and Company organized a cooperating syndicate of American banks to accept that portion of the loan offered in the United States. It did so without the customary managerial fee from the Austrian government and without a guarantee on the loan by the State Department. The firm, Lamont told a Senate Committee in 1931, considered the loan operation a "public duty."[22]

Lamont attributed the success of the Austrian stabilization scheme to the fact that it had been devised by "men of affairs," "plain men of business" who could handle complicated international economic problems efficiently because they were "technical experts" unhampered by political directives.[23] Ever since the Lamont-Davis memorandum of 1919, he and other American leaders had favored this "business" approach to European recovery, including German stabilization. Reiteration of their formula, with its stress on private management and finance, cooperation and expertise, orthodox economic policies and the limitation of reparations, had become commonplace by the end of the Wilson administration, and it remained the core of American policy during the Republican ascendancy. In 1922, for example, J. P. Morgan and a committee of private, multinational banking experts convened under the auspices of the Reparation Commission to analyze the financial reforms Germany would have to make in order to attract private foreign investment in its economic reconstruction. The bankers soon concluded that Germany could scarcely inspire confidence in the investing public unless its reparations bill was reduced below $33 billion, the figure set by an Allied conference in London the previous year. When the French refused to reconsider the London Schedule of Payments, the bankers' committee disbanded.[24]

For Americans, however, the committee's record lent credence to the belief that disinterested experts, if unhampered by government restrictions, could produce a scientific solution to the reparations imbroglio. Lamont and Secretary of State Charles Evans Hughes talked at length about reconvening the bankers' committee or appointing another committee of experts to examine Germany's capacity to pay.[25] In public speeches and in correspondence with the French, Hughes called repeatedly for a "practical, businesslike solution" to the reparations problem, one arranged by private banking experts who would be free from "any responsibility to Foreign Offices and from any duty to obey political instructions."[26] Still the French remained adamant, and when the Allied governments determined in January 1923 that Germany had defaulted on its reparations transfers, French and Belgian troops invaded the Ruhr in a desperate effort to force Germany to comply with the Versailles treaty.

A number of factors, however, soon made the French more pliable. The cost of the Ruhr occupation exacerbated the already unstable value of the franc and made the Bank of France more dependent upon foreign credits to bolster its faltering currency. Morgan and Company was the leading source of outside financial assistance for the French government; and Lamont made it clear that any long term credits depended upon a reasonable settlement of the reparations issue. The eventual collapse of passive resistance in Germany and hints that Washington would deal more generously with those of its debtors who adopted a liberal reparations policy no doubt smoothed the way for French compliance. So did British support for the American plan and the disquieting fear of diplomatic isolation among French officials. For these and other reasons, the French accepted Hughes's proposal and the Inter-Allied Reparation Commission appointed another committee of experts, the so-called Dawes Committee, to consider methods of stabilizing the German economy.[27]

/The Dawes Committee and its report symbolized the triumph of American reparations and reconstruction policy. The committee was composed of cooperating, multinational financial experts who had no official attachment to their governments. As urged in the Lamont-Davis memorandum five years earlier, the experts were to devise a stabilization scheme founded on orthodox fiscal and monetary reforms in Germany, the limitation of reparations transfers, and the nonpolitical supervision of both these reforms and transfers in order to entice private capital to underwrite Germany's recovery. In accordance with this prescription, the committee's report called for a balanced budget, currency stability, increased taxation, and a new bank of issue in Germany. It did not reduce Germany's reparations bill below that fixed in the London Schedule, but it did establish a new slate of annuities geared to fluctuations in the German economy. It also established a new Transfer Committee, chaired by an agent general for reparations payments, with responsibility for managing Germany's transfers in a fashion that did not undermine the German currency. /The agent general, as well as the members of the Transfer Committee, was to be an independent economic expert rather than a political appointee. Finally, the experts called for a $200 million foreign loan to Germany. Its proceeds would provide the new bank of issue with an adequate foreign currency reserve and finance reparations in kind long enough for Germany's domestic stabilization program to take hold.[28]

Opinion in both America and Britain generally applauded the Dawes Plan. But its implementation required the approval not only of the Allied and German governments but also of the major international investment houses, particularly J. P. Morgan and Company, whose support would be needed for the projected Dawes loan. Even before the Dawes Committee had adjourned, Owen D. Young, chairman of the board of General Electric Company and one of the American experts on the committee, solicited the firm's opinion on the requirements for raising a large German loan on the American market. In response, Lamont and his partners demanded that Allied troops be removed from the Ruhr, that the Dawes Plan and the Dawes loan be warmly supported in Germany and the Allied countries, that the loan be secured by a first lien on Germany's revenues with repayment ahead of reparations transfers, that the proceeds of any loan be used to stabilize Germany's currency rather than finance reparations, and that Germany's annual transfers not exceed its capacity to pay. In addition, the Morgan partners could not shake a suspicious view of the Transfer Committee as an ingenious political expedient contrived by the experts to convince Germany that it would not have to pay and France that it would be paid. As they put it, the experts thought they had found a way "for Germany to have her cake and France to eat it."[29] To provide investors with the additional protection they needed, Lamont wanted the Allied governments to disavow any intention of taking action against Germany which might impair service on the loan. He also demanded that the Transfer Committee be separated from the Reparation Commission and staffed only by independent business experts from the investment community.[30]

Many of the bankers' requirements remained unfulfilled when the Allied leaders gathered in London to consider the Dawes Plan in mid-July 1924. Lamont was therefore on hand to press these requirements before opinions crystalized in a fashion that might wreck the chances for floating a German bond issue.[31] In addition to the terms outlined to Young earlier, Lamont and his partners, together with Governor Montagu Norman of the Bank of England, wanted the French-controlled Reparation Commission stripped of its power to declare default. This power was to be placed with the Transfer Committee, which the Anglo-Americans could expect to dominate. Should a flagrant German default require sanctions, the bankers also wanted the Allied governments to guarantee that German revenues pledged as security against the Dawes loan would be protected. These provisions became the bankers' major demands during the course of the London Conference. Through them they hoped to insure their potential investment in Germany's recovery and prevent the French from again using the authority of the Reparation Commission to cover essentially independent actions against the German government.[32]

British Prime Minister Ramsay MacDonald ruled out a government guarantee of payment on the Dawes loan as politically inexpedient. Otherwise, British and American officials supported the bulk of the bankers' demands at the London Conference. Frank B. Kellogg, the United States ambassador in London, headed the American delegation to the conference. At key moments, Hughes and Treasury Secretary Andrew W. Mellon were on hand to confer with Lamont. They tried to mediate his differences with the British and French delegates, hoped nervously for a compromise, but carefully avoided dictating to the bankers. As for the French, aside from the question of guarantees and the procedures for declaring default, they worked harmoniously with their British and American counterparts to make substantial progress on a large number of issues whose resolution was essential to a relaxation of tensions in Europe. Lamont was nevertheless despondent during the opening days of the conference. He considered French Premier Edouard Herriot irresolute, adjudged MacDonald "nice" but naive, and thought it very unlikely that French opinion would suddenly reverse course and "throw the Reparation Commission overboard."[33]

Lamont's partners in New York were even more pessimistic. At one point, piqued by the reluctance of the conferees to accept their dictates regarding the Reparation Commission and guarantees, they demanded that the conference adjourn long enough for the Allied finance ministers to consult with the leading investment bankers. This, they explained with contemptuous sarcasm, would "bring the Conference down out of the clouds and direct attention to the real task of getting the new money essential for initiating the Dawes Plan."[34]

It did not occur to the importunate bankers that the "real task" of the conference involved far more than appeasing the investment community. Lamont was not so ingenuous. Although still disappointed that Herriot refused to scrap the Reparation Commission, he believed that the premier was going as far as French public opinion would permit, that the French delegation was demonstrating a readiness to compromise on other issues, and that any stultifying stubbornness by the bankers might wreck the conference and stymie progress toward a new and peaceful European order. Although officially he stuck by Montagu Norman and demanded a total abrogation of the Reparation Commission's authority to declare default, this seems to have been largely a negotiating ploy designed to win the best business terms for any German loan. Privately, he was urging his partners in New York to back a series of compromise proposals, the most important of which was sponsored by Belgian Premier Georges Theunis. Taken collectively, these proposals affirmed the Reparation Commission's power to declare default, provided that it first consult the agent general for reparations, a representative of Germany's foreign bondholders, and a permanently constituted committee of experts. An American would sit on both the expert's committee and the Reparation Commission. Finally, in the event of sanctions being imposed on Germany, the Allied governments would protect all German revenues pledged as security against the Dawes loan and consider these, and other German assets that might fall under their control, a first lien against the service of the loan. As Lamont saw it, these "moral safeguards" denuded the Reparation Commission, virtually ruled out unilateral sanctions by France, protected investors, and thereby made compromise possible.[35]

In Lamont's opinion, since more was at stake than the special interests of the investing class, the bankers could take a financial risk comparable to the political risk assumed by Herriot. They could accept a compromise which gave them less than ironclad guarantees. But Lamont's partners rebuked him. Saving the Dawes Plan and patching up Europe, they argued, was a government responsibility and not the duty of investment bankers. The bankers' job was to protect the interests of potential investors and, in their view, the safeguards offered bondholders under the various compromise proposals were inadequate.[36] In short, the Morgan partners were acting the part of a functional elite concerned with the parochial interests of its narrow clientele. Lamont, on the other hand, had transcended this role. He was speaking as a quasi-public official, a private statesman self-consciously impressed with his firm's larger responsibility to the goals of public policy and with the long-term confluence of these public goals and the private interests of the investment community.

Despite his private feelings, however, Lamont doggedly defended the firm's policy until he could swing his persistent partners behind a more enlightened view. He reiterated the bankers' demands to the Allied premiers, at one point even dispatching what he called an "ultimatum" to Prime Minister Mac-Donald: unless the bankers' requirements were conceded, there would be no support for the Dawes loan among private investors. At the same time he applied subtle economic pressure against the French. To stabilize the franc, Morgan and Company had established a $100 million revolving credit for the Bank of France. This credit was due to expire in September 1924 and French Finance Minister Etienne Clémentel wanted it renewed. He also hoped to arrange a substantial long term loan from Morgan and Company. Lamont never explicitly threatened to sever this financial lifeline unless the French became more cooperative on procedures regarding default, but on several occasions he implicitly linked the two issues in a way that Clémentel could scarcely fail to comprehend.[37]

No doubt the need for the bankers' support to protect the franc and underwrite the Dawes Plan finally persuaded Herriot to offer one final concession. In addition to the procedures and guarantees specified in previous proposals, he now suggested that if any member of the Reparation Commission dissented from a majority vote in favor of default, he could appeal the decision to a special arbitral committee chaired by an American. As even the inveterate Francophobe Montagu Norman admitted, the French had made a great concession which, together with the other limitations, effectively torpedoed the Reparation Commission. Lamont agreed. Although the concession was not as explicit as the bankers would have preferred, he believed that under the procedures outlined sufficient guarantees against unilateral action by the French now existed to make a German bond issue marketable in the United States.[38]

Still thinking as parochial functional elites, however, the other Morgan partners deprecated the new compromise. Because it theoretically left the French free to impose sanctions unilaterally, the partners claimed that it could hardly appeal to those "sober-headed business men of the world" whose support would be needed to float a German bond issue. Yet, as Morgan partner Russell Leffingwell noted, for all practical purposes investors would decide however Morgan and Company advised. He admitted that other investment bankers were more sanguine about market requirements for a German loan — "Sunny Jims" he called them — but Morgan and Company had more experience and, besides, without its support no other firm could successfully market a German issue. In the United States, in other words, J. P. Morgan and Company was the market; and unless appeased by new concessions it would refuse to cooperate.[39]

These sentiments notwithstanding, delegates at the London Conference endorsed the compromise formula on 2 August 1924. This forced the bankers to support the proposed loan on terms they deemed inadequate or accept responsibility for undermining the work of the Dawes Committee and the London Conference — perhaps even the peace and stability of Europe. Bitter about their unhappy predicament, Lamont, J. P. Morgan, and others warned that American investors still considered the Reparation Commission a "black beast," castigated Owen Young and his associates for being too anxious to compromise, and unflinchingly reiterated their demands.[40] Despite this display of defiance there were signs that Morgan and Company would support the Dawes loan even without the full assurances originally demanded. If the personnel of the Reparation Commission, the Transfer Committee, and the Arbitral Board were wisely selected, Leffingwell wrote Lamont on 9 August, it might "make practical an otherwise unconvincing compromise."[41]

Several factors persuaded the partners to give their grudging support to the London Conference agreements. The New York bond market, formerly depressed, had rebounded; and this "brilliant" market seemed to insure a successful reception for any German issue — so successful in fact that Morgan's New York rivals were threatening to proceed without the firm's support.[42] The Morgan partners also hoped that additional concessions might still be won in later negotiations regarding the loan with the British, French, and German governments.[43] Then too, President Calvin Coolidge, Ambassador Kellogg, and Secretaries Hughes and Mellon all urged Morgan and Company to help underwrite the German loan. Hughes tried to arouse in the Morgan partners the class-conscious sense of social duty, the awareness of how national interest and personal advantage could coincide, which Lamont had already shown. Failure to go forward with the loan, he warned them, would produce "widespread economic distress" from which those "who have substantial interests in this country would not wholly escape."[44]

Most importantly, Lamont continued to nudge his partners toward a larger view of their responsibilities. Although never breaking publicly with the firm's position on default procedures and security, he lectured his colleagues to stop expecting "politicians to enact just the sort of documents that we wish." Besides, the provisions included in the compromise formula were sufficient to protect investors. Beyond this, the conference had reached other momentous agreements. The Allies had practically dumped the Reparation Commission. They had agreed to evacuate the Ruhr and other occupied areas. They had made it extremely unlikely that the French could invoke separate sanctions except in the case of a flagrant German default. For the first time in the postwar period, they had negotiated a mutual accord with Germany on the difficult reparations problem. These results were suffusing Europe with a new spirit of cooperation. In this atmosphere Lamont simply did not believe that the bankers' demands were still of great importance. Morgan and Company could nourish or dessicate this fledgling spirit of European goodwill; and in his view the firm should "take up this German Loan matter and . . . the sooner we take hold . . . the better business it will be for all concerned, including ourselves."[45]

Lamont felt that by advancing the cause of European peace and stability, J. P.

Morgan and Company could advance its own interest. Public policy and private gain coincided. Persuaded at last, the partners at Broad and Wall streets finally swung their firm's enormous influence and managerial skills behind the Dawes loan. Cooperating with a syndicate of European investment houses led by its affiliates — Morgan, Grenfell in London and Morgan, Harjes in Paris — the House of Morgan managed a group of American banks which marketed more than half of the $200 million bond issue.[46]

As Lamont and other Americans saw it, the success of the Dawes loan seemed to prove that in Germany, as in Austria and China, private "experts" and bankers could collaborate on a multinational basis to devise stabilization programs founded on a business basis, financed through private banking channels, and managed and regulated by private leaders. This kind of private and cooperative multinationalism had been the center of America's European reconstruction policy since 1919, when Lamont drafted the Lamont-Davis memorandum for President Wilson. Not surprisingly Lamont now believed that the Dawes Plan and loan inaugurated the long-delayed process of stabilizing Europe economically and politically. The curtain, it seemed, had been raised on a new era for Europe, with Lamont and other private leaders working behind the scene to produce the unfolding drama.

Lamont, of course, always understood that the Dawes Plan and loan were only initial acts designed to set the stage for a final denouement of the German problem. He was heartened by subsequent developments, especially the decision of the American Debt Commission to adopt the capacity-to-pay principle in funding negotiations, the collaboration of multinational banking groups in other European stabilization schemes, and the successful launching of the Young Committee in 1929. For Lamont, in fact, the Young Committee vindicated once more his faith in private enterprise and management. It reduced Germany's reparations liability to a figure Americans had always considered desirable. It ended all foreign political controls over Germany. It commercialized and thus depoliticized Germany's indemnity payments. And it established the Bank for International Settlements, in part to handle Germany's reparations transfers, in part to institutionalize the kind of business self-regulation and cooperative multinationalism which Lamont and his partners had championed. Indeed, J. P. Morgan was one of the American experts attached to the Young Committee, and Lamont, who attended the Commission's meetings as an alternate, played an important part in founding the Bank for International Settlements.[47]

Later developments, specifically the world depression, the collapse of the international debt structure, the enervation of the Bank for International Settlements, and the coarse recrudescence of mercantilism in the 1930s did not dim Lamont's commitment to cooperative multinationalism. He urged President Herbert Hoover to launch the moratorium on war debt payments in 1931. He served as a delegate to the World Economic Conference in 1933 and supported Cordell Hull's reciprocal trade agreements program. Had Lamont lived beyond 1948, he no doubt would have joined those members of the banking community who championed, if not the Bretton Woods Agreements and the World Bank, at least a modernized version of the sort of voluntary self-regulation and cooperative multinationalism that characterized much of the 1920s.

The commitment of policymakers to the concept of private and cooperative multinationalism helps to explain Lamont's important role in American diplomacy. Any assessment of his influence, however, must also take account of other factors. As the spokesman for J. P. Morgan and Company, the preeminent private investment firm of the decade and one with long-standing ties to private European financial centers and government authorities, Lamont was bound to become a central figure in the financial diplomacy of the postwar period. The wide area of collaboration between Morgan and Company and the government only increased the scope of Lamont's influence. He and his firm established a record of close cooperation with the government during the war years; and after the war the pattern of cooperation widened to include the organization of the China financial consortium, support for the State Department's loan control program, Morgan's leadership of the bankers' committee that investigated the German reparations problem in 1922, the firm's management of the Austrian stabilization loan in 1923, and the pressure which Lamont and his partners exerted to bring the French into line with the reparations policy of the American government.

Despite this record of cooperation and mutual interest, had another Morgan partner been the firm's spokesman the results might have been different. Lamont, after all, had worked with the reparations problem and the difficulties involved in European reconstruction since the Paris Peace Conference. His authorship of the Lamont-Davis memorandum in 1919 made him one of the original formulators of American stabilization policy; no other member of his firm could match Lamont's familiarity with that policy and with the great leaders of European finance and diplomacy. Once more, his belief in the public responsibility of private leaders endeared Lamont to officials like Hughes and Hoover; the broad coincidence of their views on reconstruction matters made Lamont a trusted, if unofficial, agent of government policy. When Hughes, Mellon, and Kellogg refused to dictate to him at the London Conference they were acknowledging not only the power of private finance but also their personal confidence in Lamont. Because he shared their views, Lamont became the instrument through which they could exert influence on the politics of European stabilization at a time when isolationist sentiment in the United States limited official government involvement. The result was a form of public-private power-sharing, one which entrusted a private leader with the responsibility for protecting the public interest.

It would be wrong, however, to interpret the stress in American diplomacy on privatism, self-regulation, and power-sharing as simply a convenient way for

American politicians and diplomats to circumvent isolationist sentiment at home. Men such as Lamont were indeed private proxies for their public principals, but they were not mere understudies ready to fill in temporarily during the postwar decade. Also involved here was the assumption, shared widely by both public and private officials, that business and banking "experts" could *and* must play a part, perhaps the leading part, in managing public policy. This assumption reflected not mere expediency but the deeply held conviction that private leaders, working in voluntary collaboration with each other and informally with their governments, could manage the domestic and international economies more efficiently, more equitably, and with less of the oppressive paternalism and waste that supposedly characterized statist schemes.

For over three decades Lamont exemplified this emphasis on privatism in the new corporatist age. His death, however, did not signify its passing. Even today, the apparently gargantuan dimension of the central state often conceals a pattern of public-private power-sharing that places much of the state's authority in the hands of organized functional groups. According to the current theory very reminiscent of the one that emerged during the Progressive Period, these private groups are more responsive to popular needs, better equipped to manage economic policy, and more likely to forge a truly harmonious and democratic society than elected officials in the government.

❦

Alanson B. Houghton

Alanson B. Houghton

1863	Born 10 October in Cambridge, Massachusetts
1886	A.B. Magna cum laude, Harvard College
1886–89	Graduate studies in Göttingen, Berlin, and Paris
1891	Married Adelaide Louise Wellington of Corning
1903	Second vice president for sales, Corning Glass Works
1904, 1916	Republican presidential elector
1910	President, Corning Glass Works
1918	Chairman of the board, Corning Glass Works
1918	Elected to House of Representatives, 37th New York District
1920	Reelected to House of Representatives
1922	Appointed ambassador to Germany
1925	Appointed ambassador to Great Britain
1928	Republican candidate for U.S. senator from New York
1928	Trustee, Brookings Institution
1929	Resigned as ambassador
1934	Chairman of board of directors, Institute for Advanced Study, Princeton, New Jersey
1941	Died 16 September at summer home in South Dartmouth, Massachusetts

CHAPTER 2

Alanson B. Houghton and the Ruhr Crisis: The Diplomacy of Power and Morality

Kenneth Paul Jones

America had a decisive influence upon German diplomacy during the days of the Weimar Republic. As Lord D'Abernon, dean of the diplomats to Germany in the 1920s, has noted, this influence "would . . . have remained inoperative if the U.S.A. had not been represented during the critical post-war period by men of unusual authority, . . . peculiarly in touch and sympathy with German life."[1] This is particularly true of Alanson Bigelow Houghton, America's ambassador to Germany from February 1922 to February 1925.

Houghton was an excellent choice as America's first ambassador to the Weimar Republic. He spoke fluent German as a result of graduate studies in Germany. As Republican congressman from New York's 37th District since 1919, he had served on the House Foreign Affairs Committee and possessed some knowledge of the diplomatic process and the limits the legislature placed on the executive in foreign affairs. As chairman of the board of his family's prosperous Corning Glass Works, he personified the Republican administration's desire to find a business-like solution to the problems which hindered the economic recovery of Germany and the restoration of economic ties with America.[2] Although he was a political appointee, he left for Berlin with an endorsement from William R. Castle, Jr., the chief of the Division of Western European Affairs.[3] Castle praised Houghton's reports and showed them to Secretary of State Charles Evans Hughes who thought they "were the best ever and that our Ambassador there was the best representative we had." Presidents Warren G. Harding and Calvin Coolidge agreed. By 1926, Houghton, who had meanwhile become ambassador to Great Britain, emerged as the probable successor to Frank B. Kellogg as secretary of state.[4]

It is only in recent years that historians have begun to give Houghton the attention he deserves.[5] This essay fills part of the void by describing his role in America's efforts to avert and then resolve the Ruhr-reparations crisis of 1923–24. It is an instructive example of what recent scholarship has argued concerning the legend of American isolationism — Republican policymakers were deeply involved in the search for peace in Europe. The nature of that involvement was circumscribed, however, by their self-imposed restrictions as well as those imposed by Congress. They were fearful of congressional opposition to direct, governmental intervention in Europe's squabbles and convinced that the private sector could provide a business-like solution to Europe's difficulties. They therefore delegated considerable authority to semi- and unofficial diplomats like Owen D. Young and Thomas W. Lamont and to official diplomats like Houghton. The essays in this volume document the important role played by Young and Lamont. This essay will give testimony to the keen observation of one scholar that America's intervention in European affairs during the 1920s "was carried on more actively at the level of the ambassador than in the State Department, in part with the toleration of the State Department, in part without" its knowledge.[6]

Prior to his departure for Berlin, Houghton gave a number of speeches and press interviews which exemplify the prevailing sentiment within the Republican administration concerning the role America must play in the economic reconstruction of Europe. Houghton emphasized the interrelationship between American economic prosperity and European financial stabilization and economic recovery. "If Europe is not prosperous," he argued, "it is obvious that we cannot be prosperous." He warned of unemployment in the United States if Europe's difficulties continued. America must do what it could to help. The European nations, however, must also do their part. Houghton emphasized the importance of setting aside the passions of war. Victor and vanquished must recognize that the problem of economic recovery was a common one and that they were economically interdependent. The recovery of France and Britain would be impossible as long as Germany continued to suffer from hyperinflation and economic stagnation.[7]

Houghton typified the Harding administration's belief that European political reconciliation and economic recovery depended upon a financially sound answer to the German reparations question. He saw it primarily as a problem of depoliticizing the issue in order to find a business-like solution. Many Americans agreed with French Premier Raymond Poincaré that the Germans had not tried hard enough to fulfill the schedule of reparations payments set up in 1921.[8] Like Houghton, however, they thought the demands France made upon Germany were too severe and were politically motivated. If one could disentangle economics from politics by delegating the problem to supposedly neutral businessmen, a solution would be quickly found. To Houghton and others it was clear that Germany needed both a moratorium and a foreign loan in order to stabilize its currency and revive its economy. And the obvious source for a loan was America. Houghton knew, however, that American financiers would not open their coffers until they had received adequate assurances that the French would no longer make irrational, politically-motivated demands upon Germany which could endanger their loans.[9]

Like the Republican policymakers in Washington, Houghton feared that the irrational demands of the French would lead to one of two equally abhorrent consequences. Poincaré's reparations demands could lead to the economic collapse of Germany and the triumph of bolshevism. Even if the Germans did not turn to bolshevism, there remained the danger that they might turn to Bolshevik Russia. Indeed, shortly after Houghton arrived in Berlin, in April 1922, Foreign Minister Walther Rathenau signed the Rapallo Treaty with the Soviet Union.[10] Houghton therefore committed himself to bringing Germany back into the family of Western nations. He advocated this not only because of his fear of bolshevism and of economic recession in the United States, but because of his commitment to peace between nations. Although he and his Republican colleagues in Washington had limited confidence in the League of Nations, they had a Wilsonian belief in the unique role America should play as the moral arbiter of peace. Like Wilson, they looked forward to the day when the European arms race and balance of power politics would end, and believed that American economic power should be used to push the nations of Europe toward this noble goal.[11] It is this amalgam of power and morality which guided Houghton's actions as ambassador to Germany and determined his solution to the Franco-German reparations imbroglio.

Once in Berlin, Houghton initiated contacts with a wide circle of politicians, labor leaders, businessmen, and financiers.[12] He quickly won respect and confidence because of the sympathy and sincerity he demonstrated as well as his stature as the American ambassador. One example of his ability to gain respect quickly is the famous meeting he arranged on 23 June 1922 between Foreign Minister Rathenau and his leading critic, the industrialist Hugo Stinnes. The two came together at Houghton's home to discuss Rathenau's policy of fulfill-ment on reparations because "both men felt a peculiar confidence in Houghton; both realized that he understood their views and sympathized with their patriotic aspirations; both knew that he was discreet and reliable."[13]

Houghton perceived that Rathenau was the dominant influence in German political life and set out to get as close to him as he could — a task he enjoyed, for he had never met a better mind. Recognizing that Rathenau desired to cultivate their budding friendship, he saw hope for a resolution of the reparations riddle under Rathenau's leadership. But his hope and their friendship were cut short by Rathenau's assassination the morning after his meeting with Stinnes.[14]

Deeply disturbed by Rathenau's death, Houghton lamented Chancellor Joseph Wirth's inability to provide the necessary leadership in foreign affairs to find a way out of the emerging reparations crisis. German diplomacy entered a period of drift, unable to take the lead or respond adequately to outside encouragement. Meanwhile, the value of the mark plummeted and inflation spiralled as the German government continued to meet its reparations obliga-tions, but had neither a favorable balance of payments nor a surplus in the budget to cover them. On 12 July 1922, Germany requested a moratorium for the rest of that year and the next two years. Houghton supported this appeal, urging Washington to put pressure on Premier Poincaré who insisted the Allies should assert control over Germany's coal-rich Ruhr valley in return for any moratorium. By the end of August, Houghton expressed alarm because France seemed "entirely willing, if necessary, to disregard England" in order to assert control in the Ruhr valley. He wrote, "as long as France pursues her present policies, Germany's position is helpless and hopeless."[15]

Houghton's warnings were heeded in Washington where President Harding had been "watching for an opportunity to make a friendly gesture" and Secretary Hughes was "restless" under his "enforced inactivity." However, they were hesitant to act given the isolationist sentiment in Congress and Franco-British efforts to connect war debts with reparations.[16] When the German chargé presented a note to Washington appealing for help, President Harding commented, "It is apparent Germany needs help; . . . [but] unless we are further advised I do not understand what course we might helpfully and consistently pursue."[17]

Houghton did understand the proper course. He encouraged the creation of a new coalition government in Berlin which would include the German People's party (DVP). Its leader was Gustav Stresemann; but, more important, it was the party of Stinnes and other industrialists whose support was necessary for a reparations settlement. Heartened by news from Stinnes of a possible economic accord with France which would end his opposition to the government's fulfillment policy, Houghton looked forward to DVP participation in a coalition committed to settlement of the reparations question. With leading industrialists supporting the cabinet, no one could question the seriousness of any German offer to accept a feasible reparations settlement. Houghton therefore continued to cultivate his ties with Stinnes and other industrialists and encouraged their participation in a new cabinet. He also began to court another prominent figure in the German economy, the shipping magnate Wilhelm Cuno. Once again, Houghton demonstrated his talent for discerning the foci of political power, for Cuno emerged as chancellor of the new coalition government, including the DVP, created on 22 November.[18]

Houghton, however, had concluded it would not be enough for the Cuno government to offer France another reparations proposal. The French search for security was intertwined with reparations. Indeed, Houghton learned from Stinnes that Poincaré apparently would accept a reparations settlement based on Germany's capacity to pay, *if* it were combined with a security agreement endorsed by the United States.[19]

On 23 October, Houghton sent Secretary Hughes a letter setting forth his solution to the Franco-German problem. He proposed a fifty-year denunciation of war by the four leading European nations. They should also incorporate in their constitutions the requirement that a nation could only go to war as the result of a plebiscite. Finally, as a natural consequence of the above, they would agree to "substantial disarmament." Houghton believed the American people would respond enthusiastically to this peace plan. In fact, they would gladly cancel the Allied debts to America in return for Europe's commitment to peace and disarmament. On the other hand, Houghton predicted economic chaos with the "bolshevist tide" beating down the "barriers of European civilization" in Germany and sweeping "resistlessly to the Atlantic" should the war debts be added to the existing burdens weighing down the peoples of Europe. Here was Houghton's panacea for the troubles of Europe and the Western world. An effective anti-communist cordon sanitaire, a war debts-reparations settlement, European economic recovery, and world peace were all intertwined and could be achieved if America would show the way by applying the proper mixture of economic power and moral leadership.[20]

To a later generation, disillusioned by misuse of plebiscites, it is difficult to understand Houghton's enthusiasm. However, the concept of "Ballots before Bullets" (as one historian has phrased it) was a natural corollary of the widespread American desire to reduce use of military force in diplomacy, i.e., by extending the principle of popular control from domestic politics to international politics. Thus, the State Department professional William Castle, who had no love for the Germans, wrote an accompanying letter endorsing Houghton's peace plan.[21] Even Secretary Hughes supported Houghton's idea of a peace pact. When he responded negatively to Houghton's proposal on 14 November, he did not attack the flaws in the proposed plebiscite. Instead, he spoke of the impossibility of connecting debt reduction with any reparations settlement because of congressional opposition and emphasized the need to keep the security question separate and subordinate to the more immediate issue of German reparations. In other words, the reparations imbroglio must be depoliticized. Hughes shared Houghton's pessimistic view of Germany's future if a settlement were not reached. France, he agreed, was the key, and he informed Houghton that the Department of State had begun informal exchanges with the French government in an attempt to get Poincaré to support an international committee of independent financiers who could determine, on a "businessman's basis," what Germany could pay.[22]

Upset, but undaunted by Hughes's reply, Houghton turned to the German chancellor. At his urging, Cuno instructed Ambassador Wiedfeldt to present to Secretary Hughes a proposal for a peace pact. Wiedfeldt proposed that the United States should "in a sense be a 'trustee' to see that the arrangement was carried out or to take any action in the matter that the United States thought to be practicable." Houghton's hand in this proposal is unmistakable.[23]

This time Hughes responded favorably because there was no mention of Allied debts to America, and the peace proposal was theoretically independent of the present negotiations for a reparations settlement. He conveyed the German peace proposal informally to the French Ambassador Jules Jusserand on 18 December. But Premier Poincaré quickly lost interest in the German offer when Hughes divorced the United States from any role as trustee of such a pact. On 21 December, and more emphatically on the 26th, Jusserand reported Poincaré's rejection of both Wiedfeldt's peace pact proposal and Hughes's proposal for an international committee to settle the reparations dispute.[24]

Hughes's hope that Poincaré would seize upon or be won over to his proposal for getting France out of the reparations impasse had been dashed. The Germans, the British, and many of Hughes's American advisers had all urged him to publicize his solution.[25] These entreaties, plus the domestic political pressures he felt, led Hughes to deliver his famous speech at New Haven on 29 December 1922 before a meeting of the American Historical Association in which he spelled out the necessity for a settlement of the reparations issue by independent financiers.[26] Similarly, Chancellor Cuno publicized the German peace offer and outlined how far Germany would go to reach a reparations settlement. Houghton naturally supported the proposals by Hughes and Cuno, but evidence indicates that both publicized their plans simply to convince domestic and world opinion that they were not responsible for the apparent collapse of the efforts to avert French occupation of the Ruhr valley.[27] Unwilling to serve as trustee of any peace pact guarantee and unable, because of Congressional opposition, to promise a major war debts cancellation, Hughes simply lacked the means to divert Poincaré from his chosen path. Moral persuasion had failed and France's monetary problems had not yet reached the level where they would be vulnerable to American economic pressure.

Thus, the French, accompanied by the Belgians, carried out their threat by occupying the Ruhr valley on 11 January 1923. The Germans responded by withdrawing their ambassadors to the two countries and by encouraging a policy of passive resistance in the occupied territory. Washington showed its displeasure by withdrawing from the Rhineland the remaining American occupation forces. America could do nothing more, according to Secretary Hughes, except maintain a neutral attitude and await the moment when both sides realized the futility of their actions.[28]

Although Ambassador Houghton recognized the necessity for the American position, he could not repress his frustration over the course of events. He had met frequently with Cuno in the closing weeks before the breakdown in negotiations and had observed the chancellor's success in rallying the important forces in Germany behind his offer for a solution of the reparations and security questions. Houghton had, on his own initiative, gone to the French Foreign Ministry in December (while on vacation in Paris) in order to urge conciliation. The almost contemptuous manner in which Poincaré rejected Cuno's offer convinced Houghton that the premier had entered the Ruhr in search of security, not reparations.[29]

A month after the occupation had begun and the military nature of it had become more predominant, Houghton began criticizing the State Department's refusal to do more than instruct him to monitor any interference with American trade. He thought the Germans had demonstrated their readiness to reach a settlement based on Germany's capacity to pay reparations. On the other hand, the French were using reparations as a smoke screen for their fear of Germany and desire for security. The French had the Ruhr and obviously intended "to keep possession of it in one way or another." The Germans were equally determined to resist. The result would "be a simply appalling situation" with revolution and the dismemberment of Germany possible.[30] America had to intervene, according to Houghton, and words would not be enough. Indignant over the injustice of Poincaré's position, Houghton advocated a heavy dose of American economic power. On 6 March 1923, he pointed out to Secretary Hughes:

> The plain truth . . . seems to be that, having destroyed any balance of power in Europe and left France for the moment all powerful, we have simply let loose a great elemental force which inevitably seeks to satisfy itself. It is a force. It can only be dealt with as a force. The franc . . . suggests the obvious point of weakness. If it were possible, directly or indirectly, for either or both Britain and ourselves, to remove or to overcome the artificial support now given the franc, the franc would fall.

And before long, Houghton believed, Poincaré would either fall or be forced to honor his assertions that France only wanted reparations from Germany.[31]

To Houghton's chagrin, the State Department rejected his advice. In letters written during March and April, and in conversations with him after his return trip to the United States in May, both Hughes and Castle disputed his judgment. Whereas Houghton depicted the French in moral terms as "devils" for entering the Ruhr, they thought the French were "fools." Hughes shared Houghton's appraisal of the overwhelming power of the French who "could overrun the whole of Germany if they desired. . . ." However, the fact that they had not and that they were moderate in their occupation supported Hughes's conclusion that the French had entered the Ruhr in a foolish but understandable attempt to "get what they thought they were entitled to."[32]

Although Hughes and Castle shared Houghton's belief in the futility of the Ruhr occupation and did not shrink from the application of America's economic power to buttress its moral leadership, they argued that American intervention at this time would be counterproductive. From Houghton's reports, as well as Ambassador Herrick's from Paris, it was obvious neither Germany nor France was ready to respond favorably to any suggestion. Certainly France was the major hurdle, but Houghton would simply have to understand that America dare not intervene until French public opinion had realized the futility of coercion as the path to reparations. If America intervened before then, Poincaré could argue that his policy would have brought success had he not been diverted by outside pressure. Furthermore, Hughes could not count on support in America where public opinion had swung away from its pro-German stance in January to a more distinctly pro-French sentiment. No, America must maintain a neutral position benevolent toward neither side.[33]

Houghton could appreciate these arguments even if he did not entirely agree. What most disturbed him was Castle's belief that he took "an exaggerated point of view as to the situation in Germany" as a "result of intensive and rather adroit propaganda" to which he had been subjected. At one point, Castle even wondered if Houghton's pro-German sentiments had caused him to hold back "information which might bring about criticism of the German standpoint."[34] Castle believed that Houghton failed to apply a healthy skepticism to the various German assertions that they would never give in — that war or revolution was inevitable if France did not compromise. Above all, Houghton failed to realize that the Germans deserved at least equal criticism for the present impasse. Houghton was doing a disservice to the Germans in not making clear to them America's reluctance to intervene until they showed a real willingness to cooperate.[35]

Certainly much of this critique of Houghton's attitude toward the Ruhr occupation was warranted. He did fail to recognize that neither France nor Germany had a monopoly on right or wrong, that both acted from self-interest. He had shown a tendency to accept unquestionably the German assertions about the ruthlessness of the French occupation forces, and he had overstated the danger of war, bolshevism, or massacre. Finally, he had created false hopes of American intervention during the first months of the Ruhr occupation. Only when sentiment in both Germany and France began to move toward compromise could anything be done.

And yet, Houghton's emphasis on the French search for security as well as reparations could not be ignored. His warnings of Germany's possible political and economic collapse, combined with French separatist tendencies in the Rhineland, warranted more attention. He did not deserve the suspicion that he had become too pro-German to represent properly the American position.[36]

During Houghton's absence from Berlin, the German government did move toward compromise. In January, the Germans had refused to negotiate until the French withdrew from the Ruhr. Then on 2 May 1923, two days after Houghton sailed for America, Germany presented a reparations note to the Allied powers. Although Hughes shared the Allied criticism of this note, he seized upon the fact that the Germans had started what could become an exchange of views if open diplomacy were replaced by "the most direct and intimate negotiations with France."[37] When Germany submitted a second note on 7 June, Hughes thought Germany had finally accepted his advice because one paragraph referred to the need for direct conversations with the French. Informally, he urged the French to negotiate the terms of Germany's surrender. He even encouraged efforts to entice Poincaré into conciliation on the reparations issue by supporting some form of autonomous state in the Rhineland in order to appease the French search for security.[38] However, Hughes's efforts to bring the two sides to a compromise were to no avail. The German notes only strengthened the French desire for Germany's unconditional surrender.

Meanwhile, Houghton had returned to Germany refreshed and with a clear understanding of Secretary Hughes's attitude. Nevertheless, he found it "a little hard to maintain that spirit of buoyant optimism which [he had] carried away from America." He found the situation in late July bleaker than it had been before his vacation, with "complete collapse and chaos" certain before too long if no one intervened. He saw no sign that the French would exit from the Ruhr, nor would the Germans voluntarily try to buy their exit by approving some form of autonomy in the Rhineland.[39]

When Gustav Stresemann replaced Cuno as chancellor of Germany on 13 August, Houghton aptly described the new cabinet as "a Government of surrender." Confronted with the imminence of economic collapse and continued Anglo-American inaction, Stresemann had put together a Great Coalition extending from his German People's party (DVP) on the Right to the Socialists (SPD) on the Left. Showing greater maturity as a diplomat, Houghton ignored the German assertions to the contrary and correctly predicted that Stresemann would approach France to find some face-saving way to end passive resistance.[40] Even Castle found the terms Stresemann offered Poincaré "very liberal." He did not "see how France could refuse to accept them, at least if she hopes to have the world believe that the Ruhr adventure was for the purpose of collecting reparations." However, as Houghton predicted, Poincaré refused to make any concessions, and Castle acknowledged: "Well, Houghton has been right all the time."[41]

On 22 September, Stresemann conveyed to Houghton that his government had no choice but to give in despite the consequences. Hugo Stinnes revealed just how serious the consequences could be when he came to see Houghton immediately after the ambassador left the chancellor. Stinnes told him that within a month Germany would have a right-wing dictatorship which would come to power after likely Communist disturbances. Although Houghton carefully stated that he felt "completely at a loss to know how seriously to take Stinnes's statement," the State Department reacted with quite proper concern.[42]

When Stresemann reluctantly halted passive resistance on 27 September, events began to unfold as Houghton had predicted. Poincaré refused to negotiate. Within a month, Germany was near political and economic collapse. The bottom had fallen out from under the mark. The Communists did attempt to seize power; the Bavarians did move toward secession; the French did support the separatists in the Rhineland; and Stinnes almost got his overthrow of the Weimar Republic.

As these events occurred during October and November, Houghton documented them in a series of telegrams and letters.[43] This time there was no denying the accuracy of his reports and his predictions. Hughes responded to Houghton's appeals. Hughes promptly seized upon a British attempt to revive his New Haven proposal for an international committee of experts to resolve the reparations question. After Belgium and Italy joined Britain and unconditionally accepted such a proposal, Hughes saw ground for optimism. But, on 5 November, he exploded in "a certainly momentous interview" with Ambassador Jusserand who had the unpleasant task of reporting Poincaré's crippling conditions for French approval of a committee of experts. What appeared to be the final scene in the tragedy came on 9 November when Hughes described as unacceptable Jusserand's elucidation of Poincaré's terms.[44]

Nevertheless, Houghton took consolation in the fact that the American people could see how the French had sabotaged Hughes's efforts to get a reparations settlement. Furthermore he recognized that the Ruhr occupation had proved costly to the French who would sooner or later have to accept American terms in order to be bailed out of a burgeoning financial crisis. Houghton therefore urged the Stresemann government to do what it could to preserve its parliamentary system and stabilize its currency. He held out the prospect of a reparations conference as pressure built up on the isolated French. He had won the confidence of Stresemann as he had earlier with Rathenau and Cuno; thus, the chancellor heeded his advice.[45]

The denouement came on 19 November when the British threatened to withdraw from the Conference of Ambassadors and other inter-Allied bodies if France did not desist from its destructive course in the occupied territory.[46] Meanwhile, James Logan, the American unofficial observer on the Inter-Allied Reparation Commission, joined with the official Allied delegates to put together a compromise proposal which Hughes felt compelled to accept. The Reparation Commission created two committees to determine Germany's capacity to pay reparations. On 12 December Washington announced American approval, and by the 14th Charles G. Dawes and Owen D. Young had been selected to serve on the important First Committee which quickly became known as the Dawes Committee.[47]

The Dawes Committee made a major contribution to the resolution of the Ruhr crisis. This outcome was not obvious, however, at its inception. The wording for the powers of the committee which Logan and his Allied cohorts had foisted on Secretary Hughes offered no more than "vague whispered suggestions" that Poincaré would not reimpose his stifling limitations. Two factors influenced the fruitful outcome of the Dawes Committee deliberations. The first is that the French franc, as Houghton had expected, now experienced a sharp decline on the foreign exchange market. This forced Poincaré to give greater latitude than he had originally intended to the French members of the Dawes Committee in order to get a more sympathetic ear from Anglo-American bankers. Secondly, Logan's independent action in December was only a prelude to the more extensive contribution by other official and unofficial diplomats who were delegated or usurped the role policymakers in Washington would have assumed had it not been for their self-imposed restrictions, as well as those imposed by Congress, concerning direct, official involvement in Europe's problems.[48]

Owen Young deserves major credit for the success of the Dawes Plan. Alanson Houghton, however, contributed significantly to the making of the plan and especially to its acceptance by the German cabinet and Reichstag. At the request of Young, who already knew the ambassador and had a high regard for him, Houghton travelled to Paris to meet him and Dawes shortly after their arrival. He apparently gave Young information and advice about the German situation and about Poincaré's efforts at that time to pressure the Germans into a bilateral agreement which would consolidate the French hold over the Ruhr.[49] When the Dawes experts came to Berlin at the end of January 1924, Young naturally turned to Houghton who arranged meetings for him with the most important political and economic figures. Particularly important were the series of meetings he arranged with Hugo Stinnes in order to assure support from German heavy industry for the emerging Dawes Plan versus Poincaré's bilateral scheme.[50]

Toward the end of March, Houghton hurried to Paris when he received news of possible complications in the drafting of the Dawes Plan. As he feared, he found the American technical advisers in a state of near rebellion. They had been left in the dark until suddenly confronted with the fait accompli of a reparations schedule, approved by Young, which they were certain Germany could not fulfill. The ambassador shared their conviction, but tried to convince them that the Germans would accept the plan anyway because it provided machinery for readjustment when it became necessary. Although he could not cure their pessimism, Houghton did assuage their "sense of resentment," thus nipping in the bud an open denunciation of the plan.[51] The final text of the Dawes Plan appeared 9 April 1924—the unanimous recommendation of the committee.

When Houghton returned to Berlin, he made use of the close ties he had established with Foreign Minister Stresemann to urge approval of the plan. As a result, the Marx cabinet promptly announced its unqualified acceptance of the Dawes Plan, using verbatim the wording suggested by Houghton. Nevertheless, Houghton put off his vacation to the United States in order to be certain this was so.[52] The decisive factor remained the attitude of the Nationalists party (DNVP). The Dawes Plan necessitated special legislation which required two-thirds approval in the Reichstag. After the expected swing to the right in the upcoming elections, the DNVP could easily sabotage the work of the Dawes experts. Houghton stayed in Berlin during the next two months, keeping in contact with Stresemann and doing what he could to assure support from industry and banking. His most significant meetings were with Professor Otto Hoetzsch of the DNVP and Hermann Buecher of the Federation of German Industry. Both assured him the Nationalists would approve the necessary legislation in spite of their election propaganda against the plan. Still, he justifiably worried about the gap between these private assertions and the DNVP's irresponsible public statements. Finally, near the end of May he informed Castle: "the acceptance of the experts' plan is now, I think, assured."[53]

Houghton's plans for a vacation, however, had to be put off. By the time he arrived in New York on 1 July, Secretary Hughes had approved American participation in the upcoming London Conference at which the Allies and Germany would negotiate the terms for putting the Dawes Plan into force. Hughes recognized the invaluable role Houghton could play in coordinating contacts with the Germans, and ordered him back to Europe.[54]

During the London Conference, 16 July to 16 August 1924, Houghton fulfilled Hughes's expectations. When the American and Allied representatives met alone during the first phase of the conference, Houghton kept the Germans informed of the course of the negotiations and allayed their fears of a dictated settlement.[55] For the second phase of the conference Houghton provided Frank Kellogg, America's ambassador to Great Britain and delegate to the London Conference, with a clear understanding of Germany's minimal conditions. Thus, on the decisive question of how soon the French should end their military occupation of the Ruhr, Kellogg supported the French promise to get out within one year. As Houghton had predicted, the German delegation demanded evacuation within three to six months and then gave way.[56] On 16 August, the London Conference ended with the German and Allied delegations in agreement on the schedule for setting in operation the Dawes Plan and for dismantling the occupation of the Ruhr.

One last hurdle remained before reaching the end of the Ruhr-reparations crisis. The German Reichstag still had to approve the London agreements. Houghton remained optimistic that the necessary votes could be found. On 17 August, he cabled the secretary of state for permission to leave on the 22nd for his much-deserved and long-delayed vacation in America.[57] Then, on 20 August, the German Nationalists endangered his vacation plans. "This has been the day of days," he wrote in his diary. Indeed it was, for Houghton had to draw upon the credit he had stored up in Germany in order to obtain support by the Nationalists for the upcoming Reichstag vote on the Dawes Plan legislation. The German state secretary, Ago von Maltzan, rushed into Houghton's office that morning, "somewhat excitedly," to ask the ambassador to meet with leaders of the DNVP concerning their terms for approving the Dawes Plan. Houghton recorded in his diary:

> I told Maltzan that I could not, of course, receive these gentlemen and that he should know better than to ask me. I could have and would have nothing whatever to do with German domestic politics. Maltzan then went away somewhat dejectedly. In half an hour or so he returned to say that he bore a request from the President urging me to receive the delegates from the Nationalists Party. I again told him sternly that I could not and would not do any such thing. He said it was important and that he hoped I would change my mind. But I again said I

could not and would not. And for the second time he departed more dejected than before. A half hour later he appeared for the third time and said he bore from the President and Cabinet a statement that the situation was very dangerous and that in all probability, unless I talked with the representatives of the Nationalists Party they would vote against the acceptance of the plan and would probably defeat it. . . . By this time I had reached a decision. It was plain to me that although the interview suggested was to be confidential and personal and under no circumstances to be divulged, that in reality the leaders of the Nationalists Party were probably trying to find a way out of the awkward position in which they found themselves. An interview with me would be reported to the Party and that might or might not make a difference in their attitude. At any rate it would offer an excuse. Without further demand, I told Maltzan that in view of the necessity of the situation as outlined by him and the government, I would receive the Nationalists delegates this afternoon.[58]

When the Nationalists arrived, Houghton warned them that rejection of the Dawes Plan would turn American opinion against Germany and make any loans difficult if not impossible. On the other hand, he held out the assurance that not only would the $200 million loan provided for in the Dawes Plan be subscribed, but that considerably larger amounts would immediately become available. In other words, American economic power could be used as a carrot or a stick to bring Germans as well as Frenchmen into line. With this, the meeting ended.

As scheduled, Houghton set sail for America where he arrived 31 July. According to his diary entry for that date, he then learned that his conversation had indeed been reported. Although other factors were involved, his meeting with the DNVP delegates no doubt played an important role in the fact that a sufficient number of Nationalists voted for the Dawes Plan to give the government the necessary two-thirds vote.[59] The French legislature also approved the London agreements, bringing an end to the Ruhr-reparations crisis which had been brewing since Houghton arrived as ambassador to Germany in 1922.

For Houghton, however, the Dawes Plan had not resolved the primary cause of the Ruhr occupation—France's fear of a revived Germany. After being appointed ambassador to Great Britain in January 1925, as a reward for both his diplomatic services and his efforts in the Midwest during Coolidge's presidential election campaign, he impressed upon the German foreign minister the need to allay France's fears. At a key moment, he served as the Coolidge administration's fulcrum to pressure France and Germany into a rapprochement on the security question. The result was the Locarno agreement of 1925 which earned for its major participants the Nobel Peace Prize.[60] Yet the Locarno security treaties did not satisfy Houghton. He considered America's search for peace incomplete. Locarno provided a temporary respite, but "pretty much everyone in Europe," he wrote President Coolidge, "believes that war is coming; and not so very far off." He still believed his plan for peace by plebiscite offered the best chance for lasting peace. He had tried unsuccessfully to get

Coolidge to use the idea in his election campaign. In August 1925 he submitted a more detailed explanation of his proposal, minus any mention of war debts, but again could not get Coolidge to take it up as his own.[61] Finally, in a commencement address at Harvard University in 1927 (with much discussion in the press concerning the outlawry of war), he offered his solution to the world and received a mixed reaction from the press. A watered-down version of his proposal did emerge in the Kellogg-Briand Pact of 1928, but Houghton no doubt felt only limited satisfaction.[62]

Houghton's diplomatic career ended officially in 1929 and unofficially in 1928 when he returned to the United States for an unsuccessful campaign as the Republican senatorial candidate from New York. During the election campaign and lecture tours during the 1930s, he continued to urge his war referendum proposal. He also worked for permanent peace through membership in a number of organizations. Most notably, he served as an officer of the Carnegie Endowment for International Peace and was elected, in 1934, chairman of the board of directors for Princeton's Institute for Advanced Studies. He died at his summer home in South Dartmouth, Massachusetts on 16 September 1941. His hopes for lasting peace had failed, and, as he had predicted to Coolidge in 1925, the Locarno treaties had fixed the "point where the next great war [would] begin, i.e., the German-Polish Frontier."[63]

Our own assessment of Houghton's contribution must be more positive than his. As Lord D'Abernon noted, Houghton's "unusual authority" made possible the decisive influence America had upon German diplomacy during the Ruhr-reparations crisis and the making of the Dawes Plan. Chancellor Cuno had, for example, geared his reparations and security proposals to Houghton's suggestions. Cuno and then Stresemann had hung their hopes on his words of encouragement during the Ruhr crisis. When the Dawes Plan was announced, Stresemann followed Houghton's advice for prompt acceptance. After Hughes sent Houghton to the first phase of the London Conference, it was the Germans who urged him to return to England for the second phase. His meeting with the DNVP representatives in August 1924 is the most dramatic example of the respect and authority he had gained in Germany. Although his status as ambassador for the economically powerful United States explains much of this influence, it was also the man. Even when he moved on to London, Foreign Minister Stresemann continued to turn to him for advice and support.[64]

Houghton had also won the confidence of the State Department. During the first part of his career when Hughes and Castle were at times "intellectually out of sympathy with him," they still acknowledged the value of his "excellent information so vividly expressed" and the importance of his close ties with all the major figures in German politics.[65] None of the correspondence Castle and Hughes received from their other representatives in Europe excelled the quality of Houghton's letters, particularly during the month of severe political and economic crisis in Germany from mid-October to mid-November 1923.

Houghton had returned from his trip to the United States that summer with the proper mixture of sympathy for Germany's struggle to restore its sovereignty over the Ruhr and frank advice about the price which would have to be paid. Castle would occasionally get angry with him but he would always be "a little ashamed" afterwards, especially when he had an opportunity to discuss the issue during one of Houghton's trips home. In 1925, Castle responded to "rumors of the probable pro-German attitude of the Ambassador" by remarking, "Mr. Houghton was, of course, sympathetic with the German dilemma, but he never for one moment forgot that he was an American and his restrained sympathy during the last part of his time in Berlin made him of almost inestimable value to the Department."[66] It is difficult to weigh the influence of different people upon Secretary Hughes's actions during the reparations negotiations of 1922–24. Clearly, at key moments such as Hughes's intervention in late 1922 and in October to November 1923, Houghton's reports and advice had a significant impact. Perhaps the best example of the immense confidence the administration had in his judgment came when President Coolidge, after a warning from Houghton about the likely repercussions in Germany, vetoed the candidacy of Dwight Morrow (of J. P. Morgan and Company) as the first agent general for reparations under the Dawes Plan.[67]

Houghton's actions during the Ruhr-reparations crisis demonstrate both the extent of American involvement in European affairs under the Republicans and the important role played by American official and unofficial diplomats. The Harding and Coolidge administrations were committed to the economic and political stabilization of Europe out of self-interest and a desire to serve as moral arbiter. But they were unwilling as well as unable, due to legislative restrictions, to become too directly involved. Both by intent and default a significant role in America's involvement in European affairs passed into the hands of diplomats like Houghton. Among the several examples provided in this essay, this is particularly evident in the negotiations concerning the making and final approval of the Dawes Plan, for Hughes had to delegate broad authority to Houghton and others in order to maintain the facade of American nonintervention. It was through them that American economic power was used to push the nations of Europe toward a resolution of the Ruhr-reparations crisis.

Owen D. Young

Owen D. Young

1874	Born 27 October in Van Hornesville, New York
1894	Graduated with A.B. from Saint Lawrence University
1896	Received law degree from Boston University and joined the law firm of Charles H. Tyler in Boston; later Tyler and Young
1912	Employed by General Electric Company as vice-president and head of the law department
1919	Organizer and chairman of the board of Radio Corporation of America (RCA)
1922	Chairman of the board at General Electric
1923	Appointed by President Harding as chairman of committee on business cycles and unemployment
1923	Appointed to the Expert Committee on Reparations (Dawes Committee) in December
1924	Attended the London Conference of premiers to ratify Dawes Plan, July– August
1924	Appointed agent general for reparations (ad interim), October– November
1925	Chairman, American Section of International Chamber of Commerce
1928	Appointed to Second Expert Committee on Reparations (Young Committee), December; elected chairman of committee
1929	Final draft of Young Plan signed 7 June
1930	Young Plan goes into operation 17 May; Bank for International Settlements is established and Dawes Plan ends
1933	Adviser to Franklin D. Roosevelt
1947	Appointed by President Truman to committee of industrialists to advise on America's role in European recovery
1962	Died 11 July in Saint Augustine, Florida

CHAPTER 3

Owen D. Young and German Reparations:
The Diplomacy of an Enlightened Businessman

John M. Carroll

Owen D. Young served as a semi-official American financial expert on two reparations committees during the 1920s in an attempt to resolve one of the most difficult economic problems of the postwar period. The German reparations question and the associated issue of inter-Allied war debts were direct results of the Great War and constant reminders of the national rivalries and hatreds the war had generated. Thomas W. Lamont, an American economic expert at Versailles, wrote in 1921 that "reparations caused more trouble, contention, hard feeling, and delay at the Peace Conference than any other point of the Treaty of Versailles."[1] In late 1923, the unresolved reparations dispute, and to a lesser degree, the war debts issue continued to arouse hatred and bitterness in the former belligerent countries and helped to lead Europe to the brink of economic collapse and renewed armed conflict. French troops occupied the Ruhr. German inflation and the accompanying social disorder threatened the very existence of the nation. International trade broke down, and the specter of bolshevism gripped Europe. Under these circumstances Young first became involved with the problem of international indebtedness, a task which occupied a good deal of his time and energy between 1924 and 1930.

As an independent business expert on the first reparations committee (1924) and later as chairman of the second reparations inquiry (1929), Young attempted to settle on a just and amicable basis one of the most emotion-charged controversies resulting from the war. He believed that it was the duty of his generation to resolve the reparations issue and other economic problems associated with the war before passing the reins of leadership on to a new generation.[2] His approach to the reparations problem was based on his own experience in international business affairs and the prevailing American policy which held that the reparations dispute should be settled on a business-like basis reflecting Germany's actual capacity to pay.[3] Young was convinced that if governments would only face the economic facts that often underscore a given political problem, a reasonable and just solution would result. He maintained that "you can not make progress toward high ideals until you get your money matters straightened out first."[4] In this sense, Young believed that a business solution to the reparations problem might relieve Europe of a great financial burden and in turn create a climate for the establishment of lasting political cooperation.

An examination of Young's career shows that he played an important role in extinguishing the hatred and bitterness that resulted from World War I. His activities as a reparations expert also demonstrate the degree to which Republican administrations of the 1920s relied on business diplomacy and semi-official diplomats to resolve European problems.

Young utilized the techniques of the gentry class in shaping compromises at the reparations conferences during the 1920s. Born in rural New York in 1874, he was an unlikely individual to confront one of the most complex international financial problems in the post-World War I era. His early life was typical of a nineteenth century farm boy with daily work in the fields and a modest education at the local one room schoolhouse. The 160 acre Young farm in Van Hornesville made the family one of the most prominent in the region, but provided only an adequate income by the standards of the day.[5] As one of the first families to settle in the Mohawk Valley, the Youngs considered themselves part of the New York gentry. In his youth Owen D. Young imbibed the ideas of the gentry which included a leadership role in the community and a personal obligation to family, tenants, and neighbors. The gentry endeavored to solve problems in private conferences and to execute the decisions publicly. The gentry had to weigh all the solutions, be just, and find the best compromise under the circumstances.[6] Throughout his life Young took pride in his role as a village leader and frequently returned to Van Hornesville to help solve local problems.

Despite the financial sacrifice involved, his family and friends encouraged him to attend Saint Lawrence University where he emerged a first-rate student and campus leader. Upon graduation, Young delivered the class oration and articulated for the first time his belief that the world would progress steadily in social and economic affairs if leaders of high moral character were called upon to serve in government. This idea of evolutionary progress in society remained a constant in Young's thought throughout his career and can be partially traced to his upbringing in the gentry class.[7] After a successful college career, Young entered Boston University Law School where he excelled as a student and worked both as a bill collector and in a settlement house. His experiences as a law student confirmed and refined Young's basic belief in an evolutionary process toward a better world.[8]

As an attorney Young entered the law practice of Charles H. Tyler in Boston which led him into the burgeoning electrical industry and sharpened his views on the interaction of business and government in society. After becoming Tyler's partner in 1907, Young devoted more and more of his time to the firm of Stone and Webster, a new but important company in the electrical industry.

His work on behalf of Stone and Webster brought Young to the attention of Charles A. Coffin, the president of the General Electric Company, who convinced Young to join that firm in 1912.[9] The move to General Electric set Young on the course to a career in international business and offered him the opportunity to observe and analyze the interaction of big business and government within the sphere of international affairs.

World War I brought dramatic changes and created new challenges for General Electric. The defeat of Germany opened new markets for General Electric and the postwar readjustment in the world balance of power put the American firm into a leadership role in the innovative and expanding electrical industry. General Electric and the newly formed Radio Corporation of America (RCA), which Young organized and headed beginning in 1919, were in a position to shape the course of the anticipated worldwide surge in business activity based on the refinement of electrical equipment. Scientific advancement in communication and transportation, accelerated by the war, seemed to offer opportunities for global business expansion and prosperity unprecedented in history. In Young's view, these advances and the accompanying increase in business activity would usher in an age of greater international cooperation in almost every field. During the Great Depression, Young maintained he had firmly believed in the 1920s that the compression of the world and the close contact among its people, resulting from scientific and technological achievements, would lead to a global society "more closely integrated in peaceful effort, in business interchange, in financial stability, in economic development, in psychological neighborliness."[10]

Although the war opened up vast new opportunities for international firms like General Electric, it also created new problems. Young believed that one of the greatest dangers institutionalized during wartime was the tendency of governments to engage in business activity. Both during and after the war, more and more countries took control of major industries and supervised the operation of both domestic and foreign business affairs. As a firm believer in the capitalist system, Young opposed this trend toward government monopolies, trade restrictions, higher tariffs, and an increase in intense nationalism. In his view, the end result of this process had already appeared in Russia where it was proposed that all business be done by political agencies. Young warned that if government control of business went unchecked it would result in international regulations which would destroy the American political and economic system.[11]

Having served as a business adviser to the government during the war and as an organizer of RCA, Young did not believe that the laissez-faire system of the nineteenth century or the statist system taking shape in Russia were the only alternatives open to society in the postwar era. Like Thomas W. Lamont and others, he was impressed by the potential for government-business cooperation which had been demonstrated during the war and had continued afterward.[12] Most notably, Young saw the advantages of cooperation first hand as the director of RCA, a government-supported but privately run company which held a monopoly over radio communications between the United States and other countries. Young believed that this form of voluntary cooperation between government and business could expand world trade, promote prosperity, and create a climate in which international peace would be maintained.

For Young, however, the cardinal principle behind this kind of voluntary cooperation was that international business activity should indicate the direction of progress toward greater global integration. He maintained that the progression of world business expansion and the accompanying interrelationship of economic units was a fact of life in the twentieth century which political entities and their leaders could not retard. Governments desiring international cooperation in the political field should, therefore, shape their policies to coincide with the movement of economic forces rather than to impede them. "After all," Young told an audience in 1928, "that is the normal way of development. As business becomes more international, we shall necessarily develop not only a more international point of view, but more international machinery; but it will come through the evolution of need."[13] During the 1920s, Young attempted to apply to the complex reparations problem the economic theories which crystalized during the postwar years and the gentry techniques he had learned as a youth.

By the early 1920s, American policymakers believed that the greatest impediment to European economic recovery and future peace was the unresolved problem of German reparations. The United States had an important interest in European recovery and political stability for several reasons. First, Europe, and especially Germany, was an important trading partner. Without a prosperous Europe, American trade, foreign investment, and eventually its entire economy would suffer. Second, the economic breakdown of Europe and the accompanying social upheaval invited the spread of bolshevism on the continent. As the leading capitalist nation, the United States opposed such a development for both ideological and strategic reasons. Finally, the Allies owed America $10 billion in war debts and the prospects for repayment would increase with European recovery.

The major stumbling block to recovery was the huge reparations debt ($33 billion) the Allies had imposed on Germany. This lien on German resources, which many contemporary observers believed could never be paid, discouraged American businessmen from sending the capital needed to begin reconstruction. The small amount of capital flowing from America to the Old World not only retarded recovery, but also posed a threat to the United States in the form of inflation and unemployment at home.[14] In Europe, France was the main obstacle impeding the reconstruction of Germany. The French insisted upon the strict enforcement of the Treaty of Versailles including the collection of reparations to the last centime. In the early postwar period, it was clear that France was attempting to use the reparations issue to keep Germany weak and thus ensure French security. Between 1920 and 1922, France and Germany engaged in a diplomatic struggle that retarded European recovery, increased the possibility of worldwide depression, and endangered peace in Europe. In late 1922, Secretary of State Charles E. Hughes suggested a plan to call a committee of independent financial experts to assess Germany's capacity to pay and to set reparations quotas in a business-like manner. The implementation of the Hughes plan was delayed, however, until after France had exhausted its financial strength during the Ruhr occupation of 1923. By the end of that year, the French reluctantly agreed to support the appointment of an expert committee to study and suggest a temporary solution to the reparations problem.[15]

With the advice and approval of the State Department, the Inter-Allied Reparation Commission appointed Charles G. Dawes, Henry M. Robinson, and Young to serve on two separate expert committees. The primary committee to study reparations was headed by Dawes, an outspoken Chicago banker and first director of the budget, whose name is associated with the expert report of 1924.[16] Young, who had extensive business contacts in Germany, was appointed on the recommendation of Secretary of Commerce Herbert Hoover. Young was the leader of the American delegation and dominated the proceedings at Paris during the winter and spring of 1924. From his perspective, the settlement of the reparations tangle through the application of business principles was only the first step in the overall effort to solve the economic and political problems which resulted from the war. Many European controversies stemmed from the phenomenon of international political indebtedness because reparations and war debts served as a reminder of wartime rivalries and hatreds. Young believed that political disharmony in Europe could be reduced once the open wound caused by the debts was eliminated by commercializing the reparations and war debts.[17]

In late December 1923, Young and Dawes received their instructions from President Coolidge. After an initial round of ceremonial meetings, the president "opened up" to Young and presumably informed him that the committee was to deal exclusively with the reparations problem and not with the related issue of Allied debts. Young supported this strategy because he believed that it would help limit the scope of the conference and thereby increase its chances of success.[18] If the business approach to the reparations problem proved to be effective, Young hoped that the way might be open for the further application of business principles to the entire question of international political indebtedness. Because Coolidge and especially Secretary of Commerce Herbert Hoover had great confidence in Young's abilities as a negotiator and administrator, the president gave Young and Dawes a good deal of latitude in their approach to the Paris conference. Coolidge simply told the experts: "Just remember you are Americans."[19]

Young was optimistic about the prospects for a successful conference for several reasons. First, he believed that the greatest impetus toward the settlement of the reparations problem was the pervasive view that the continuation of economic chaos on the continent would invite the spread of bolshevism. After the conference, Young explained that by the end of 1923 the "Red Terror" had "reached its threatening hand toward chaotic Germany, until finally democracy itself, not only in Europe but here, recognized the ultimate fact that its existence depended upon a right-about-face and upon really facing all the facts of the problem dispassionately and impartially as they affected the world as a whole."[20] Second, by agreeing not to discuss Germany's total reparations bill and avoiding the war debts issue, Young hoped to curtail the kind of acrimonious debates that had led to the failure of previous reparations conferences.[21] Finally, the weakness of the franc made France more receptive to serious discussions of the reparations issue. To arrest the decline of the franc which threatened to undermine the French position of leadership in Europe, France needed the support of Anglo-American bankers, who refused to rescue the franc until France accepted a reasonable reparations settlement. Young and Hughes agreed that the success of the Dawes committee hinged on the rise or fall of the franc. In early 1924, Young was encouraged by the continuing decline of the franc and the support the British government and experts gave to the American delegation.[22]

Despite the favorable climate for a compromise on the reparations issue, Young had to use considerable skill as an administrator to devise a plan which would be acceptable to both the Allies and Germany. Drawing upon his business experience, Young first attempted to sell the idea of a business solution to the world before he started to negotiate a plan. Young believed that he had to go over the heads of the political leaders and gain public support for the experts' mission in order to assure a reasonable chance of governmental acceptance of any reparations formula. In his view, "it was not enough to manufacture a product, even a good product. It must be sold." To accomplish this task, Young turned to General Dawes who rallied world opinion behind the experts.[23]

The main features of the Dawes report, hammered into final form by early April, were not new or unique. Many of the ideas incorporated in the report had been discussed at previous conferences or had been used in the plan for Austrian stabilization in 1923. The plan called for the balancing of the German budget based on a formula of taxation commensurate with the Allied nations. It proposed a method to stabilize the German currency, called for the establishment of a new Reichsbank to aid in the collection and transfer of reparations, and recommended a sizable private loan to help revitalize the German economy.[24] The most important provision of the plan was the transfer clause which provided that Germany was obligated to collect reparations and deposit the sums in the Reichsbank, but was not responsible for transferring the funds to the Allies. An agent general for reparations would be appointed to supervise the German economy and make the transfer of reparations. Young maintained that Germany should only be held accountable for producing and setting aside a surplus and that the Allies must decide how much of that amount they could afford to accept, based on their willingness to receive German exports. "To be precise," Young declared, "we preferred not to speculate on what Germany could pay; we sought a machine which would demonstrate both her *ability* and her *will* to pay."[25]

By placing the burden of transfer on the agent general and the Allies, Young opened the way for a breakthrough in the reparations negotiations. The transfer formula was also a first step in taking the reparations problem out of the realm of politics and putting it in the province of business and financial reality. Beyond this, the report stipulated that if reparations on account at the Reichsbank could not be successfully transferred, as Young suspected would be the case, then these sums would be automatically cancelled. Thus, the plan contained within itself the potential for further reducing reparations below the standard annuity of $625 million which Germany would be expected to pay in 1928, 1929, and thereafter. The transfer mechanism, if it worked as Young envisioned, would not only reduce reparations, but help provide Germany with the needed capital for recovery and lessen its dependence on foreign loans.[26]

Throughout the conference, Young engineered a series of compromises on important issues that averted a breakup of the meeting and eventually led to the unanimous approval of the report on 9 April 1924. The masterful role Young played in negotiating the compromise which produced a final figure for reparations during a standard year might serve as an example of his skill in directing the conference. Young sought to establish a reparations sum high enough to satisfy the French yet low enough to gain the approval of the Germans and the British. As Alan Goldsmith of the American staff of advisers observed, Young accomplished this by quietly placing his own ideas in the mouths of others and allowing them to take credit for the suggestions. Realizing that France posed the greatest obstacle to the final approval of the plan, Young first appeared to support the French position by encouraging Dawes, an admitted Francophile, to win French confidence by pursuing what one American observer described as a "sitting at your feet" policy. Young clearly recognized that countervailing forces such as the fall of the franc and pressure from the British and Germans would force France to settle for less. As the conference progressed, Young, while ostensibly remaining in the French camp, allowed other experts to reduce gradually his initial figure until it was actually less than the original British proposal.[27] By employing this strategy, which was based on his gentry training, he soothed sensitive French feelings and gained their approval of a standard annuity which was far below what they might have accepted under different circumstances. Later, Young worked together with Ambassador Alanson B. Houghton to gain German approval of the standard annuity and the Dawes Plan.[28]

After the unanimous ratification of the report by the experts in April, Young remained in Europe to aid in gaining approval of the report by the interested governments and by the private bankers who were expected to raise a loan for Germany. At the London Conference, which was held during July and August, Young teamed up with a group of American official and unofficial participants in an effort to convince the French and German governments to accept the

Dawes Plan. The Americans, working in conjunction with the British and Belgian delegates, skillfully played on French economic weakness and the threat that this was their last effort to help Europe, to bring about the necessary compromises by the respective governments. The French agreement to evacuate the Ruhr within a year and Germany's acceptance of that time limit paved the way for the ratification of the report by the concerned powers.[29]

The last obstacle before the plan could go into operation was the task of negotiating an agreement with international bankers to float a loan for Germany. J. P. Morgan and Company, the dominant firm in international finance, was hesitant about contracting the loan because of the ambiguous language in the London Agreements concerning the powers of the Reparation Commission to declare Germany in default and the right of the bankers to have a first lien on German resources ahead of reparations payments. The bankers, in effect, wanted a revision of the treaty that would prohibit France from interfering in German affairs.[30] After the French Senate officially ratified the London Agreements in late August, Young focused his attention on the necessity of curbing the powers of the Reparation Commission in order to satisfy the bankers. He realized that the "Commission had great powers under the Treaty, and unless the Treaty was amended so as to abolish the Commission, it necessarily had great control over the Dawes Plan." Because "it was then too early to amend the Treaty," Young attempted to revise unofficially the Versailles document by undermining the powers of the commission. At the London Conference, Young had been instrumental in writing a section of the agreement which provided for an American to sit on the commission "with substantially full powers." In Young's view, the American member, Thomas N. Perkins, would "have great influence, if not indeed pretty much the final say on any questions affecting the Dawes Plan."[31] During the late summer of 1924, Young attempted to convince the bankers that Perkins would stand as a bulwark against any dangerous interference by the French-dominated Reparation Commission in the internal affairs of Germany. In early October, Young made a further effort to satisfy the bankers' requirement that the Dawes loan be a first charge on German resources. He appeared before the Reparation Commission with a set of stipulations which would guarantee this principle. According to one witness, he handled the meeting brilliantly, and by the evening of 10 October the commission had agreed to his proposals.[32]

A short time later, Morgan and Company agreed to offer a loan to Germany. On 14 October American subscribers took $110 million in Dawes loan bonds while another $400–$900 million worth of prospective subscriptions had to be turned down. European investors took what was left of the $191 million loan. The Dawes loan was an unqualified success and the plan was ready to go into operation.

Young had meanwhile been chosen agent general ad interim in order to set up the Dawes Plan machinery for the permanent agent general, Seymour

Parker Gilbert, a former under secretary of the treasury. During his short tenure as agent general, Young, in conjunction with Perkins, was able to "maintain the independence of executive action by the Agent General" and reduce the Reparation Commission to a kind of board of directors on broad policies. After six weeks on the job, Young reported that there was now a "new spirit determined to restore tranquility in Western Europe." If this spirit continued, he maintained, then the Dawes Plan would work: "It will work irrespective of whether it is as good as its most ardent supporters believe or as bad as its worst enemies charge."[33] And work it did. Germany recovered rapidly from the economic chaos of 1923 and Europe attained a high degree of prosperity by 1928. In addition, the plan paved the way for the Locarno Pacts of 1925, Germany's entrance into the League of Nations in 1926, and the reestablishment of the gold standard in Europe.

In later years, the massive loans to Germany which followed the Dawes loan became one of the most controversial parts of the reparations plan. From 1924 to 1928 large amounts of short-term credit, mainly from America, provided Germany with the necessary budget surplus to make reparations payments. Young and the other experts have been criticized for shaping a plan which, in effect, supplied Germany with American money to meet reparations quotas, which was subsequently transferred back to the United States in the form of war debts payments. Critics of the Dawes Plan have emphasized that this tripartite system was dangerous in that any curtailment of short-term loans from America, which occurred in the late 1920s, would cause the plan to collapse and seriously disrupt the international economy.[34]

It should be pointed out that Young never envisioned that the loans would be used, even indirectly, to provide Germany with the surplus to maintain a reparations account for the Allies. He maintained that loans should be supplied for reproductive purposes and then only for a short period in order to allow Germany to expand its economy and thus raise reparations from its own resources.[35] Young anticipated that reparations would build up in Germany due to the unwillingness of the Allies to accept transfers and that this reserve might be used by Germany as capital to rebuild its economy. The experts did not consider the problem of large-scale foreign lending to Germany because there was no evidence that investors would be attracted to the German market on the basis of its performance in early 1924.[36] Young might be justly criticized for being too optimistic about the ability of Germany to recover from the war on its own and for failing to anticipate how the transfer mechanism would actually work. But it is important to note that he viewed the plan as a temporary solution to the reparations problem and that he recognized from the beginning that it would have to be revised to conform with the economic reality which it would help to reveal. The transfer crisis which developed in 1927 and 1928 was not the fault of Young or the other experts, but of the excessive optimism which the plan generated in both Europe and America.

During the first two years of the Dawes Plan, Young was both encouraged and troubled by the course of European recovery. Germany and Europe had emerged from the financial crisis of 1923 into a period of prosperity which contributed to a new spirit of political conciliation. But this success revealed a number of problems that threatened to undermine European recovery and upset the international financial system. In addition to the problem of German short-term loans, Young was concerned about Europe's ability to discharge its large war debt to America. He believed that it was America's responsibility to make concessions on trade and/or war debt policies which might lighten the financial burden on the debtor nations and help lay the basis for long-term economic and political stability in Europe. In October 1925 Young outlined what he conceived to be America's obligation to the world in a letter to Joseph Tumulty, President Wilson's former secretary. He stated that the United States, as the creditor nation of the world, could no longer consider its tariff, fiscal policy, or agricultural problem as separate domestic issues isolated from international events. "We can no longer act solely for ourselves," Young wrote, because "our every act involves something in the nature of a trusteeship for others." Young recommended that America meet the problems affecting the whole world with wisdom, courage, and generosity.[37]

Expanding on this theme in early 1926, Young wrote to Herbert Hoover, criticizing America's trade and tariff policies. In reviewing the interrelated problems of European war debts and artificial trade restrictions, Young told Hoover, who spoke for the Coolidge administration on these matters, that "our position would be much stronger in criticizing their artificial restraints if we did not indulge in them ourselves, and at the same time demand extraordinary payments." Young argued that "the establishment and maintenance of sound currencies abroad, the export of our gold for that purpose, the creation of export markets for our agricultural and other produce, is so much more important, in my mind, than the collection of these war debts that I regret their very existence." As a solution to the war debts problem, Young suggested that the debts should be reduced and commercialized.[38]

By early 1928, other financial leaders in both America and Europe shared many of Young's concerns about the international financial system. With reparations payments scheduled to rise to the standard level the following year, there was a growing fear that Germany might default. Benjamin Strong, chairman of the Federal Reserve Bank of New York, was particularly concerned that a default might cause a suspension of service on the substantial American loans to Germany and a financial crisis in America. In late 1927, Strong encouraged Gilbert to sound out Allied and German leaders concerning the possibility of seeking a final settlement of the reparations problem in the near future.[39] During early 1928, Gilbert laid the groundwork for the organization of a new expert committee. He gained British and French support for a new settlement by agreeing that the total reparations sum should be more than enough to cover their war debts obligations to America. Gilbert proposed that an expert committee similar to the Dawes committee should set a final sum for Germany to pay, that transfer protection be eliminated, and that bonds be issued which might allow for the future commercialization of the reparations debt. On 16 September the Allied and German governments formally accepted Gilbert's formula and called for a new committee to meet in early 1929.[40]

During 1928 Gilbert had kept Young informed on the progress of the negotiations leading to the appointment of the committee. He urged Young to support the long-standing American position that reparations and war debts were not interconnected and that the reparations question must be settled on its own merits. After that had been accomplished, he told Young, the United States might be willing to revise the war debt agreements. Although Gilbert assured Young that the circumstances surrounding the creation of the new inquiry were "not very different" from those which had prevailed in 1924, it was clear that the forthcoming conference would be severely restricted by political agreements made prior to its appointment. In an effort to gain both Allied and American support for a new settlement, Gilbert seemed to both affirm and deny any direct link between reparations and war debts.[41] It was mainly due to his assurance that the war debts would not be officially discussed by the new committee that Coolidge approved American participation in the inquiry. The president once again asked Young to serve as an unofficial American expert, and he was appointed on 19 January 1929.[42]

The task before Young and the other experts was more difficult than that which they had faced in 1924. During the previous conference an atmosphere of crisis had gripped Europe; any reparations settlement seemed preferable to none at all. By 1929, however, Europe had entered into a period of relative prosperity and political stability which lessened the apparent urgency for a new reparations plan. In addition, the Coolidge administration was divided on the subject of whether or not the war debts issue should be discussed at the conference. Young believed that the war debts would have to be considered in any settlement and hoped that the experts would propose a plan for the mutual reduction and early commercialization of both reparations and war debts.[43]

When Young was appointed chairman of the expert conference on 9 February, the American government was placed in a difficult position with regard to its stand on the war debts issue. Coolidge had instructed the American experts to play a secondary role at the conference with the objective of aiding the European powers in setting a definitive reparations schedule. Young had assured the president that the experts' task would be only to revise the Dawes Plan. In early February Coolidge informed White House reporters that while he could not prevent the Allies from discussing the war debts in Paris, any decision that they might reach on the subject would not be binding on the United States.[44] With Young as chairman of the conference, however, it would be difficult for the American experts to dissociate themselves completely from any discussion of the war debts issue. The resulting confusion over the precise mission of the American delegation later led to a serious controversy between Young and Hoover when the new administration took office.[45]

Even before he was appointed chairman, Young viewed his instructions from Coolidge as only a general guideline for the American experts. Despite his public statement to the president that the "new Plan would be merely supplementary to the Dawes Plan," Young thought that the experts should determine what was necessary to revise the reparations system. Apparently, Young still held out some hope that Allied pressure at the conference might force the United States to alter its position on the war debts issue and thus open the way for a general reduction and early commercialization of the international political debts.[46] Shortly after the inquiry began, however, Young became convinced that "the Allies really did not want the debts to be cancelled." He later explained to his assistant, Everett N. Case, that the Allied experts' acceptance of the war debts as an established fact determined the nature of the final settlement right from the start. The Allies wanted to stand by the pre-conference agreements and link the new reparations settlement to the existing war debts structure. That kind of solution, Young recalled, was one with which "I was personally not in sympathy, so far as the debt situation was concerned." But Young concluded that if the Allies wanted a reparations settlement based on the premise that the war debts were going to be paid in full, he would accept that fact and try to work out a plan along those lines.[47] It appeared that the expert committee had been assembled to ratify the political decisions made prior to the conference.

During the first weeks of the inquiry, however, Young developed an idea for a new world bank which changed the focus of the conference and directed the reparations problem toward a business rather than a political solution. The inspiration for the creation of the Bank for International Settlements (BIS) came from several sources. On 22 February, the Belgian expert Emile Francqui suggested to Young a scheme for establishing a bank to handle reparations receipts and war debts payments. The following day Hjalmar Schacht, the German representative and president of the Reichsbank, placed before Young a tentative proposal for a new credit bank to help increase German and world trade. Although he had some objections to both suggestions, Young and his advisers studied the matter and were convinced that a bank should be an integral part of the plan. The Americans had not been caught unprepared because Shepard Morgan and J. A. M. Sanchez, two financial advisers assigned to the delegation, had discussed a similar organization during the summer of 1928. In typical gentry fashion, Young decided to combine some features from both the Francqui and Schacht proposals with the ideas of his own staff to create the BIS.[48] During late February, Young and his advisers worked frantically to draft a blueprint for a new bank which would rid the world of all war agencies associated with reparations and replace them with "machinery essentially commercial in character." The final version of the BIS went far beyond the initial proposals. As a bank for central bankers under business control, the BIS could serve as a clearinghouse for international accounts, earmark gold, swap foreign exchange between central banks, and solve problems inherent in the gold exchange system. For Young, the BIS was an instrument which might help to remove the reparations problem from the sphere of politics and allow business leaders to make decisions that would eventually eliminate all international political indebtedness associated with the war. The BIS might serve as an organ through which economic force and business activity could overshadow the selfish nationalism of the postwar years in setting the course of future world development. It is little wonder that Young later regarded the bank as "the most constructive job done in our generation."[49]

While the experts worked out the details of the new bank, Young opened negotiations concerning the amount, schedule, and distribution of reparations payments. In these discussions, he found that the creditors were determined to link reparations and war debts. To avoid a deadlock on the linkage question, Young suggested a two-tier system of reparations: a smaller amount of reparations bonds which would be unconditionally transferable and thus suitable for commercialization, and a larger share of bonds which would be conditionally transferable and thus postponable during economic emergencies. The reparations annuities were to run for fifty-nine years, the same as the American war debts schedules. During the last twenty-two years the German obligations would correspond with the Allied payments to America. For the first thirty-seven years reparations would average $512 million dollars per annum which was close to the amount Gilbert had mentioned in the pre-conference agreements. In addition to lowering the annuities, the proposal held another advantage for the United States. The service on regular private loans to Germany would have priority over the conditional reparations annuities. The danger of a "transfer crisis" which had worried Strong and other financiers under the terms of the Dawes Plan was now minimized.[50] In March, Young cabled the State Department to report on the discussion of reparations figures he had suggested and to outline the idea for establishing a new bank which he described as having great possibilities in resolving all future debt settlements.[51]

On 8 April the recently installed Hoover administration responded to Young's reports in such a negative and insulting manner that Young nearly resigned from the expert committee. The controversy that erupted between Young and Hoover over the war debts issue and the BIS highlights one of the fundamental weaknesses of America's European diplomacy in the 1920s. Young, as an independent agent appointed with the approval of his government, had attempted to deal with the reparations problem in a manner that would protect American interests and at the same time conform with the realities of international finance. Hoover, who saw the war debts as a political lever to influence European affairs, feared that the close linkage between war debts and reparations in the proposed schedule might place unwarranted pressure on the United States to further reduce or cancel the debts. The president was also concerned about congressional reaction to a reparations plan which appeared to make America the ultimate creditor of Germany and called for Federal Reserve participation in an international bank.[52] The Hoover-Young dispute demonstrates the difficulties the United States confronted in attempting to conduct European diplomacy under the aegis of unofficial representatives. America's European economic policy was often imprecise and sometimes contradictory. Although the Hoover-Young controversy was largely resolved in 1929, it would become more difficult to coordinate American public and business policies toward Europe after the Depression began in the 1930s.

After reading the reports from Paris, Hoover was convinced that Young had made a "complete departure" from his instructions. In a telegram drafted by Under Secretary of the Treasury Ogden Mills and approved by the president, Secretary of State Henry Stimson criticized Young and his associates for failing "to maintain the position consistently taken by their Government" and warned that their action "may have unfortunate consequences in the future in so far as the protection of America's interests are concerned." Stimson stated bluntly "that under no circumstances" would an official of the Federal Reserve be permitted to serve as director of the BIS or to name a director and that "our Government would consider it most unfortunate . . . if the proposed payments by Germany are divided into two categories, one of which is to be made to correspond exactly to payments by Allied Governments to this country."[53] Young was shocked by both the tone and content of the cable and considered resigning from the committee at once. He did not understand how Hoover, whom he considered a personal friend, could have approved such a derogatory message as his first official communication with the experts. After a meeting with Republican elder statesman Elihu Root in Paris, Young decided to continue his work with the committee. But he made it clear to Root, who was departing for America, that unless there was some change or modification in the administration's position on the war debts and bank issues he would resign and give a plain disclosure of the reasons therefore.[54]

Several days later, Young sent two cables to Washington that were remark-ably mild and explanatory considering his anger and humiliation. In the official reply to the State Department, he attempted to clear up some misconceptions contained in Stimson's message. Young maintained that if a coincidence existed between the reparations and war debts payments "it is a coincidence of fact which is inherent in [the] situation which [the] Committee of Experts cannot escape." He also pointed out that the BIS would not short-circuit reparations receipts into war debts payments and that official Federal Reserve participation was not necessary if private American bankers could be appointed to the bank's board of directors. In a second private message to Secretary of the Treasury Andrew Mellon, Young stated pungently that "such an indictment by one's country . . . cannot fail to hurt, and it is difficult for us to believe that it was not intended for that purpose."[55]

As the Hoover administration considered its options, Young and Thomas Lamont, a Morgan partner and alternate American expert, kept pressure on the government to modify its position on the two important issues. Young made it known through the American embassy in Paris, and presumably through Root, that the Allies might use the new American objections to the proposed settlement as an excuse to break up the conference and place the blame on Washington. As tempers cooled in early May, Young and the State Department worked out a compromise which prevented a premature ending of the conference. The administration gave its qualified support to the BIS and approved private American participation on its board of directors. Washington also agreed to waive a percentage of Army costs due the United States as part of the expense for occupying the Rhineland after the war. For his part, Young managed to delete from the official report a section which stated that Germany would receive a reduction of reparations to the extent of two-thirds the amount of any diminution of Allied war debts.[56] Although war debts and reparations were still linked in fact, the deletion of this passage served as a cosmetic which the administration believed would lessen congressional opposition to the Young Plan.

Young's clash with his own government was but one of many crises which threatened to break up the conference. Schacht of Germany protested against the reparations schedules on a number of occasions and temporarily withdrew from the conference in mid-April. When tension built up within the committee, Young quickly ended meetings before delegates made rash statements which might jeopardize the success of the conference. He later recalled that "whenever I saw Schacht's neck getting red or hands trembling I adjourned the conference." In the end, it was Young's idea to create the new and dynamic world bank by assimilating German and Belgian concepts into a vastly superior organization that made the eventual settlement, in his words, "too dear to take, yet too cheap to leave."[57]

On 7 June 1929 the experts signed the Young Plan and submitted it to the Reparation Commission. With the conference successfully concluded, Young turned his attention to the problem of convincing the various governments to accept the report without major revisions. He immediately returned to America and made an appointment with Hoover to discuss the report and iron out the personal differences between them. On 25 June, Lamont and Young met with Hoover and Stimson in a tense conference at the White House. Young later recalled that by the end of the meeting Hoover realized that no government decree in the world could stop the participation of the Federal Reserve in the BIS. The president adamantly maintained, however, that the Federal Reserve should have no official connection with the new bank and that the United States was not going to have a hand in the plan in any way. Although he was relieved to learn that Hoover would not openly oppose the report, Young was disappointed with the administration's decision not to ratify it. Young told his assistant that "what they ought to do if they think it is harmful — and I would have some respect for them if they did it — is to say that I should be shot as a traitor; otherwise they ought to welcome me with open arms for having done a good job."[58]

The ratification of the Young Plan by the European governments was delayed for almost a year due to a series of disputes among the Allies and Germany concerning the distribution of reparations payments and sanctions against Germany in case of default. Britain, under the leadership of Chancellor of the Exchequer Philip Snowden, created the most difficult problem by demanding a larger percentage of reparations than was provided for in the report. Young was convinced that the lack of enthusiasm for the plan in Washington "served more or less as an encouragement to Snowden." The disputes over the distribution of reparations and sanctions were finally resolved at two separate conferences in the Hague during August 1929 and January 1930, with Germany making substantial concessions in both cases.[59]

France and Britain also had objections about the private character of the BIS and the proposed American control over the new bank. During the summer of 1929, Young worked in concert with Lamont and J. P. Morgan to make it clear to the Allied powers that, unless the BIS remained a private organization outside the control of governments and under American directorship, the United States would not cooperate in the bank project. Lamont echoed Young's view when he informed Snowden that in the event of the BIS scheme being changed "we shall see no American cooperation of any kind." The pressure the Morgan partners and Young exerted on the Allied governments resulted in an agreement at Baden-Baden, Germany in October 1929 in which the BIS was organized along the lines Young had originally envisioned. What should have been Young's final triumph in his long struggle to resolve the reparations problem came on 17 May 1930 when the major interested powers, with the exception of the United States, officially ratified the second expert report, bringing the Young Plan and the BIS into operation.[60]

From the perspective of 1930, the reparations plans of 1924 and 1929 were a success. The settlements helped to provide Europe with a degree of economic and political stability which in turn reduced the hatred and bitterness associated with the war. Europe was relatively prosperous in early 1930 and had made great strides toward solving war-related problems through mutual cooperation. Although the Young Plan did not provide a final solution to the problem of international political indebtedness, it was a step forward. Reparations were at last definitively set, yearly payments were further reduced, and the reparations control agencies were removed from Germany. With the establishment of the BIS, the apparatus existed for the eventual commercialization of reparations bonds and war debts claims. In addition, the new bank offered the prospect of streamlining the system of international exchange and providing more efficiency and stability in world-wide commercial operations. The French evacuation of the Rhineland in 1930, moreover, was linked to the ratification of the

Young Plan and offered further evidence of the growing spirit of conciliation in Europe.

During the early 1930s, however, the Young Plan collapsed under the weight of the worldwide depression of 1929. In the following decades, the words *reparations* and *war debts* became almost synonymous with the alleged shortsightedness of America's European diplomacy in the 1920s. Historians criticized government leaders and businessmen alike for dealing with the indebtedness problem in a selfish and inept manner and for contributing to the economic collapse of the 1930s.[61] Although Young remained active in political affairs for a number of years after 1930, his reputation as an international financial expert suffered because his name was inextricably linked with the ill-fated reparations plan of 1929. Until recently, historians have passed over him as a minor figure associated with America's unsound economic diplomacy in the 1920s.[62]

This brief examination of Young's role as a reparations expert shows that he made an important contribution toward the reduction of European tensions in the postwar decade. Young attempted to utilize America's economic power to help reconstruct Europe and thereby stabilize and pacify the war-torn continent. He believed that if governments would only follow the natural economic movements instead of trying to shape them, the result would be greater prosperity, political cooperation, and world peace. From his perspective, the settlement of the reparations problem through the use of business methods was only the first step in an overall effort to resolve the economic and political problems resulting from the Great War. By commercializing the international wartime indebtedness, Young believed that much of the bitterness associated with the war would diminish and open the way for a new spirit of cooperation to take hold in Europe. He also maintained that by improving and streamlining commercial operations, through such institutions as the BIS, world prosperity would increase, economic problems could be more easily solved, and political tensions reduced. In the process, Young hoped that national leaders would see the wisdom of solving international economic issues through business methods and that they would construct policies on such issues as reparations, war debts, tariffs, and foreign loans to conform with the business interrelationships that would shape world commerce in the coming decades. If this could be accomplished, Young maintained, the source of many international disputes could be eliminated and his generation could pass the reins of leadership to a new generation, confident that it had constructed a solid foundation for future peace. By 1930, Young had made considerable progress toward the achievement of these goals.

Young's service as a reparations expert also demonstrates the strengths and weaknesses of America's unofficial economic diplomacy in Europe during the 1920s. United States policy was predicated on the close cooperation between business and government leaders who together hoped to stabilize conditions in Europe. When the two groups had similar objectives and worked in relative harmony, as in the case of the Dawes Plan, economic diplomacy worked well. The first reparations plan marked an important advancement in America's attempt to ameliorate war-related tensions in Europe. Between 1924 and 1929, American government leaders were content to exercise only a small amount of control over businessmen and unofficial diplomats who were attempting to promote European recovery and stability.

Toward the end of the decade, however, the cooperative efforts of business and government leaders began to break down as evidenced in the Hoover-Young dispute of 1929. Hoover became increasingly convinced that there was a disparity between the objectives of the American international business community and the national interests of the United States. More than any other president in the postwar decade, Hoover questioned the assumption that the advancement of international business always benefited the United States and that government leaders should subordinate other national priorities in favor of international business objectives. By the early 1930s, the cooperative relationship between Washington and Wall Street, which had been tenuous at best during the 1920s, further deteriorated in the face of the mounting economic crisis.

It should be noted that American economic diplomacy worked reasonably well in the postwar decade. The Republican administrations, with the aid of unofficial diplomats like Owen D. Young, played an important and constructive role in European affairs with a minimum of domestic political risk and helped to lay a foundation for future peace on the continent. The Great Depression destroyed this foundation and has helped to obscure the nature of America's European diplomacy and Young's role in carrying out that policy. It is Young's historical misfortune that the foundations of economic and political stability he helped to construct at the reparations conferences of the 1920s were swept away during the economic crisis of the 1930s. Historians have only recently begun to appreciate the positive side of America's European diplomacy in the postwar decade.[63]

John B. Stetson, Jr.

John B. Stetson, Jr.

1884	Born 14 October in Philadelphia, Pennsylvania
1906	A.B. from Harvard University
1912	Founded Defiance Manufacturing Company
1917–20	Pilot and captain, U.S. Army Air Service
1920	Published translation of *The Histories of Brazil* (by Pero Magalhaes)
1925–29	Minister to Poland
1930–36	Member of New York Stock Exchange
1936	Retired
1952	Died 15 November in Elkins Park, Pennsylvania

CHAPTER 4

John B. Stetson, Jr. and Poland:
The Diplomacy of a Prophet Scorned

Frank Costigliola

In 1926 John B. Stetson, Jr., the American minister to Poland, prophesied:

> Germany will use American capital for her political ends which will threaten the integrity of Poland and cause war. War in Europe will jeopardize American investments and probably give Europe over to Bolshevism.[1]

Stetson regarded as inviolate the Versailles treaty and its territorial arrangements including the German-Polish border. He urged Washington to launch a program of massive economic and political action to safeguard Poland's territory. Stetson was an accurate prophet, but he lacked credibility in the State Department. Department officials shared Stetson's concern for European peace and stability. Yet they opposed political entanglements and disagreed with Stetson on the Versailles treaty issue. On the one hand, Washington officials feared that rigid enforcement of the treaty would lead to an explosion of German resentment and possibly another war. On the other hand, they were unwilling to undertake the risk or responsibility of initiating treaty change. Administration Republicans preferred a course of subtly encouraging moderate, peaceful treaty revision. As minister to Poland from 1925 to 1929, Stetson learned the limits of America's commitment and Poland's tractability. His education highlighted the nature and dilemmas of United States foreign policy in the 1920s.

Washington's caution stemmed from domestic political restraints and foreign policy strategy. In the 1920 presidential campaign, Republican candidate Warren G. Harding wobbled successfully enough on the League of Nations issue that he won votes from both League opponents and advocates. After Harding's victory, however, senators irreconcilably against the League threatened to wreck the new administration unless the president renounced the international organization and formal political involvement with Europe.[2] Harding's compliance disappointed his chief foreign policymakers, Secretary of State Charles E. Hughes and Secretary of Commerce Herbert Hoover. Hughes and Hoover believed that the League, freed of the Article X collective security provision, could be an effective instrument to stabilize Europe, revive important markets, and reform the Versailles treaty.[3]

Despite the setback, the Harding administration adapted tools of unofficial, economic diplomacy to accomplish these objectives. Hughes restored American representation on the Reparation Commission with unofficial observers. Such delegates, Hughes believed, "represent[ed] the government as 'completely'" as official ones.[4] He signed a separate peace with Germany which skirted congressional obstruction and secured the rights of Versailles without the responsibilities. Hughes then stage-managed the Washington Naval Conference to limit the naval race, buttress the open door in China, and abrogate the Anglo-Japanese alliance.[5] Hoover, who accepted the commerce post on the condition that he would share in foreign policymaking, geared up the Bureau of Foreign and Domestic Commerce as an efficient engine promoting foreign trade.[6] Hoover was also head of the private American Relief Administration (ARA). In this capacity he undertook a food relief program to Russia during the 1921–23 famine. Hoover was frustrated in his hope that the ARA would provide the inspiration for capitalist reconstruction when the Bolshevik regime collapsed. Yet Hoover's adept financing and direction of the $87 million venture testified to the utility of unofficial, economic diplomacy.[7] In 1924, Hughes and Hoover crowned this success with the Dawes Plan. The plan's dependence on businessmen and private loans epitomized the unofficial, economic approach. The scheme stabilized German finances, smoothed the path for Locarno, and, most significantly, loosened Versailles's grip on Berlin.[8]

This kind of gradual, peaceful revision of the Versailles treaty, undertaken in an atmosphere of political good feeling and economic good times, is what Americans favored throughout the 1919–32 period. Americans believed peaceful change and international reform was the happy medium between the extremes of revolutionary upheaval and sterile rigidity — which might also lead to a blow up. In the relatively stable and prosperous 1920s, American advocacy of peaceful change was implicit in support for the Dawes Plan and Locarno pacts which meliorated Germany's status. In 1931–32, with worsening political extremism in Europe, the Hoover administration called explicitly for peaceful treaty revision, particularly on the German-Polish border. Peaceful change — not Stetson's idea of treaty enforcement nor Woodrow Wilson's dream of collective security — remained the Republican formula. Once domestic opposition killed the issue of participation in the League, Hughes and Hoover pursued pacific, stabilizing change through economic, unofficial diplomacy.[9]

Apart from the domestic political restraints, administration Republicans believed that foreign policy strategy dictated a policy of cautious, limited involvement in Europe. America's position as the most powerful nation in the world was a cliché of the 1920s.[10] This reputation rested primarily on America's economic might, easily translatable into military power as World War I had demonstrated. The United States also earned credit as a disinterested mediator by remaining aloof from European quarrels. Washington officials saved this asset, and in the Dawes Plan negotiations they drew on it to secure a vital European settlement. Europeans also respected America's apparent success in solving the problems of machine age, mass society. They looked to the United States for ideas, institutions, values, methods, and gadgets to cope with the modernization indigenous to both continents but most advanced in North America. Whether delighted or disgusted, many Europeans believed their continent was becoming "Americanized."[11] This cultural leadership, coupled with America's political neutrality and economic preponderance, generated prestige or what people in the 1920s termed moral power. Moral power was a valuable but inexpensive tool in international relations. Administration Republicans shrewdly calculated that they could safeguard American strength and protect the national interest most efficiently with limited, judicious application of their superior power. It was essential, Hughes recalled, to "safeguard prestige of the U.S.A. and not lower it by futile acts." If America lost its reputation for success, he explained, it would "be less effective in international affairs."[12]

The extent to which America used — or did not use — its preeminent power was a crucial factor in the German-Polish border issue. In his Fourteen Points, Woodrow Wilson called for an independent Poland with secure access to the sea. This led to the separation of East Prussia from the rest of Germany, the detachment of Danzig, and the creation of the Polish corridor. The territorial arrangement rankled Germans after World War I and provided the spark which set off World War II.

Unlike Minister Stetson, most American political and business leaders who commented on the issue sympathized with Germany. Alanson B. Houghton, ambassador to Berlin and London in the 1920s, pointed to the border as "the point where the next great war will begin."[13] Sharing with other Americans a low opinion of Polish capabilities, Houghton condemned the border as "uneconomic" since the Poles were incapable of developing their resources. "Economic needs," he asserted, "will require . . . [a] peaceful readjustment of the eastern frontier."[14] Although many Americans did not fully share Houghton's pro-German feelings, they agreed that Poland's borders were probably not permanent. "The fact of Russia on one side and Germany on the other . . . does not seem to indicate the brightest possible future for Poland," predicted State Department official William R. Castle, and "if something should happen to start trouble, . . . the nutcracker would inevitably crack."[15] With massive German investments, American bankers were prone to agree with Thomas Lamont of J. P. Morgan and Company that "it might settle a lot of things if Germany could have back the darned old Polish corridor."[16]

In 1931–32, the Hoover administration tried to strengthen German moderates against rising extremists by escalating American support for peaceful treaty revision. Washington rejected Paris's attempt to link financial aid to Berlin with a ten year moratorium on Versailles revision.[17] Secretary of State Henry L. Stimson concluded that:

> the political questions of the Eastern Boundary of Germany underlay the whole question, not only of disarmament but of the economic rehabilitation of Europe and of the whole peace of Europe.[18]

Acting on this analysis, Stimson and President Hoover urged visiting French Premier Pierre Laval to press his Polish ally to accept peaceful border revision. Laval refused, but this did not alter American opinion of the 1919 settlement. "I don't like Versailles," Hoover told Stimson, "I never did."[19] Washington was less eager to appease Berlin after the accession of right-wing Franz von Papen in June 1932 and Adolf Hitler in January 1933. Yet in the 1920s and early 1930s, the United States tilted toward Germany and peaceful border change.

Despite this sentiment, Washington did not make political or military commitments on the border issue. That would have generated domestic opposition and foreign entanglements. Instead, Washington counseled moderation and encouraged American bankers to stabilize with loans the German and Polish economies. Americans hoped rising prosperity would ease political tensions and peaceful change. Here, too, America favored Germany over Poland.

United States bankers loaned money to both Germany and Poland, and former treasury officials became financial advisers in Berlin and Warsaw. However, the parallel was only superficial. American loans to Germany from 1924 to 1929 were eight times those to Poland in the same period.[20] S. Parker Gilbert, the agent general for reparations under the Dawes Plan, had served as undersecretary of the treasury and remained a confidant of key Washington officials.[21] Charles S. Dewey, the financial adviser to Poland under the terms of the 1927 stabilization loan, had left his post as assistant secretary of the treasury partly out of pique at being passed over for the position of undersecretary. While in Poland he never enjoyed Gilbert's intimacy with Washington leaders.[22] These differences symbolized the American approach to German-Polish rivalry.

United States leaders were unwilling to become entangled in the German-Polish dispute. Yet they appreciated Germany's stability, profitability, and compatibility with American institutions. Consequently they tended to sympathize with German revisionist ambitions. Ironically, this sentiment contrasted sharply with the opinions of the United States minister in Warsaw.

John B. Stetson, Jr., was a man of varied talents. Although he inherited a good part of the John B. Stetson Company, a leading hat producer, he founded his own business, the Defiance Manufacturing Company. In World War I, the Philadelphian flew in the Air Service. Soon after, he translated into English the two-volumed *Histories of Brazil* by Pero Magalhaes. Stetson was a curator of Portuguese literature at Harvard, from which he graduated in 1906. But John Stetson was foremost a progressive businessman. In July 1925, President Calvin

Coolidge rewarded the 41-year-old manufacturer with the Warsaw post for his political loyalty and contributions.[23] True to his entrepreneurial instincts, Stetson tried to aggrandize the far-off post into a major center of United States political, economic, and cultural influence.

Shortly after arriving in Warsaw on 30 August 1925, Stetson recommended to the United States government a far-ranging program of financial and political action. Ravaged by war, inflation, and disorganization, the Polish economy needed, he explained, foreign capital and control. He urged that the Federal Reserve System, in close cooperation with the State Department, grant the Polish government a large loan. It was essential that Americans supervise the loan's expenditure. Stetson insisted: "control should be positive and sweeping. Poland needs to learn self-restraint, self-discipline, and how to work."[24] In addition to indoctrinating Poles with the work ethic, Stetson wanted to introduce American business methods, particularly "business financing and accounting. . . . The Poles must change their [banking] law to bring it into harmony with ours," the minister decided.[25] The expansion into Europe of American branch plants and the business ideology of Frederick Taylor and Henry Ford were transforming Old World concepts of the work ethic and worker efficiency. What Stetson wanted was the United States government itself to oversee the modernization of a backward European state.[26]

Such American intervention was necessary, Stetson asserted, because Poland and the United States faced, in different degrees, the same threats: aggressive Germany and Bolshevist Russia. Rebuilt with American loans, Germany already was pressuring Poland economically and would soon do so militarily.[27] The Reich determined to retake the Polish corridor, the minister predicted, and that meant war. Consequently it was "necessary for someone to hold Germany back." Washington could do it by forbidding any further loans until Berlin renounced territorial revision in the east as it had done in the west through the Locarno pact. "The United States cannot give free rein to American bankers," Stetson emphasized, "without fomenting a war in Europe." War would wreck American investments and European capitalism.[28]

The former businessman believed that European capitalism's safety depended on American aid to Poland. Failure to help that capitalist outpost threatened "the turning of the country to Bolshevism, thereby breaking down the wall between the [U]SSR and the rest of Europe." He linked Russian Bolsheviks with home-grown Polish leftists. The danger from the left underscored the loan's importance. The money would, Stetson hoped, "vindicat[e] . . . the Right parties and . . . diminish the power of the Socialists and Radicals." In sum, he argued that Poland needed United States money and management in order to uphold its precarious position between Germany and Russia.[29]

America also stood to benefit from such aid, the minister promised. Old Worlders were obsessed with America's economic predominance which they believed had "drained . . . all the wealth of the world . . . out of Europe."

Consequently, Europeans wanted to "imitate... American business methods." Simultaneously Europe was "jealous of and hate[d] the United States." Stetson foresaw a tariff union of England, France, Germany, and Japan that would copy American mass production methods while shutting out American goods. To outflank this group, he recommended that America encourage a union of the eastern European agricultural producers centered on Poland. By controlling the sources of most of western Europe's food imports, Washington could "prevent the three western manufacturing states from boycotting the United States." Stetson dreamed that from its base in eastern Europe, America could win "control over the Asiatic market" once the Russian Bolsheviks fell.[30] The hat king did not think small.

Stetson's ideas were grandiose, but they rested on a solid foundation. He understood Washington's opposition to political entanglements. Yet official policy flowed counter to the flood of American loans. "All money which comes to Europe," he observed, "turns at once into a political force. . . . Therefore, whether we admit it or not, we are participating in European politics."[31] Washington officials realized this, and in fact used private loans as a club to get Europe to adopt war debt settlements, the Dawes Plan, and the Locarno pact.[32] Yet they rejected heavy responsibility and remained confident in the soothing benefits of general economic growth. Consequently the State Department rejected Stetson's bid for "a new policy" of official intervention.[33]

Similarly Benjamin Strong, governor of the Federal Reserve Bank of New York (FRBNY), dismissed Stetson's proposal of granting a large loan in return for direct FRBNY control. Strong shared Washington's aversion to potential political entanglements. The banker was also sensitive to European resentment of "American financial domination." Such hostility endangered the long-range prospects for American expansion. Nor did Strong accept Stetson's warning of another European war. "Europe was too exhausted," the banker believed, to go to war for many years.[34] Once again the minister to Poland was accurate in his prediction, but unable to convince either Washington or New York.

Although Washington and New York differed with Stetson, they did appreciate the importance of a stable Poland. Therefore the Calvin Coolidge administration quietly blessed a financial stabilization plan formulated by American bankers in cooperation with the French.

In 1926–27, Stetson helped American bankers hammer this plan together. He facilitated the economic study of Princeton Professor Edwin W. Kemmerer, invited by the Polish government at the suggestion of American financiers. After returning from Poland, Kemmerer congratulated the State Department on the ability and influence of its minister in Warsaw. Stetson used his contacts with Poles to combat German and British efforts to defeat the American stabilization plan and substitute another scheme. Sympathetic to German ambitions, Bank of England Governor Montagu Norman hoped to trade a stabilization loan to Poland for border concessions to Germany.[35] Many Americans favored peaceful revision of the border. Yet the Anglo-German pressure was too blatant for Strong's taste. Moreover he thought that stabilization of the Polish currency on the gold standard was too important a goal to be lost in political arguments. Finally, neither Strong nor Washington wanted the responsibility of rearranging Europe's frontiers. Thus by promoting the American plan for stabilization, Stetson furthered his goal of defending Poland against German designs.[36]

His efforts met success when in 1927 the FRBNY organized an international central bank loan of $20 million to the Bank of Poland. Bankers Trust formed a consortium which lent $72 million to the Polish government. These loans were the heart of the stabilization plan to put the zloty on a gold basis and open Poland to Western capital.[37] Thus, although Washington did not make government-to-government loans, it came close to doing so since the FRBNY and the Bank of Poland were the financial arms of their respective governments.[38] In October 1927, the plan went into effect. Charles Dewey became Poland's financial adviser and liaison with Wall Street. Dewey's influence was not authoritative, as Stetson had earlier recommended. Instead it was limited by his ability to procure further loans for Poland. This proved difficult after the stock mania hit Wall Street in mid-1928.[39]

Meanwhile, Stetson was proud of the stabilization plan whose negotiations he had nurtured.[40] He also demonstrated a new understanding of the limits of American foreign policy. The bankers' scheme followed the formula, he recited, of aid "in the economic restoration of postwar Europe" and avoidance of the "political entanglements against which [George] Washington . . . invoked a warning."[41] Appropriately, the minister now focused on the economic and cultural aspects of Polish-American relations.

The financial link "begins a new epoch in Polish history," Stetson declared; "opportunity is calling Poland." The American minister welcomed the dictatorship of strong-man Jozef Pilsudski, who came to power in a coup d'etat in May 1926.[42] Pilsudski's efficient, progressive authoritarianism, Stetson reported to Washington, was a happy compromise between the Polish reactionaries and radicals.[43] The minister believed this strong government could modernize Poland, i.e., adopt modern "American ideals in business as well as in government." The minister hoped that the "propaganda" of Dewey and other Americans coming into Poland would "reinforce the ideas I have tried to plant in the minds of statesmen."[44]

Some Poles welcomed this propaganda. On a trip to the United States in 1925, Foreign Minister Alexander Skrzynski appealed for American advice and answers to help his country cope with modernization. Skrzynski called for "the Americanization of Europe."[45] Similarly, Sigismund Heryng, the Polish economist, told Stetson that even more important than "Ford dollars" (American loans) were "the Fords themselves to push our production into new, proper ways." He hoped American industrialists would come to Poland with their "organizing talent." Heryng explained to the minister that Poles were particularly interested in the principles which had worked so well for the John B.

Stetson Company — "low prices and high wages with the participation of labor in the management and in the profits."[46]

Anxious to promote both Polish education and American profits, Stetson assisted U.S. business expansion. He worked hard helping the Averell Harriman interests acquire Polish mining and electrification properties. Harriman's difficulties demonstrated the point that Stetson had unsuccessfully conveyed to Washington and New York. In tension-ridden central Europe, Americans could not separate economics and politics. Harriman's economic partnership with German interests ran afoul of Warsaw's determination to, as Stetson put it, "degermanize and polonize [sic]" important economic enterprises. Despite efforts by Stetson and Harriman's lawyers (John Foster Dulles and Allen W. Dulles), Poland vetoed Harriman's plan to acquire much of its electrical generating industry.[47] Stetson's other efforts to help American business were more successful. At the request of the Coolidge administration, angered by the Franco-German potash cartel, Stetson aided negotiations between Warsaw and New York bankers to develop Polish potash deposits.[48] By the end of the 1920s, Americans held 16 percent of the foreign investments in Poland, ranking behind France (27 percent) and Germany (22 percent). Americans made most of these investments from 1925 to 1929, the years of Stetson's ministry.[49] Yet America's third place position suggested Stetson's difficulty in making Poland an American outpost.

By 1928, Stetson himself was disappointed with Poland's capacity to accept American teachings. He concluded that "the mentality of the Poles as regards capital is eastern rather than western." Each class in Poland struggled for its own narrow interest. He had tried to introduce the American notion of "government, capital and labor" working together, Stetson reported to the secretary of state. Yet the Poles "cannot conceive of a stability based upon an equilibrium . . . which we call cooperation."[50] Nor could Stetson conceive that the American road might not be the fastest or easiest for other, very different countries.

In this respect Washington, which tried not to become directly entangled in feud-ridden Europe, was more realistic than Stetson about the effectiveness and benefits of overt intervention. Administration Republicans tried to stabilize Europe and protect American interests while avoiding foreign quagmires and domestic protest. Partly because of this restraint, their formula of prosperity and peaceful change failed. The Depression, World War II, and the Cold War discredited the Republican policy of economic unofficial diplomacy and limited intervention.

This failure fulfilled the prophecies made by Stetson in 1925—26. His vindication, however, was private. In mid—1929, he resigned the Warsaw post and reentered business. Although loquacious in his diplomatic despatches to Washington, the ex-minister maintained until his death in 1952 public silence on Poland and other foreign policy issues. Stetson's ministry in Poland was most significant not for what he did, but for what he represented. Stetson embodied 1920s Republican confidence in economic diplomacy, liberal capitalism, and the American way. Yet, unlike administration leaders, he questioned the government's refusal to assume economic and political commitments to the European status quo. This businessman-diplomat thus foreshadowed the new generation of foreign policymakers who emerged from World War II supremely confident in America's power and mission.

Hugh Gibson

Hugh Gibson

1883	Born 16 August in Los Angeles, California
1907	Graduated from *Ecole Libre des Sciences Politiques*
1908	Entered the diplomatic service as secretary of legation in Honduras
1911	First secretary of legation in Cuba
1914	Secretary of legation in Belgium
1916–18	First secretary of embassy in Great Britain followed by various assignments in Washington and Europe connected with American diplomacy during World War I
1919	Minister to Poland
1924	Minister to Switzerland
1926	Chairman of the American delegation to the Preparatory Commission for the General Disarmament Conference
1927	Ambassador to Belgium
1927	Chairman of the American delegation to the Geneva Naval Conference
1930	Member of the American delegation to the London Naval Conference
1932	Acting chairman of the American delegation to the General Disarmament Conference
1933	Ambassador to Brazil
1937	Ambassador to Belgium
1938	Retired from the diplomatic service
1940	European director, Commission for Polish Relief and Commission for Relief in Belgium
1951	Director, Provisional Intergovernmental Committee for the Movement of Migrants from Europe
1954	Died 12 December in Geneva

CHAPTER 5

Hugh Gibson and Disarmament:
The Diplomacy of Gradualism

Ronald E. Swerczek

Witty, dapper, urbane, and fluent in major European languages, Hugh Gibson was thoroughly at home on the European diplomatic scene. The disarmament negotiations of the late 1920s and early 1930s marked the pinnacle of his career as a professional diplomat. A look at his participation in formal conferences and interim meetings, including the Preparatory Commission for the General Disarmament Conference, the Geneva and London Naval Conferences, and the General Disarmament Conference itself, provides an excellent opportunity to assess the role of a professional diplomat in the implementation of American foreign policy. The disarmament talks represented an important aspect of Republican involvement in European affairs, and Gibson utilized his skill, experience, and knowledge to help keep them alive, particularly through his ability to seek out areas of compromise and concession in the periods between formal sessions.

As an internationalist, Gibson welcomed the willingness of the Republican administrations of the post World War I era to become involved in the disarmament effort. Disarmament appealed to the Harding, Coolidge, and Hoover administrations both as a domestic economy measure and as a means of fostering economic and political stability abroad. In addition, the anti-arms race atmosphere prevalent after the war enabled these administrations to participate in a popular international movement without becoming enmeshed in the workings of the League of Nations. American policymakers during these years evidenced no desire to pursue disarmament to a degree detrimental to American defense.[1] Gibson, essentially a pragmatist, preferred a deliberate and measured approach to disarmament. While he was occasionally frustrated by the unwillingness of his superiors to approve a more prominent role for the United States, he agreed with the basic American policy of gradual arms limitation.

As a career man accustomed to the give and take of diplomatic negotiations, Gibson worked comfortably within the limits imposed by the competing interests of the major powers and by the procedural as well as substantive constraints of American policy. Disarmament nevertheless provided a formidable challenge to his belief in the ability of dedicated, well-trained diplomats to settle disputes and to advance the cause of peace. An optimist and a realist, Gibson never expected more than modest gains and eventually regarded the mere continuation of negotiations as a form of success. In so doing he failed to perceive the inherent limitations of his gradual approach.

Gibson's gratification from such a minor achievement as simply keeping negotiations alive is understandable given the limits within which he worked. The demands of individual nations for security, equality, parity, or superiority sharply narrowed the areas of potential agreement. In addition, Gibson often faced an unwillingness in Washington to take any steps that could be construed as American initiative, despite the obviously deep involvement of the United States in the disarmament effort. Despite his professional experience and training, Gibson did not enjoy the luxury of freedom of action. Because he saw his role as that of a mediator, he accepted such limitations and worked assiduously within them to find areas of compromise upon which agreements could be built. But compromise was never easy and, by the time Gibson left Geneva in 1933, he realized that there was little likelihood that the differences over arms policies could be resolved by negotiation. Thus, Gibson's experiences in these years illustrate vividly the limitations and frustrations encountered by well-intentioned diplomats who sought to lend their skills to the cause of disarmament. His experiences also reveal a lack of leadership and commitment on the part of the United States that contributed to the inefficacy of the disarmament movement.

When Gibson arrived in Berne as minister to Switzerland in 1924 his career seemed to be carrying him steadily toward the highest levels of the diplomatic service. He was enjoying the fruition of years of preparation. Plagued by illness as a child, Gibson, with determined guidance from his mother, worked diligently to prepare for a career in diplomacy. The Gibson family was not wealthy, but Frank Gibson, cashier of the First National Bank in Los Angeles, bequeathed an estate sufficient to allow his widow and son, an only child, to live comfortably and to travel and study abroad. After private tutoring and two years at Pomona College, Gibson and his mother sailed for Europe in 1903. There he spent more than a year touring, attending theater and opera performances, and studying with language tutors. With the intention of preparing for a diplomatic career, he entered the *Ecole Libre des Sciences Politiques* in Paris. He graduated with high honors in 1907 and returned to the United States to seek admission to the diplomatic service. The following year, at the age of twenty-five, he achieved his goal, and accepted the position of secretary of legation in Honduras.[2]

During the years succeeding his initial appointment, Gibson moved frequently from post to post. The necessity of making part of the trip to his first post in Tegucigalpa on the back of a mule did not dampen his initial enthusiasm.[3]

He took on other assignments almost as eagerly, confident that valuable experience could be gained and important lessons learned from each. From Honduras he moved to the embassy in London, then to the State Department in Washington where he impressed his superiors with his appetite for hard work and his high spirits.[4] Gibson never cared for departmental work, however, and always avoided staying in Washington any longer than required. He returned to the field as first secretary of legation in Havana in 1911, then moved to the embassy in Brussels in 1914. Gibson welcomed this transfer from Cuba to Belgium because it returned him to the familiar surroundings and comfortable social circles of western Europe. He arrived in Brussels just months before the outbreak of World War I. For most of the next two decades he was deeply involved in European affairs.

Gibson's wartime experiences, while at times frustrating and unpleasant, proved in the long run to be the key to his advancement in the diplomatic service. The aggressive and articulate young diplomat served in key posts during the war years in Brussels, London, Washington, and Paris, and worked with such agencies as the Commission for Relief in Belgium and the Committee on Public Information (Creel Committee). In the process he became acquainted with and favorably impressed major Wilson administration officials, including Walter Hines Page, ambassador to Great Britain, Herbert Hoover, director of the Food Administration, and Colonel Edward M. House, Wilson's adviser. Consequently, in 1919, Wilson appointed him the first American minister to Poland. He had not yet reached the age of thirty-six.

Gibson tackled problems awaiting him in Warsaw with characteristic zeal and poise. Still, the frustrations of dealing with the many difficult issues raised by the rebirth of Poland put those qualities to a severe test. By 1924 he was ready to leave the relative isolation of the Polish capital for the more serene atmosphere of Berne. In addition, he had married in 1922, and the death of his first child during delivery probably influenced his desire for relocation.[5]

Between assignments Gibson journeyed to Washington in order to testify at hearings that eventually culminated in the Rogers Act of 1924. The law merged the consular and diplomatic services into a foreign service with a single personnel board to oversee appointments, transfers, and promotions. Gibson, who served as spokesman for the career diplomats in the hearings, used the opportunity to voice his and his colleagues' opinions on the virtues of professionalism. Originally opposed to amalgamation with the consuls, whom he regarded as social inferiors, Gibson accepted the inevitable and used the hearings on the Rogers Bill to express his belief that a corps of elite, well-bred, well-educated men could best conduct the foreign relations of the United States.[6]

By 1924 Gibson had established a reputation as an experienced, adaptable, diligent professional. He had risen through the ranks to the level of minister and considered himself eminently qualified for virtually any diplomatic assignment. The Berne post offered little more than routine work, but his involvement with disarmament over the next several years provided a severe challenge and considerable frustration.

By the mid-1920s American interest in disarmament was manifest. President Wilson had included reduction of armaments as one of the Fourteen Points for peace in January 1918 and President Harding had hosted the Washington Conference of 1921–22.[7] The Coolidge administration hoped to extend the limits agreed upon in Washington, at least in areas that would not adversely affect American defenses. But the League of Nations was now the sponsoring organization for further arms limitation negotiations and the United States had formally rejected the League along with the Treaty of Versailles. Thus, Gibson inherited an observer's role from his predecessor as minister, Joseph C. Grew. State Department officials expected Grew and Gibson to keep them informed of the League's activities while avoiding close contacts with it, a requirement both found exasperating.[8] The situation had changed but little by the time the League Council sent invitations to the meetings of the Preparatory Commission for the General Disarmament Conference in 1926. President Coolidge accepted the invitation only after carefully assuring Congress that sending a delegation would not commit the United States to anything.[9]

From the beginning of his involvement in disarmament, Gibson worked within narrowly constructed guidelines. Throughout the six sessions of the Preparatory Commission between 1926 and 1931, the United States refused to accept any kind of international supervision because it implied interference by the League or some other international body in America's internal affairs. In addition, American policy, as set forth by Secretary of State Frank B. Kellogg in his instructions to Gibson as chairman of the American delegation, ruled out arms limitations based upon potential war strength or limitation of expenditure. The former would have meant limits based upon such factors as industrial capacity and population, which could have put severe restraints on American armaments. The latter would have interfered with congressional control of appropriations.[10]

It neither surprised nor dismayed Gibson that the early meetings of the Preparatory Commission in 1926 and 1927 produced nothing beyond the reading, at the third session, of a draft convention. He saw disarmament as a matter requiring long, careful study and resisted attempts to hasten the convening of a general conference. At the same time he feared the formulation of plans which appeared plausible in theory but could not be applied in practice, although he did not make clear what he considered practical. From the outset, in other words, Gibson did not have high expectations. He sought small gains, painstakingly achieved through careful negotiation within limits imposed by the requirements of the participants.[11]

In the spirit of proceeding gradually, Gibson strongly supported Coolidge's proposal for a separate naval conference in 1927. At the Washington Conference in 1922 the United States, Great Britain, Japan, France, and Italy had achieved only a beginning in the limitation of naval armaments. The Five Power Treaty had placed limits (within a ratio of 5:5:3:1.67:1.67) on capital ships and aircraft carriers, but not on auxiliary craft such as cruisers, destroyers, and submarines. President Coolidge, acting at least partly on Gibson's advice, assumed that the provisions of the treaty could be extended with relative ease. He hoped this would break the stalemate in the Preparatory Commission, while contributing to his administration's drive for economy measures. So, with virtually no advance diplomatic preparations, the Geneva Naval Conference began in June 1927.[12]

The Conference opened inauspiciously. France and Italy refused to participate, claiming that there was little to be gained from a piecemeal approach to disarmament. In addition Italy maintained that its unfavorable geographic position made consideration of further naval limitation impossible.[13] Consequently only the United States, Great Britain, and Japan sent delegates.

A deadlock developed immediately between the United States and Great Britain primarily over limits on cruisers. The British, with their large empire and extensive commercial routes to protect, wanted cruisers limited to 7,500 tons with six-inch guns, permitting more vessels within an overall tonnage limit. The United States insisted that larger cruisers (10,000 tons) and guns (eight-inch) should be permitted. Gibson, acting as head of the United States delegation, but under orders from the State Department not to concede on this issue, pressed the American argument vigorously, while Viscount Robert Cecil did the same for the British position. At one point the debate became so heated that Gibson, normally a cool, even-tempered negotiator, threatened to walk out of a session.[14] Nevertheless, despite the obvious hopelessness of the situation, Gibson continued to search for a compromise. He suggested that the United States propose an agreement including a political clause which would allow an individual signatory to call a new conference if it believed the cruiser allotments needed adjustment. Although Secretary of State Kellogg approved the suggestion, the British delegates, under orders to make no concessions, rejected it.[15] The conference ended, on 4 August 1927, having accomplished nothing.

Gibson wrote his mother that he was pleased he had "prevented it from ending in a free fight which would have rendered further discussion hopeless. . . . I'm sad we could not agree, but we have done our honest best."[16] He sharply criticized the British delegates for their intransigence, failing to perceive that they had no choice but to adhere to their country's position. They could not accept the larger cruisers (10,000 tons) and guns (eight-inch) any more than Gibson could accept the lesser tonnage (7,500) and gunnery (six-inch). In light of the basic differences between the American and British positions the conference probably never should have been called. Yet Gibson, who was not above carrying a personal grudge, placed undue blame on his British counterparts.[17]

The Geneva Naval Conference represented only one episode in Gibson's involvement in arms limitation attempts. He missed the fourth session of the

Preparatory Commission in the autumn of 1927, as his delicate health forced a temporary respite from all except ceremonial duties in his new assignment as ambassador to Belgium. That session lasted only four days, however, and produced only the creation of a committee on security and arbitration. By the time the fifth session began in the spring of 1928 Gibson was able to return to his position as head of the American delegation.

The fifth session was nearly as brief and unproductive as the fourth. It consisted of little more than an acrimonious debate over a Soviet proposal for immediate and total abolition of armaments. Gibson joined the majority of the other delegations in condemning the plan. He agreed with the American position that total disarmament was undesirable. Furthermore, he found the proposal to be contrary to his deliberate approach as well as inimical to his sensibilities as a professional diplomat. Gibson harbored a long-standing distrust of the Soviets and resented their unwillingness to abide by the conventions of European diplomacy. He therefore saw no contradiction in denouncing the Soviet plan as impracticable, while simultaneously expressing faith in the proposed multilateral pact outlawing war (the Kellogg-Briand Pact). The anti-war pact would, he claimed, set the stage for disarmament, but total disarmament would not prevent war.[18]

When the fifth session of the Preparatory Commission adjourned without accomplishing anything, Gibson felt discouraged by the lack of progress toward disarmament. In fact, he saw little point in sending delegates to the next session if they would have "nothing to do except listen to bolshevik propaganda and quarrels between the French and Germans about the Treaty of Versailles."[19]

Gibson was not alone in his misgivings. The Coolidge administration believed there was little purpose in proceeding with formal negotiations until Anglo-American disagreements could be reconciled. American officials were particularly disturbed by the announcement in June 1928 of an Anglo-French naval agreement. Clearly directed against the United States, the agreement called for limits on ten thousand ton, eight-inch gun cruisers, but not on light cruisers or small submarines.[20] Anglo-American differences vis-à-vis naval armaments thus remained a major barrier to further progress. At American urging, the Preparatory Commission did not meet for another year.

By the time the sixth session of the Preparatory Commission convened in April 1929, Herbert Hoover was president. Gibson and Hoover had been friends since their work together on the Commission for Relief in Belgium during World War I. Their friendship gave Gibson an opportunity to participate in the preparation of a new approach to naval armament questions. Hoover, who believed in disarmament for economic reasons as well as from personal conviction, called Gibson home for consultation before the inauguration. Gibson remained at the White House for a week in March and worked with the president and the Western European Division of the State Department in drafting a statement designed to break the stalemate in the Preparatory Commission.[21]

The speech Gibson delivered to the Preparatory Commission on 22 April 1929 contained what became known as the "yardstick" proposal. In this proposal the American government announced a willingness to give up its long-standing insistence on tonnage as the only basis for limitation and accept a combination of variables, such as age of vessels and caliber of guns, along with tonnage, in the formulation of a yardstick.[22] The yardstick concept was no panacea, but it did help clear the way for partial adoption of the draft convention. It provided a plausible reason for postponing consideration of the naval section of the convention once the delegates agreed to omit limitations on trained reserves for land armies and to accept a Gibson proposal that publicity be adopted as a means of encouraging limitation of expenditures. On both of these points the Hoover administration reversed earlier American policy, although the concession on expenditures proved minor indeed. Gibson found even such limited progress sufficient to rejuvenate his innate optimism. The diplomatic process seemed to be working and he, as a professional, played a major role in making it work.[23] To Gibson, the disarmament talks seemed much more promising than they do in retrospect.

In effect, the disarmament negotiators appeared in 1929 to have overcome the inertia of the preceding years. The yardstick proposal helped make possible another naval conference even though, contrary to general assumptions, no formula yet existed. Gibson now turned his attention to preparations for the coming London Naval Conference and the prerequisite of Anglo-American cooperation. Historians have paid little attention to his participation, but his correspondence shows that he played a key role in the preparations. Traveling between Brussels and London, and working mostly behind the scenes, he endeavored to educate Charles G. Dawes, Hoover's ambassador to Great Britain, concerning the intricacies of disarmament and to prepare the way for a successful conference. Gibson, remembering the abortive Geneva Naval Conference of 1927, served as the voice of caution and restraint. He complained to Assistant Secretary of State William R. Castle that whenever he tried to prevail upon Dawes to avoid haste, Dawes brushed aside his warnings as "gahdam nonsense." British Prime Minister Ramsay MacDonald also seemed eager to have the conference under way. Hoover and Secretary of State Henry L. Stimson, however, shared Gibson's concern for caution and prevailed upon MacDonald to proceed slowly.[24]

By late July 1929, Dawes and Gibson had made substantial progress in talks with MacDonald and Albert V. Alexander, First Lord of the Admiralty. Gibson served essentially as a mediator, relying upon his experience to gauge the tenor of the negotiations. Convinced that MacDonald was sincerely anxious for a meaningful agreement, Gibson nevertheless could not forget the Geneva Naval Conference. He urged that there be a firm guarantee beforehand that the British admiralty would not hold a veto power over any agreement. Eventually, a preliminary agreement emerged. It recognized British demands based on naval necessity and American claims to parity, but provided only for limitation, not reduction, of armaments. In October personal discussions between Mac-Donald and Hoover (the Rapidan Conference), which Gibson had strongly advocated, brought to a climax the Anglo-American rapprochement.[25] This paved the way for the London Naval Conference.

When the London Naval Conference opened in January 1930 Gibson was, for the first time in his career, a member of a politically influential delegation. In addition to Gibson, the delegation included Stimson, as chairman; Dawes; Joseph T. Robinson, Democratic senator from Arkansas; David A. Reed, Republican senator from Pennsylvania; Dwight W. Morrow, ambassador to Mexico; and Charles Francis Adams, secretary of the navy. As in the advance planning, Gibson's role during the conference was primarily supportive, providing the other delegates the benefit of his knowledge and experience. Thus, to the extent that the London Naval Conference was an improvement over the Geneva fiasco of 1927, Gibson deserves some of the credit. He drafted the speech given by Stimson at the official opening and delivered one major address to the conference himself. Significantly, considering Gibson's consistent emphasis on the necessity for compromise, the speech afforded him the opportunity to announce an American concession on the issue of allowing a country to transfer tonnage from one category to another within the limits of its authorized tonnage allotment. The United States originally opposed the transfer idea when the French proposed it in 1927. Now, although still convinced that limitation by category was the best approach, the American delegation agreed, as a means of breaking the deadlock, to accept the transfer concept.[26]

Such minor concessions did little, however, to fulfill the French desire for security. The treaty produced by the London Naval Conference won neither French nor Italian approval. Yet, compared to the disaster at Geneva, the London Naval Conference was a marked success in that it extended the provisions of the Five Power Treaty of 1922 to cover auxiliary craft as well as capital ships.

Gibson was justifiably satisfied with the treaty signed by the American, British, and Japanese delegates. Characteristically, he saw the London Naval Conference Treaty as a forward step in a long, complex process. He believed the French and Italians could, given time, work out their differences. Then, he hoped, the Preparatory Commission could proceed with its work, but always by making "haste slowly."[27] Even in 1942, after the collapse of disarmament and the onset of World War II, Gibson (and Hoover) still maintained that the treaty had been valuable because it recognized the right of the American navy to parity, prevented a wasteful building program, and furthered international understanding.[28] At the time he seems to have appreciated the agreement reached in London mainly because it furthered the cause of continuing negotiation. That is, its value lay in the fact that it cleared the way for further negotiation. To a professional diplomat that was sufficient reason for praising it.

Because he was deeply immersed in disarmament matters, Gibson naturally viewed individual conferences as simply part of a continuing process. While the other delegates returned home, Gibson turned his attention back to the Preparatory Commission which had recessed to await the outcome of the London Naval Conference. In the months preceding the renewal of Preparatory Commission meetings, Gibson resumed the kind of activity that constituted his major contribution during the years of disarmament efforts — informal negotiations between the formal sessions.

Called home in September 1930 because of the death of his mother, he worked with J. Theodore Marriner and Alan Winslow in the Western European Division of the State Department to formulate a proposal aimed at reconciling Franco-Italian differences left unsettled in London. Essentially, the plan called upon each side to subordinate theoretical demands for the time being. To the French, this meant conceding to Italy theoretical parity while maintaining practical superiority until 1936. To the Italians, it meant conceding temporary French superiority while reserving the right to demand parity with France after 1936.[29]

Gibson traveled first to Paris and found Premier André Tardieu to be favorably impressed by the plan. In Rome, however, the response was less positive. Italian Foreign Minister Dino Grandi stated repeatedly that his government wanted an agreement. Yet he appeared to Gibson to be almost without hope that France and Italy could agree. Italian public opinion, Grandi said, demanded adherence in principle to parity with France.[30]

Gibson continued searching for some basis of agreement even after the resumption of Preparatory Commission meetings in November 1930. At one point he suggested that a distinction be drawn between replacement and new construction. Since much of the French building program could be considered replacement construction, Italy could plausibly claim parity in new construction. Both sides expressed interest in this proposal, but were unable to reach an agreement in direct negotiations. When both requested direct mediation, Gibson refused in order to reserve freedom of action for himself and the United States. Robert L. Craigie, chief of the American Department of the British Foreign Office, assumed the role that Gibson had declined. Later, in February 1931, Gibson changed his mind and tried to "inject" himself back into the talks for a last-ditch effort. By then, Craigie informed him, there was little he could do.[31] Direct mediation by Gibson at either time probably would not have made any difference. In March Dwight Morrow, who had played a key role in the London Naval Conference, arranged a tenuous settlement, but it proved to be short-lived.[32]

The final session of the Preparatory Commission had taken place in November and December 1930. Gibson, speaking for the Hoover administration, articulated significant concessions at that meeting, including modification of American opposition to direct budgetary limitation, international supervision, and, most importantly, a consultative pact.[33] But Gibson realized that the adoption of a draft convention, made possible in part because of these concessions, was far from an arms reduction agreement. By this time his perennial optimism, dampened by the years of nearly fruitless negotiations, was beginning to wane. He knew the difficulty of trying to achieve agreement between even two powers from his experience in the Anglo-American and Franco-Italian disputes and expected little progress at the General Disarmament Conference. He hoped for, at most, "a stabilization of existing armaments."[34]

In March 1931, Gibson took advantage of the hiatus in formal negotiations to prepare, primarily for his own guidance, several memorandums on issues which the United States would have to face at the General Disarmament Conference in 1932. He dealt with several topics including budgetary limitation (limits on the proportion of a nation's budget spent on arms), the relation of a disarmament treaty to existing treaties, the status of a permanent disarmament commission, and the outright prohibition of certain weapons. On the first issue, budgetary limitation, he noted that the United States was the only power on the Preparatory Commission to insist upon direct limits on the quantity of armaments. Gibson believed, in view of the strong pressure for budgetary limitation, that the United States would have to give careful consideration to the possibility of accepting such an arrangement as long as it applied only to the executive branch and did not restrict congressional control of appropriations. He perceived the second concern, the relationship of existing treaties to a general disarmament treaty, as requiring a more adamant stand. The United States should insist on a separate article preserving the Washington and London Naval Conference Treaties. It should also demand that the Treaty of Versailles, to which the United States was not a party, not be included in the same article. Gibson maintained that a strong stand would have to be taken against any attempt to give the proposed permanent disarmament commission the power to make investigations within countries charged with violations of the treaty. Finally, Gibson reached the conclusion that a disarmament treaty stood a better chance of acceptance if it did not include a prohibition on certain weapons such as poisonous gas. He noted that the United States had not accepted the 1925 Protocol on Gas Warfare and feared a similar fate for any new attempt at prohibition.[35]

Gibson's positions in these preparatory memorandums are revealing when viewed in conjunction with the pessimism he expressed at the close of the Preparatory Commission's sessions. He had clearly decided that, if a treaty could be drawn up at all, it would have to be extremely narrow in scope. The United States would gain little by making broad concessions on vital points. In other words, he seemed determined to be prepared for the worst. Once the conference began, however, he would revert to his characteristic optimism, and watch for opportunities to compromise.

Gibson was all but guaranteed a position on the American delegation to the General Disarmament Conference by his extensive preparation and experience. Nevertheless, the Hoover administration considered it imperative that someone of substantial political stature head the delegation. Stimson wanted someone who could make decisions on the spot, not someone like Gibson who would have to be directed from Washington. The secretary considered several possibilities including William E. Borah, the isolationist Republican senator from Idaho (a possibility which offended Gibson's sense of internationalism and his elitism); Dwight Morrow, who accepted shortly before his death in October 1931; Henry Fletcher, chairman of the United States Tariff Commission; Charles G. Dawes, who also accepted and then resigned to become president of the Reconstruction Finance Corporation; and Senator Claude Swanson of Virginia, the ranking Democrat on the Senate Foreign Relations Committee. When none of these choices proved feasible, Stimson took the official chairmanship himself. Gibson accepted the position of acting chairman of the delegation, which included Senator Swanson; Hugh Wilson, minister to Switzerland; Norman Davis, an organizer of the International Monetary and Economic Conference; and Mary E. Woolley, president of Mount Holyoke College. Stimson realized that no one was as well qualified as Gibson to direct the day-to-day work of the American delegation, even though he never considered entrusting to Gibson, a career diplomat, the responsibility for the direction of United States participation. In Stimson's mind Gibson's abilities extended only to negotiating and not to policymaking.[36]

Stimson and Gibson had previously worked together, but the arrangement the secretary of state devised for the General Disarmament Conference, whereby he as chairman remained in Washington and Gibson as acting chairman was in Geneva, produced recurring friction. When Gibson wanted to open the conference by calling for a break with the past, the State Department overruled him on grounds that to do so would put the United States in a position of insisting upon revision of existing treaties as a condition for proceeding with discussions.[37] Once the conference opened in February 1932, Gibson was anxious that the United States have a positive program to offer. Stimson did allow him to present a proposal which included a call for total abolition of submarines, lethal gases, and bacteriological warfare, as well as restrictions on aerial bombing, tanks, and heavy mobile guns. In addition, Gibson included an announcement that the United States would consider budgetary limitation as a complementary method to direct arms limitation. But when Gibson and Hugh Wilson formulated a plan designed to reconcile arms limitation with security needs, they met resistance from Stimson. Their proposal revolved around the belief that the demand for security, voiced most strenuously by France, resulted from fear of invasion. Gibson and Wilson argued that the abolition of weapons, such as mobile guns, tanks, and bombing planes, which made invasion possible, would "restore superiority to the defensive," solve the problem of security from invasion, and make possible the reduction of land armies. Stimson directed Gibson not to link aggressive weapons with land forces and to keep land weapons separate from bombing planes and submarines. Gibson encountered another State Department rejection when he proposed that the United States should offer to consider further naval reductions once land forces were reduced. Under Secretary of State William R. Castle informed Gibson that land and naval questions had to be kept distinct. Gibson, who was assidously searching for areas of concession or compromise, did not fully realize the effect such events as the Sino-Japanese conflict were having in Washington. Administration fears that the United States Navy was already inadequate made discussion of further limitation politically inappropriate.[38]

While restrained on the one hand by the State Department's determination to keep various categories of armaments separate, Gibson faced on the other hand French insistence that arms were interdependent and that such weapons as planes and ships over ten thousand tons could also be considered aggressive. Gibson's speech of 11 April 1932 before the General Commission of the conference proposed abolition of tanks, mobile guns over 155 millimeters in caliber, and poisonous gas, but said nothing about abolishing submarines and bombing planes or placing further limits on capital ships. When the French delegation, led by Premier André Tardieu, objected vehemently to the American proposal, Stimson found it necessary to go to France in an attempt to mollify Tardieu. Stimson succeeded in soothing Tardieu's ruffled feelings, but the essential disagreement remained. The conference disposed of the American proposal by passing a resolution declaring its "approval of the principle of qualitative disarmament."[39]

Gibson's difficulties in dealing with French intransigence and State Department restraints stemmed in part from a basic difference in opinion between Stimson and Gibson regarding the role the United States should play in the conference. Involved in disarmament negotiations for years, Gibson realized that unless the United States completely withdrew from the Disarmament Conference it would be unable to avoid a prominent role. If that meant making concessions, he stood ready to present them to the conference. Stimson, however, preoccupied with the Far Eastern situation and convinced that adequate American naval strength was necessary to discourage Japanese expansion, opposed any plan that suggested additional naval limitation. He believed that the United States had done all that could be asked in 1921—22 and 1930. He informed Gibson in June 1932, that "you are facing what is primarily a European peace conference."[40]

President Hoover's views, however, were nearer to Gibson's than to Stimson's. Gibson reacted with understandable pleasure when he received word on 19 June of the proposal which the president wanted him to make to the conference. Unknown to Gibson, Hoover had concluded that it was time for the United States to assume a more positive stance. His proposal, outlined initially in a memorandum to Stimson, called for one-third reductions in battleships, cruisers, destroyers, and land armies, plus abolition of aircraft carriers, submarines, military aviation, large mobile guns, tanks, and poisonous gas. Though delighted with the proposal, Gibson knew from experience the importance of preparing the way before presentation of any new plan. In particular he wanted more time to talk privately with the French delegation, now headed by Premier Edouard Herriot. But Stimson, compelled to accept a proposal he privately opposed, refused to permit any meaningful delay in submitting it to the conference. In addition, for domestic political reasons, Hoover wanted the plan before the conference prior to the convening of the Democratic National Convention of 1932. On 22 June, just three days after receiving the proposal, Gibson officially placed it before the conference.[41]

French reaction to the Hoover proposal was crucial. Gibson and Norman Davis tried vainly to convince French representatives that the plan would meet their security needs because of its emphasis on defensive over offensive weapons. In a further attempt to gain French support, the Hoover administration made another concession by reversing the American position on international inspection. Throughout the meetings of the Preparatory Commission the United States had opposed this implied authority to interfere in a nation's internal affairs. But when the Italian delegation announced a willingness to accept inspection, Gibson recommended to Stimson that the United States follow suit. Stimson agreed, realizing that to do so would give the United States "a trading point of high value with the French."[42] Nevertheless, neither the French nor the British would commit themselves to the Hoover plan. Gibson could gain nothing more than an agreement to recognize it as a basis for future discussion. This in effect consigned the plan to a lingering death. Although the General Commission of the conference did adopt a resolution which included the Hoover proposal as a statement of objectives, the plenary session of the conference rejected it. Germany and the Soviet Union voted against the resolution, denying it the required unanimous approval — the former because it contained no recognition of the principle of equality of treatment and the latter because it did not go far enough toward true disarmament.[43]

The adjournment of the first session of the General Disarmament Conference in July 1932 effectively marked the end of Gibson's period of meaningful involvement in the interwar arms limitation effort. Though he remained at Geneva for nearly another year, virtually no further progress occurred. Furthermore, once Hoover became a lame-duck president, Gibson's effectiveness as an American spokesman diminished considerably. In the meantime, the first session had ended in a fashion familiar to Gibson — inconclusively, but with a promise of continuing effort. Gibson found this acceptable if not entirely satisfactory. He told his colleagues in the American delegation that the resolution passed by the General Commission should be explained as "the level of agreement possible at the present time." By the time the conference reconvened, he hoped, "public opinion throughout the world will have made possible more substantial achievements." He realized that peace organizations would probably criticize the lack of progress and ask why the American delegation had not been more forceful in demanding positive results. That, he said, was not the way of diplomacy and would only have "made agreement more difficult."[44] In effect, Gibson regarded diplomacy as the art of the possible. He believed that making demands which might cause the breakdown of negotiations defeated the purpose of diplomacy. Gibson, ever the professional career diplomat, found than an unsavory possibility.

Gibson's participation in the session of the conference which began in January 1933 and spanned the change of administrations in Washington was largely perfunctory. Acting on behalf of the Hoover administration, Gibson remained aloof from new proposals, preferring to stand on the American plan of the previous year.[45] He could provide the new Secretary of State Cordell Hull with nothing more than recommendations that the United States support an Italian suggestion calling for no more meetings until after Easter and that the new administration take a "generally friendly stand" toward a draft treaty which Prime Minister MacDonald planned to present.[46] Thus he continued until the close of his tenure as acting chairman of the American delegation to stress policies which would keep the conference alive.

Gibson's final official contact with the General Disarmament Conference came on 27 March 1933, at a meeting where the delegates agreed to recess until 25 April. By April Gibson had left the American delegation in order to prepare for a move to Rio de Janeiro, where he would continue his diplomatic career as ambassador to Brazil. Norman Davis, a Democratic member of the delegation under Gibson, became chairman. Gibson fully approved of President Roosevelt's choice of Davis. At the same time, Davis urged the retention of Gibson, at least at a post where he could serve as an adviser to the American delegation.[47] But Gibson was too closely identified with the Hoover administration and with Hoover personally for such a suggestion to receive much attention from the new president. Considered in terms of Gibson's contribution to disarmament, it mattered little. The negotiators struggled on in Geneva until Germany's announcement in October 1933 of its intention to withdraw from the talks signaled the demise of the conference. The effort was virtually hopeless by the time Gibson departed and his continued presence would have had little effect on the outcome.

After leaving Geneva, Gibson served as ambassador to Brazil and represented the United States at the Chaco Peace Conference in Buenos Aires until 1937. He then returned to Brussels as ambassador to Belgium while awaiting retirement from the State Department in 1938. The disarmament experience remained the highlight of his diplomatic career. He never exhibited, during his last five years of service, the level of dedication that marked his performance in the disarmament negotiations. Following retirement Gibson engaged in a variety of occupations including writing, editing, and various activities on behalf of international relief agencies. He died in Geneva in 1954, still active in the city where the disarmament effort expired two decades earlier. The effort foundered because of the inability of those who met there to resolve the conflicts and fears of the European powers. No amount of American leadership could have changed the result, yet the sporadic nature and uncertain commitment of American involvement over the years clearly contributed to the failure to achieve meaningful disarmament.

Gibson made his major contributions to the disarmament effort before the stalemate developed in the General Disarmament Conference. In fact one of his most important roles came not during formal sessions but between them, when he worked largely behind the scenes to prepare for future meetings or to reconcile opposing points of view. In that role his experience and skill as a professional and his familiarity with the European diplomatic scene provided the continuity without which the delegates to the plenary conferences could not have functioned. The assistance he provided to Charles G. Dawes prior to the London Naval Conference was particularly noteworthy. In addition, his constant alertness to the need or opportunity for concession helped to keep the effort from breaking down sooner than it did. Eventually the disarmament venture collapsed because the areas of concession, patiently sought out by diplomats like Gibson, were exhausted by the irreconcilable differences among the major powers.

Rival demands placed extremely rigid limits on diplomats such as Gibson. He could do little, for example, to reconcile British requirements for a minimum number of light cruisers with the American insistence on larger, more heavily armed vessels at the Geneva Naval Conference of 1927. Nor could his patient attempts at indirect mediation bridge the gap between French and Italian differences over parity after the London Naval Conference. Above all, the clash between French security needs and German demands for equality narrowed sharply the area within which Gibson and his colleagues worked.

The competing interests of the major participants were not the only source of inhibition. The nature of American policy in this period created additional restraints. Despite the leadership of the United States in the Washington Conference, the Geneva Naval Conference, and the London Naval Conference, policymakers in Washington viewed the overall disarmament issue as a non-American problem, a view well summarized in Stimson's comment that Gibson was involved in a European peace conference. Both the Coolidge and Hoover administrations failed to recognize that, in the final analysis, naval and land armaments had to be considered together for progress to continue. Thus, until Hoover presented his plan in 1932, Gibson often worked in an ambiguous situation where he was deeply involved in negotiations in which other nations' delegates viewed him as an equal, but where the State Department treated him as little more than an observer.

Within these limits, Gibson worked diligently to advance the cause of disarmament in the 1920s and 1930s. He accepted the constraints within which he worked, perceiving the task of the professional diplomat to be that of constantly searching for areas of compromise upon which further agreement could be based. He believed not so much in the prospect of large-scale disarmament, a concept too idealistic for him, as in the possibility that sincere, skilled diplomats could formulate, bit by bit, agreements which would eventually impose limits and, hopefully, reductions on armaments. Each agreement, whatever its substance, had value insofar as it paved the way for further negotiations. In fact, Gibson apparently came to value negotiation for its own sake almost as much as for the results. As a professional dedicated to career diplomacy, he sometimes viewed the diplomatic process as an end in itself. He abhorred the breakup of a conference not only because it signified inability to agree on issues, but also because it represented the failure of the diplomatic process. This outlook was perhaps inevitable considering the limits within which he had to work. Unable to formulate policy, professionals such as Gibson nevertheless worked doggedly and skillfully to reconcile existing policy differences. Even to the realistic Gibson disarmament was not a "pipe dream," but an attainable goal to be achieved gradually. For years, through session after session of fruitless negotiations, he pursued that goal, never losing his interest and seldom losing his enthusiasm.

PART II

The Roosevelt Years, 1933 – 1941

Shading shows areas as of 1935 · · · · · · · · Czechoslovakia ≡≡≡≡≡
Austria |||||||||||||| Poland · · · · · ·
Lithuania ⧄⧄⧄⧄ Albania ▦▦▦▦▦

Europe in 1939

Prentiss Bailey Gilbert

Prentiss Bailey Gilbert

1883	Born 3 October in Rochester, New York
1900	Saw military service in Philippines until 1902; briefly attended El Colegio de San Carlos
1906	Awarded Ph.B., Philosophy, University of Rochester, Class of 1905
1907	Awarded A.B., English, Yale College; began work as mining superintendent
1910	Left mining company; obtained New York teacher's certification; traveled around world; returned to U.S. in 1915 and briefly studied at Columbia University
1916	Awarded M.A., English, Rochester; established University's Extension School
1917	Reentered army in Military Intelligence, War Department, Washington
1918	Married Charlotte Gilder of New York 9 November
1919	Entered State Department as director of the Division of Political and Economic Information 12 March
1925	Appointed assistant director of the Division of Western European Affairs; was acting director until 1927
1930	Confirmed by Senate as F.S.O. 12 June; became consul at Geneva in August
1931	Sat with Council of the League of Nations, 16– 24 October
1937	Appointed counselor of embassy, Berlin; chargé from 4 August to 30 October and from 29 December to 3 March 1938
1938	Chargé from 16 November
1939	Died on duty 24 February; buried in Geneva 3 March

CHAPTER 6

Prentiss Bailey Gilbert and the League of Nations:
The Diplomacy of an Observer

J. B. Donnelly

Prentiss Bailey Gilbert entered the State Department shortly after the 1918 Armistice and died on duty the year Adolf Hitler invaded Poland. Aged thirty-five when he started his diplomatic career, he did not achieve high rank but held positions of importance in American diplomacy between the world wars. During his seven years as consul in Geneva (1930–37), Gilbert and a series of outstanding young Foreign Service novices conducted the day-to-day American relations with the League of Nations. Briefly during the Manchurian crisis of 1931, Gilbert became the only American ever to sit with the League Council. Then, for the eighteen months before his death (1937–39), Gilbert was counselor of the American embassy in Hitler's Berlin. During more than half of that time he was chargé, most notably in the immediate aftermath of the Crystal Night pogrom of November 1938.

In these posts and while an innovative lieutenant in the State Department headquarters during the twenties, Gilbert won the lifelong admiration of the future ambassadors he trained and of leading journalists of the period. He was not influential behind the scenes in the Foreign Service. To the contrary, Gilbert was never fully accepted by more orthodox figures in the American diplomatic establishment. No policy bore his name; cautious administrations never authorized him to do more than observe the world's slide into a second global war. Even those who were not close to Gilbert, however, acknowledged him as an unexcelled teacher and reporter. These were his two long-remembered contributions to the American diplomatic tradition. At his best when dealing with the unconventional diplomatists and unprecedented diplomatic situations to be found in abundance between the wars, Gilbert prepared many future leaders to meet the new challenges of American diplomacy in the forties and after. With the background and talents of the foreign correspondents who covered and befriended him, Gilbert produced, in hundreds of cables, despatches, reports, and interviews, a shrewd and detailed political journal of the thirties in Europe.[1]

Young Prentiss had just graduated from high school in Rochester, New York, when his father, a Civil War veteran and long-time United States commissioner for his New York district, reentered the army and took his son with him to the Philippine campaign. Before young Gilbert returned to get a Ph.B. in Philosophy at the University of Rochester (Class of 1905), he witnessed American atrocities in the Islands and contracted elephantiasis and a form of bubonic plague. He barely recovered and had to bandage his right leg and retire to nursing homes periodically for the rest of his life.

While taking an A.B. in English at Yale (Class of 1907), Gilbert developed a lifelong interest in creative writing, which resulted in some essays and a charity performance of an historical drama. He developed a maverick streak early, left his family church to protest against ethnic discrimination, and later spent several years traveling around the world. He returned to the United States in time to found Rochester's Extension School in 1916 and to serve during the Great War as the head of a military intelligence office in Washington. Two days before the armistice he married a young War Department translator, Charlotte Jeannette Gilder. A polylingual and spirited member of a prominent literary family, Charlotte Gilbert became immensely helpful in her husband's new career.[2]

Captain Gilbert (as he was called for some time after the war) entered the State Department early in 1919 as the chief of the new Division of Political and Economic Information. He was commissioned to establish the kind of reporting and cataloging system for peacetime diplomatic purposes that had been used by the War Department in 1917–18. Even before the armistice, Gilbert had called for a government-wide, peacetime, nonclandestine intelligence system. In a long essay which anticipated a similar argument made in 1922 by Walter Lippmann, another world war intelligence captain, Gilbert stressed the need for seasoned observers abroad who could find the reality behind appearances. He saw an equal need for evaluators in Washington who could use the facts reported to build an accurate picture of the complex interrelationships of the modern world of nation states.[3]

Ultimately a similar system, called the National Intelligence Estimates, was established by the National Security Council early in the Cold War, but Gilbert's own project was scotched by Under Secretary Joseph Grew as involving too much paper work. Gilbert's initiative, however, was noticed, as was his ability to inspire and train newcomers to the State Department and Foreign Service. Furthermore, he was able to satisfy both nervous superiors and zealous internationalists in a series of transactions with the League of Nations.[4]

Contact with the League was not for the ambitious, but when the State Department was reorganized in 1925, Gilbert willingly took an informal League portfolio with him into the new Division of Western European Affairs. As assistant or acting chief for the rest of the decade, Gilbert also continued his lectures to entering Foreign Service classes and at the Army War College, his search for talented youth, and his drive to increase the flow of diplomatic information into the department. He additionally handled a number of touchy special assignments, such as acting as the departmental spokesman on the Kellogg-Briand Pact of 1928, which outlawed war as an instrument for settling international disputes.[5]

During one of three short overseas trips he took in his first decade in the department, Gilbert by chance stumbled onto his future. He and his wife were visiting Geneva when their host, the wealthy American consul Elbridge Rand, announced that he was leaving the Foreign Service to go into philanthropic work. Washington agreed to let Gilbert cover the League's tenth assembly in place of Rand. On 5 September 1929, the longtime French Foreign Minister, Aristide Briand, in one of the most vividly remembered speeches of the era, called for the League to start building a United States of Europe. Gilbert wrote a widely circulated report on the Briand proposal while arguing in Washington for the "strongest possible" successor to Rand.[6]

Henry Stimson, the new secretary of state, finally decided to appoint Gilbert himself. He was only the fourth departmental officer to enter the jealously guarded Foreign Service under the terms of the Rogers reform legislation of 1924. By midsummer 1930, Gilbert was on his way into what his main sponsor, Under Secretary Joseph Cotton, called the "firing line." Cotton, like Gilbert a wry humorist, added, "I fear also that I am throwing you pretty much to the dogs."[7]

Gilbert would remember Cotton's remark when nipped at by pro- or anti-Leaguers or both. But for the moment, aside from a few predictable isolationist protests, the American press strongly supported Gilbert's appointment to Geneva. Pro-League Edwin L. (Jimmy) James, the very influential future managing editor of the *New York Times*, hailed Gilbert as America's "blue-ribbon Consul."[8]

Luckily, Gilbert had a year to get his bearings in Geneva before the crises leading to World War II began in earnest. League Secretary-General Sir Eric Drummond and other social leaders rarely saw the Gilberts off duty, but the Gilberts preferred the "wonderful Latinos," newspapermen, and other regulars at the city's best beer hall. Charlotte was still a young beauty and Prentiss was in his prime at slightly under six feet, weighing 180 pounds, and possessing a full head of blond, wavy hair over a face which featured sad looking eyes and a prominent jaw. As in Washington, poker playing, sailing, and elaborately prepared practical jokes became elements of Gilbert's reputation in Geneva.[9]

During working hours, which usually lasted into the night because Gilbert and his men could only see the League people when they were not in meetings, Gilbert had a job he had unknowingly tailor-made for himself. As he had suggested in 1929, visa-stamping chores were relegated to a contingent of American and Swiss clerks. Gilbert and his embassy-sized staff were thus freed to run an intelligence-gathering operation which went beyond official League matters to include all obtainable "gossip" and "personal opinions outside dispatches." To meet the quoted needs of J. Pierrepont Moffat, head of the Division of Western European Affairs and Gilbert's chief contact in the department all during the thirties, Gilbert and his aides would fan out each day like newspaper reporters. After their return, the staff would help Gilbert to draft and redraft the comprehensive dispatches and cables for which the consulate was repeatedly commended.[10]

Gilbert vainly sought a bigger consulate entertainment budget to facilitate better relations with League ambassadors, visiting American legislators, and a legion of such scholars as Sir Alfred Zimmern, head of a Geneva summer school for specialists in international relations. Gilbert also went to great lengths to get along with Arthur Sweetser, the foremost American in the history of the League. Sweetser, nominally an official in the secretariat's information section, had strong connections with the Rockefellers and other League supporters, and had long acted as behind-the-scenes liaison between Geneva and Washington. Now Gilbert, with a strong professional staff, was operating more openly than any of his predecessors; a fact which sometimes left Sweetser less centrally positioned than he wanted. Gilbert ran into the same difficulty with Hugh Wilson, the old guard minister to Switzerland. Wilson had strongly advocated splitting the Geneva consulate to free the League specialists from routine tourist work and the like. But Wilson had wanted to maintain complete control over the Geneva professionals whereas the department had supported the contention of Gilbert and others that, except for matters of high policy, the consulate should independently keep tabs on the fifty or more League-related activities.[11]

Gilbert's major difficulties with Wilson and Sweetser fortunately did not arise until after the League phase of the Manchurian crisis had ended. Gilbert meanwhile had successfully avoided the professional and social pitfalls built into the Geneva landscape, and by the fall of 1931, had his staff operating smoothly and producing the first batch of many topical studies of League activities. To both the isolationists and internationalists, among the thousands of Americans who visited Geneva for study or recreation each year, Gilbert successfully defended the consulate's surveillance of the League as having "practical bread-and-butter importance" for the United States. Additionally, in the eyes of the department, Gilbert was performing well the kind of representational duty hitherto usually performed by Wilson alone.[12]

In fact, early in the Manchurian crisis Gilbert was left as the chief link between Secretary Stimson and Secretary-General Drummond when Wilson was recalled to Washington to help prepare for the upcoming disarmament conference of 1932. Stimson and Drummond had both been alarmed when an elite Japanese army division launched a major offensive in Manchuria in mid-September 1931 after pretending the Chinese had sabotaged a rail line near Mukden. This unit, the Kwantung Army, enraged by a long string of attacks by Chiang Kai-shek and his warlord allies in Manchuria and China proper against Japanese (and often Western) citizens and property, now swept through the province in a matter of months to the cheers of the Japanese masses and increasing numbers of Tokyo leaders.[13]

Kijuro Baron Shidehara, the liberal Japanese foreign minister, however, wanted to curb the runaway army and its militant supporters. With the encouragement of his friend Stimson, he agreed to some peaceable, if pious, resolutions at the September session of the League Council. While Hugh Wilson was on his way home, Stimson was hailing the resolutions and the efficiency of the League's peacekeeping machinery. In early October Stimson cabled Drummond a pledge of support of "League action" and expressed the hope that the League would "assert all the authority and pressure within its competence" to end the Sino-Japanese dispute.[14]

On 8 October, Kwantung Army aircraft killed nearly twenty civilians in an attack on Chinchow, the last Chinese-held city in Manchuria. Angrily rejecting embarrassed explanations by Tokyo, Stimson feared the imminent collapse of the whole network of peace treaties established since 1919. President Herbert Hoover, though preoccupied with the world economic crisis and ruling out any military or economic measures against Japan, agreed to support the treaties by allowing "our men in Switzerland" to sit with the League Council in an emergency session. On 10 October, Stimson carried out this presidential suggestion—which Drummond and others had failed earlier to get him to support—by cabling Gilbert to participate in the mid-October special meeting in Geneva. Gilbert, who felt as if he had been "hit by lightning," asked for another transmission of the cable.[15]

Gilbert soon received a torrent of telegrams and a series of lengthy transatlantic telephone calls from Secretary Stimson himself. Gilbert had hardly met Stimson in Washington and had only recently been delegated Wilson's usual task of communicating with Drummond for the secretary. Stimson's first call, on 12 October, was inauspicious. Stimson's celebrated temper was momentarily aroused by a mistaken belief that Gilbert agreed with Drummond's doubts about America's participation in the upcoming Council session, which was to be justified by the addition of the Kellogg-Briand Pact to the agenda. Drummond was afraid that Japan might take advantage of some legal complication related to the pact to evade its peacekeeping responsibilities under the League of Nations Covenant. Stimson quickly had Gilbert assure Drummond of the bland fact that Council consideration of the Kellogg-Briand Pact would involve nothing more than formally notifying China as well as Japan of the concern of the other signatories of the 1928 pact. One feature of the 12 October call was to become characteristic of the rest of Gilbert's ill-fated assignment: the rather new and expensive radio telephone hookup led to countless misunderstandings on both ends of the line.[16]

Stimson's second call from Washington to Geneva on 13 October was the highpoint of the October mission. Believing, as he often did at first, that the liberal Japanese government was about to curb the military and its political supporters, Stimson gave Gilbert almost complete liberty to engage in behind-the-scenes Council negotiations to end the crisis as long as they were conducted under the auspices of the pact and not of the Covenant. He even authorized Gilbert to hold back American support of public invocation of the pact if the mere threat would suffice to bring Japan into line. But there was another bad connection and another misunderstanding: Stimson, thinking Gilbert was concerned with "phraseology," agreed to provide Gilbert with an opening statement for his appearance at the Council. Gilbert actually was pleading for detailed negotiating instructions so that he could cope with the critical "psychology" of the upcoming session.[17]

Also on 13 October the liberal Japanese foreign minister Shidehara ordered his Geneva ambassador, Kenkichi Yoshizawa, to oppose Gilbert's appearance unless the United States agreed to participate in League consideration of all subsequent major crises. The Council president, French Foreign Minister Aristide Briand, soon admitted to Yoshizawa publicly that he hoped Gilbert's mission would become a model. By coincidence, French Premier Pierre Laval was about to visit Hoover at the White House with the request that the Kellogg-Briand Pact be amended to provide for such consultations in future crises.[18]

As the time for Gilbert's debut drew near, Stimson was beginning to feel the predictable effects of isolationist protests in the United States. But Hoover, who turned down an adviser's plea to strengthen the Kellogg-Briand Pact, nonetheless again approved Gilbert's appearance just hours before the Council met. What really worried Stimson — the increasingly intransigent attitude of liberal Japanese leaders as well as of patriotic crowds in Tokyo — resulted in large part from discovery of a sensational Japanese army plot to assassinate the entire cabinet. The young officers, who were also planning to commit hara-kiri in front of the emperor's palace to complete their protest against any government compromise over Manchuria, were caught just in time, but Stimson's hope that his move with Gilbert would be fully accepted by Shidehara was dashed.[19]

Although Gilbert quickly spotted Yoshizawa's hardening attitude, he went ahead with Stimson's earlier orders. While grappling with a crush of newsmen from all over the world and with an overburdened code room, Gilbert arranged for Briand, the Marquess of Reading (the aged British foreign secretary making his only appearance in Geneva for this occasion), and other Council members to make bland comments within the limits of Stimson's ground rules for American participation in the session. He prepared noncontroversial remarks on the Kellogg-Briand Pact to use if called upon in the Council debate and further watered down Stimson's draft of his opening statement to take into account Yoshizawa's opposition to his appearance. But when he cabled Stimson that he was making a few unspecified changes in the speech, the secretary left a cabinet meeting in a vain effort to question him at the last minute.[20]

Answering Briand's invitation shortly after 6 P.M. on 16 October 1931, Gilbert solemnly took a chair at the end of the Council's horseshoe table in the former dining room of the Hotel Nationale. Veteran spectators ever after regarded this simple act as one of the most dramatic moments of interwar diplomacy. The many dignitaries present carefully understated their welcomes but were as exhilarated as the watching crowd of journalists, scholars, and socialites. Gilbert carried out his role to the satisfaction of all American diplomatists and newspapermen there, delivering without a hitch his first — and, as it turned out, his last — speech to the Council. Given by Stimson platitudes about peace and the Kellogg-Briand Pact to utter, Gilbert made them even more innocuous. He was, after all, a consul in a room full of foreign ministers; his importance, of course, lay in his nationality and in his role as the instrument of what many thought to be a new and dynamic Stimson policy.[21]

The corridors of League-watchers therefore buzzed when Gilbert was called to a telephone room near the chamber minutes after the end of the short session of amenities. In possibly the worst connection of all during October in Geneva, Stimson quickly approved of Gilbert's revised speech. Mistakenly thinking that the Council now wanted to shift all initiative to Stimson, the suspicious secretary declared that the pact issue might as well be dropped unless invoked first in Geneva by the other signatories. Hearing only Stimson's arguments in favor of invocation and his order to go directly to Reading with the problem, Gilbert quickly got Lord Reading to lead the major European powers in invoking the pact on 17 October.[22]

Stimson then shocked Reading, Briand, and others by delaying his own invocation on a technicality, and on 19 October, by ordering Gilbert to leave the Council table. Completely confused by Stimson's apparent reversal of his earlier plan to use the pact as a lever to bring about Sino-Japanese peace arrangements, Reading finally got Stimson to allow Gilbert to remain silently at the Council table for the remainder of the now doomed session. Briand, only months away from his death in March 1932, tirelessly tried one after another formula to reconcile Japan into withdrawing Kwantung troops and entering into negotiations. Even Yoshizawa, who did not learn until later that the Mukden Incident had been faked by his own army, was now in favor of helping Briand. But Shidehara objected, so Briand gave way to a Council resolution on 24 October, ordering Japanese withdrawal, which Yoshizawa vetoed. Gilbert repeatedly cabled for precise instructions concerning Briand's maneuvers, but Stimson ironically shut him off in favor of concentrating on Premier Laval's visit to the White House. In talks there on 24–25 October, Laval asked for a stronger Kellogg-Briand Pact (plus more American cooperation in coping with Allied and German debts) and came away as empty-handed as Briand.[23]

By the time the Council next met in emergency session, in Paris to accommodate the ailing Briand, the Japanese forces had not withdrawn to their railway zone; instead, they were pressing on through Manchuria. The Tokyo government, however, expressed a willingness to accept League investigation of not just the Mukden Incident but the entire history of the long-festering Sino-Japanese controversy. In fact, the Tokyo foreign office had mentioned that compromise possibility in September and again during Gilbert's mission.

Stimson had raised and then dashed many hopes in October. Now, he carefully followed the Council's lead, authorizing American membership on the inquiry headed by the Earl of Lytton, after others had initiated the plan. Stimson could have done as much for the League through Gilbert. For the Paris session, however, he chose as his spokesman not a consul but Charles Dawes, former vice-president and the senior American ambassador. Unfortunately, Dawes dismayed many leading European statesmen by making them wait upon him in his suite at the Ritz. He alternated between denunciations of the League and a last-minute bid, scotched by Hoover and Stimson, to appear at the Council table. Dawes made full use of Arthur Sweetser as his liaison with the Council; he could also have used Gilbert less indirectly as a primary aide. Ironically, while Gilbert had been left in Geneva to appease isolationists, Dawes was endlessly preoccupied in Paris with Gilbert's precedent, calling the question of another American Council appearance the "Banquo's ghost" of the session.[24]

The Manchurian crisis continued, of course, while Gilbert reverted to his old Geneva role as the day-to-day American contact with the more routine League activities. His October mission nonetheless had changed his status and enhanced the potential of his post in the eyes of several Americans in ways which would briefly threaten his career and his operation in Geneva.

Sir Eric Drummond finally had the Gilberts to dinner after the October mission, though he appears to have resented Stimson's continued use of the consul as a liaison with him during the disarmament conference early in 1932. Hugh Gibson, the old guard Foreign Service head of the American delegation following Stimson's brief appearance at the conference, tried to get Stimson to reserve all official American contacts with Drummond for Gibson's long-time Foreign Service comrade, Hugh Wilson. But Stimson did not want to discourage Gilbert and, while recognizing Wilson's seniority, authorized Gilbert to keep in touch with Drummond officially whenever the minister was absent.[25]

Wilson had difficulty working with Gilbert in Geneva. In 1933 he finally sought Pierrepont Moffat's advice in a very confidential letter. After defending his use of a Berne legation aide instead of Gilbert at a Geneva conference, Wilson reviewed the entire situation. He said that Gilbert had been thrust into the limelight in October 1931 only because Wilson had been called to Washington. The consul, Wilson clearly inferred, had let the momentary fame go to his head. As Gibson had earlier, Wilson complained about a problem of personalities. In a telling sentence, one old Foreign Service hand, Wilson, told another, Moffat, that the problem of soothing egos would not have arisen were S. Pinckney ("Kippy") Tuck (a wealthy predecessor of Gilbert's) still in the Geneva consulate.[26]

Also in 1933 Gilbert poured out his views in confidential letters to Stanley K. Hornbeck, the influential head of the department's Division of Far Eastern Affairs though not a foreign service officer. Gilbert did not directly criticize the members of what Wilson had called a "pretty good club." But he recalled that

Under Secretary Cotton had named Gilbert as consul precisely because he was not a member of an unspecified clique trying to influence the nomination. In one handwritten postscript, Gilbert did assert that Arthur Sweetser and other influential people in Geneva wanted him to leave the consulate. Otherwise, he claimed in his letters that his sometimes estranged position did not hurt him personally (he and Charlotte disliked society events) but made him look professionally inconsequential in the eyes of Geneva. He had always had difficulties with low budgets and the ambiguous status of the Washington-League connection. Now the consulate's reportorial task, which he believed of great value to the United States, was being hampered by other Americans' resentment of Gilbert's direct pipeline to the department.[27]

Sweetser, as it developed, was campaigning with the new Franklin Roosevelt administration to upgrade the Geneva mission in order that it might be headed by an ambassador — perhaps Wilson. Premature publicity quashed any chance the proposal might have had with the new secretary, Cordell Hull. Gilbert stayed in the consulate, continually winning praise from Hornbeck, Moffat, and Hull himself. Gilbert's repeated pleas for budget increases went for nought in Depression America. His reputation as an outstanding teacher of young diplomatists continued to grow along with the list of promising juniors assigned to him. When the United States joined the International Labor Organization (ILO), Gilbert won additional recognition for guiding neophyte American delegates at the ILO meetings.[28]

Taking advantage of his consulate's research opportunities in Geneva whenever possible, Gilbert ended his years there by carefully tracing developments which were gradually transforming the League. He quickly perceived that Joseph Avenol, who became secretary-general in 1932, would be far more influenced by French political interests than Sir Eric Drummond had been by his own domestic considerations. Gilbert noticed that as the great powers became more cautious in their support of the League, the small states appeared to become more active in both Assembly and Council. But Gilbert, who had many friends among the smaller nations' delegations, was able to show Washington their underlying fears of being ignored or worse in the wake of the dictators' repudiation of the League.[29]

Gilbert also saw both the small and the great states as moving toward elimination of sanctions from the Covenant, thus turning the League into nothing more than a convenient forum for diplomatic consultations or even into just a sounding board for propaganda campaigns. Gilbert noted that Geneva hoped that a League without sanctions would be more attractive to the United States. But economy-minded plans to end the Gilbert operation had been discussed in Washington as early as 1934. Roosevelt's failure in 1935 to win Senate support for the World Court ended all hopes for any closer United States ties with the League.[30]

For Gilbert, the disillusioning climax of the Washington-Geneva relationship (and of the sanctions issue) came in the Ethiopian crisis. Late in 1934,

Italian dictator Benito Mussolini seized upon the latest of countless incidents along the border of an adjacent Italian colony to threaten to invade Ethiopia, one of the few independent non-white states in the world. Ethiopia, aided ultimately by several American scholars, businessmen, and former soldiers, appealed quickly to the League for examination of the crisis under the terms used in the Manchurian episode in 1931.

Britain and France almost desperately wanted Mussolini's continued support against Hitler's challenge to Europe, but had to satisfy domestic pro-League sentiment by invoking economic sanctions under the terms still set by the Covenant after the Italians turned down arbitration and began their full-scale invasion early in October 1935. News of a sweeping Franco-British offer to Mussolini led to the resignation of the British foreign secretary, Sir Samuel Hoare, in December 1935, just months after he defended the League in a ringing Geneva speech.

Captain Anthony Eden, his 35-year-old replacement from the "Lost Generation of 1914," had soared into fame by championing the Covenant. While foreign secretary, he continually called for collective action against Rome. Behind the scenes, however, he was reluctant to push Mussolini too hard without American support. But Roosevelt and the State Department thought they had gone as far as they could by invoking a congressionally-mandated embargo on arms to both sides and by deploring (totally legal) American oil sales to Italy. The scene at Geneva, therefore, was set as in 1931 for one more frustrating session for Gilbert as an almost powerless observer of another chapter in the League's decline.[31]

Gilbert and his staff quickly spotted Secretary-General Avenol's attempts to follow the basically pro-Mussolini policies of French Premier Pierre Laval. Gilbert devoted several reports to the small states, who saw themselves as being shunted aside — along with Ethiopia — in favor of appeasement of Italy. Overburdened with work, Gilbert and his staff nonetheless kept up their strong contacts in all important delegations and provided Washington with incisive character sketches of the delegates to facilitate better understanding of the situation. But, while Gilbert repeatedly asked Washington for precise instructions, he got little in response other than vague encouragement and orders to deny any connection between the policies of Washington and those of Geneva. In fact, the department strenuously avoided invitations to invoke the Kellogg-Briand Pact, or otherwise to repeat the initiatives of the Gilbert mission of 1931.[32]

Gilbert kept reporting every twist and turn of Geneva's diplomacy; but, in the course of being frequently reminded of October 1931, he became deeply disillusioned with the British this time, rather than with the Americans. From his contacts in the London delegation, he learned that England sometimes contemplated leading an oil embargo against Italy regardless of Washington's position and even expected an ultimate showdown with Rome for Mediterranean supremacy. Mostly, Gilbert heard talk of appeasement, that London not only ruled out war but in some diplomatic way might ultimately pull Italy out of the hole Mussolini had dug.[33]

Extremely discouraged by the spirit of depression in Geneva, Gilbert turned against Eden, still popularly regarded as Italy's main foe at Geneva. "Never trust a man with a gold tooth," he advised the American journalist, Wallace R. Deuel, in a bitter, whimsical reference to the otherwise handsome British statesman. Comparing 1931 with the current crisis, Gilbert allowed that the United States had then failed to cooperate with the League against Japan. "We were uncertain then; now we were ready to cooperate. They wouldn't do anything," he said to State Department aide John D. Hickerson shortly after the crisis. Then, in a wrap-up memorandum, he expressed pride that the United States, far from associating with what he regarded as the lukewarm efforts of London and Geneva to invoke sanctions, had been the first to announce an embargo (against both Italian and Ethiopian arms shipments) and the first to call it off. As subsequent scholarship has shown, he was not the only American in the late thirties who believed that Washington's moral "cooperation" was all that the British really needed as top nation to take action against the dictators.[34]

During a short and final trip to America in 1935, and in subsequent mid-decade correspondence, Gilbert reflected disillusionment with the whole interwar experiment in collective security. Ruefully summing up the Washington policy which had kept him on the sidelines of one crisis after another in Geneva, Gilbert said the American motto, "In God We Trust," would soon be replaced by the Pullman car sign, "Quiet is requested for the benefit of those who have retired." He nonetheless agreed with Wilbur Carr and Breckinridge Long, two very conservative assistant secretaries, that the United States should not become mixed up in the growing European crisis.[35]

In the context of Gilbert's other dispatches and conversations, his support of Carr and Breckinridge was not isolationist, per se, but the result of overexposure to Geneva. Frequently slated for transfer, he did not actually go until two years after the popular Geneva artists, Alois Derso and Emery Kelen, drew a farewell caricature of the consulate team. Meanwhile, Gilbert was describing what Kelen later called a disarray of the spirit:

> the atmosphere of Geneva and of Europe . . . is universally one of extreme pessimism. There is a disheartening lack of belief in the value of all pacts and incidental to this the feeling that the very multiplicity of arrangements operates to create involvements which are a danger to themselves. . . . The expectation of an armed conflict takes the form of a popular fatalistic belief in its inevitableness.[36]

Gilbert too, would become deeply pessimistic; for the moment, he welcomed his next assignment, a major diplomatic challenge in Berlin.

Gilbert's seven-year stay in Geneva ended in August 1937 with his appointment as counselor in the Berlin embassy. He had been promoted to "one of the three or four key posts in the Service," wrote Moffat. Gilbert told friends that he thought he was going to the "essence" of the European and even of the world situation. Old "students" (James Riddleberger, Jacob Beam, and the brilliant but short-lived Henry Leverich) were already posted in Berlin and many of the key American journalists in Germany had been his strong supporters in Geneva days. But right from the start, as Moffat observed, Gilbert was thrown "into the ocean to learn how to swim."[37]

Ambassador William Dodd, whose increasingly emotional opposition to the Hitler regime Gilbert was supposed to abate, had returned to Washington to campaign against the Nazis. Gilbert became chargé upon arrival for the first of two extended periods in the last eighteen months of his life. Gilbert had become acquainted at Geneva very early with Nazi strong-arm diplomacy, but believed that the State Department wanted him to establish the best contacts he could as long as the United States maintained formal relations with Germany. Thus, when Hitler invited the diplomatic corps to a technically nonpolitical event at the 1937 Nuremberg party rally, Gilbert accepted along with the other major envoys. He was backed by the department and by the American newsmen covering the event, despite Dodd's protests.[38]

Glad that he had been criticized by the Nazis for his delay in accepting the Nuremberg invitation from Hitler, Gilbert observed that some German officials befriended him, apparently for having attended the rally. He was encouraged to look forward to a conference with Hermann Goering before the end of his stint as chargé. Gilbert planned to be blunt with Hitler's right-hand man and warn him that the Nazis were in danger of turning a nation of 125 million against Germany, as in 1917. Gilbert never did get a private interview with Goering but he did deliver a similar message, about Italian fascist excesses in America, to an old friend, Mussolini's ambassador to Berlin.[39]

Gilbert reported the intensification of anti-Jewish pressures, but carefully noted that the activities of some American Jews in Germany (such as a journalist's false use of a Berlin dateline, which Gilbert kept secret from the Nazis) would be criticized in any country. He also told Washington that some American consuls were afraid to report such Jewish improprieties — partly out of sympathy for the persecuted and partly out of concern for their own careers. Then Dodd returned for a brief period before retiring in December 1937. Gilbert was left in charge until Hugh Wilson took over in March 1938.[40]

Whatever their past relationship, Gilbert and Wilson now arrived at a smooth working arrangement. The new ambassador gave Gilbert special recognition for a number of long background studies done during the next months. Then came the "Night of the Broken Glass," 10 November 1938, during which the Nazis carried out a pogrom against the Jews throughout the Reich. When Roosevelt recalled Wilson in mid-November in protest, Gilbert was again chargé; no ambassador would return until after the war.[41]

Turning aside from weekly poker games with newsmen and an occasional sail on a nearby lake, Gilbert now particularly worried about the safety of the embassy's Jewish employees and about the morale of the staff generally. As during the Ethiopian affair in Geneva, he resorted to bitter whimsy in long walks and talks with American reporters. John Whitaker, of the *New York Herald-Tribune*, reported that Gilbert would talk about the mounting Nazi outrages by addressing all of his remarks to an imaginary companion, "McGonicle." Gilbert and Whitaker, who copied him, were succumbing to what another reporter called the "Berlin Blues."[42]

In a remarkable number of long cables, despatches, and letters to Washington, Gilbert unfolded the story of growing terrorism. As had occurred so often in Gilbert's career, there was scant policy guidance and little he could do but watch. But he tried. Gilbert shook up a few Nazi generals by telling them:

> One can very easily gain an erroneous impression of the temper of the United States, particularly during the postwar era, because of our steadfast emphasis on peace. I said, however, that the American people were those who had the initiative and character to leave their homes and go to a new country . . . and that they (the Germans) might think they were tough, but if we really ever got going, the American soldier, as I had seen him in the Philippines and elsewhere, would make their soldiers look like lilies.[43]

Gilbert also struck a blow or two in behalf of the mission of the American lawyer, George Rublee, who was shunted from one Berlin underling to another in his futile effort to negotiate the safe emigration of at least some of the German Jews. Gilbert made sure that consular reports about Jewish applicants for emigration got quickly to Washington. He cultivated a contact who frequently conversed with Hitler. He held clandestine meetings with numerous German opponents of the regime. And he met personally with as many of the "desperately unfortunate" Jews as possible among the crowds waiting each day at the embassy.[44]

Mainly, however, he felt that he could do nothing except convey prompt but meaningless protests against each new German "legal" measure against the Jews. He was repeatedly praised for these actions by Washington. Once, after Gilbert declared that unless he heard from Washington he was about to send a protest of his own to the German foreign office, he was quickly provided with a strong note written by Under Secretary Sumner Welles. Still, in that bitter-whimsical mood which now characterized him, he acknowledged to journalist friends that he had no real comeback when German officials taunted him about racial prejudice against Jews and other minorities in America.[45]

He made the painful prediction that still more drastic measures would be taken against the Jews. Behind the regime's anti-Semitic "nervous screaming," however, Gilbert detected that many Germans were ashamed of the pogrom. Even some Gestapo agents were sheltering or feeding Jews, he found. With the support of Jewish contacts, then, Gilbert often took a moderate course in order to help non-Nazis in the foreign office to avoid giving extremists any excuse to increase the terror.[46]

Now that he felt his career was drawing to a close, Gilbert was engaging in more diplomatic activity (however unorthodox and ultimately futile) than had ever been possible before. His voluminous reports were being increasingly noted, even by the president, much to Gilbert's satisfaction. Two long despatches in February 1939 were particularly farsighted. One accurately described German plans for economic pressure on the Balkans. The other logically concluded that Hitler should spend 1939 consolidating his diplomatic triumphs and restoring Germany's economic strength. But he repeated an earlier prediction:

> Should the regime in Germany because of a factual deterioration in German economy, or because of popular discontent, turn to radical means, such means might be sought either in the internal or in the external field and might be unexpected in their direction and explosive in their character.

In the February despatch, Gilbert also reported that Hitler "could easily shift his policy" in order to win Russian support and "will most certainly impose a radical adjustment of some nature" on Poland.[47]

Gilbert finished these two despatches on 24 February but did not live to sign them. Exhausted by his efforts, he had neglected a flareup of his old Philippine sicknesses. A foreign office doctor clumsily injected the leg inflicted with elephantiasis. The puncture did not heal, but Gilbert would not stop work. He collapsed at his desk on the afternoon of 24 February of a heart attack and died at 9 that night. To journalist John Whitaker, he was one of the first American casualties of World War II.[48]

Though he had more scope for action and more authority in Berlin than he had had in Geneva, except for that fleeting moment in 1931, Gilbert's thoughts in his last weeks turned back to Geneva. He had once concluded that "all propaganda methods are a boomerang. . . ." He was now writing to the refugee artists Derso and Kelen that he preferred "reality however small to unreality however pretentious." He looked forward to leaving the unreality of Hitler's Berlin to return to Geneva to do something, however modest, for peace.[49]

He was buried there on 3 March, against a low wall in the Petit Seconnex Cemetery, which overlooks the hills and valleys surrounding the old city.

Gilbert died on the eve of World War II. He therefore did not take part in the vast expansion of the State Department after 1939. But many of the people he trained, James Riddleberger, Llewelyn Thompson, Jacob Beam, and more, filled key positions and helped the United States to carry out a program of global scope in the postwar world. Because American policy between the wars was often antipathetic to Europe, Gilbert rarely got the opportunity to display the talent for decision-making and action which he proved he had in the last months in Berlin.

He made marks in the diplomatic record, in Geneva and in Berlin, and he left a voluminous account of the interwar period. Cordell Hull said there was no finer reporter in the Foreign Service. What makes his work still valuable is that he came to know as well as one could two opposite poles of the thirties: an often absurdly weak Geneva and an always absurdly murderous Berlin. He showed these scenes with compassion and an extraordinarily free spirit.[50]

Gilbert also represented an interwar type often overlooked by historians, for he was neither an isolationist nor an all-out internationalist, neither a pacifist nor a disciple of realpolitik. He was no opponent of the League, yet he was never moved to unreserved praise of the institution. Like many foreign correspondents of the period, Gilbert received few instructions from his "editors" other than to report the news. Events, rather than preconceived views or orders from the State Department then, taught him by the time of his death to despair for peace.

He had looked to the British in the early thirties, and like many anglophiles, had grown disillusioned with the appeasement policies of the latter half of the decade. He tried to find some way in Germany to soften Nazi policies; then, like many other searchers for an alternative to a second Great War, Gilbert became a fatalist in the wake of Crystal Night and early 1939 rumors of Hitler's next moves. Had he lived a few more weeks, until Hitler marched into Prague, Gilbert would have come to know—as even isolationists and appeasers soon were forced to realize—that it would be years before anything could be done for peace, however small, in Geneva or anywhere else.

George S. Messersmith

George S. Messersmith

1883	Born 8 October in Fleetwood, Pennsylvania
1900	Graduated from Keystone State Normal School
1900–14	School superintendent in the Delaware public schools
1912–14	Vice-president of the State Board of Education, Delaware
1914	Consul in Ft. Erie, Ontario
1916	Consul in Curacao
1919	Consul in Antwerp
1923	Consul general in Antwerp
1928	Consul general in Buenos Aires
1930	Consul general in Berlin
1934	Nominated as minister to Uruguay
1934	Minister to Austria
1937	Assistant secretary of state for administration
1940	Ambassador to Cuba
1941	Ambassador to Mexico
1946	Ambassador to Argentina
1947	Retired from the Foreign Service in August
1947–60	Honorary chairman of the board of the Mexican Light and Power Company, Ltd.
1960	Died 1 February in Mexico City

CHAPTER 7

George S. Messersmith and Nazi Germany:
The Diplomacy of Limits in Central Europe

Kenneth Moss

From early 1933 until the summer of 1937 George S. Messersmith was the State Department's most insightful commentator on Nazi Germany. While serving as consul general in Berlin until mid–1934, his reports were Washington's best source of information on German internal affairs. After appointment as the American minister to Austria, he watched Germany expand its influence into central and southeastern Europe. Until President Franklin D. Roosevelt brought Messersmith home in 1937 to become assistant secretary of state, his Vienna despatches contained a penetrating, first-hand analysis of German foreign policy. Other diplomats, like Ambassador William Bullitt in Moscow and William Dodd in Berlin, stand out in their reports about Germany, but on a daily basis Messersmith supplied the most knowledgeable analysis to Washington. By autumn 1933 Messersmith's analyses were read in the White House as well as in the State Department; Undersecretary of State William Phillips found the despatches so important that he passed on parts of them to the president.[1]

Messersmith's influence on American policy was greatest between 1933 and 1936. During these first three years of Adolf Hitler's rule, American-German realtions deteriorated because of trade disputes, anti-Jewish demonstrations, and rearmament. As a consul Messersmith was involved in the first two issues and gained insight into domestic considerations behind Nazi policy. American policymakers in Washington trusted Messersmith and learned from him that German foreign policy was a response to internal economic problems as well as a fulfillment of Hitler's expansionist dreams. Messersmith helped Washington understand the political implications of American policy. American trade policy during 1934–35 became a weapon cautiously aimed at undermining Hitler's government by worsening economic conditions.[2]

Regardless of their interpretations of American policy, historians use Messersmith's statements to justify their conclusions. Writers, like Arnold A. Offner, who believe American leaders were tragically shortsighted and naive about German aspirations, regard Messersmith as a voice in the wilderness, a prophet who saw truth while others refused to accept it. Offner believes Washington excluded Messersmith's arguments and thereby put American policy on a disastrous course. "Revisionist" historians, who emphasize the economic causes for the breakdown of German-American relations, argue that Messersmith played a central role in American policymaking. The German historian Hans-Jürgen Schröder, for example, insists Messersmith's interpretation of German economic policy was behind the uncompromising course of Washington's Open Door diplomacy—the demand for equal treatment of American exports by German importers.[3]

Neither interpretation of Messersmith is fully correct. While one can applaud Messersmith's realistic predictions about the expansionist aims of Hitler's regime, it is difficult to excuse his misconceptions about the weakness of Germany's economy and the strength of Hitler's opposition. His prophecies about Germany sometimes deserved neglect. Nor was Messersmith as strictly concerned with commercial issues and the Open Door as some insist. He perceived commercial affairs in a political context and argued that American trade policy could thwart Hitler's European dreams. Although many in Washington conceived trade policy primarily in terms of the Open Door, others agreed with Messersmith and sought to define it from a political perspective as well.[4]

Based on his understanding of German policy, Messersmith insisted that effective European collective security reinforced by American economic pressure could stop Hitler. None of his ideas were fully implemented by European or American statesmen during the mid–1930s. By mid–1937 Messersmith conceded that Germany had become stronger. Still, this did not stop him from believing that Germany was economically vulnerable. He maintained this conviction until September 1939, when the crash of guns made further discussion meaningless. Messersmith's reports were a mixture of reality and illusion; it was never easy to separate the valuable from the misleading.

Born in Fleetwood, Pennsylvania in 1883, Messersmith attended school in Pennsylvania and Delaware. His professional goal was to become a secondary school teacher, and thus he attended Keystone State Normal School and Delaware State College. Settling in Delaware, he taught civics, wrote a textbook about Delaware's government, and eventually became a high school principal in Felton, Delaware. While living there he became engaged to Marion Mustard, the daughter of a well-to-do family active in state politics. Because his income was low, his fiancee arranged for him to take a room with the family of Dr. John Bassett Moore. Moore was one of the country's foremost authorities on international law and held the post of counselor of the Department of State. The meager salaries of high school principals in the early 1900s made Messersmith wonder whether he and Marion could exist on such paltry earnings, so he questioned Moore about a career in the State Department. Moore advised him to avoid the diplomatic branch and join the consular service where salaries were better. Moore probably suspected Messersmith would have trouble winning acceptance from the diplomats, whose regard for others too often depended on social and educational background. Persuaded by Moore's counsel, Messersmith took the required entrance examination for the service and in 1914 received appointment as a consul.[5]

Throughout Messersmith's career his uncompromising personality determined the quality and nature of most of his work. He once told George F. Kennan that his years as a high school principal taught him never to yield to an opinion simply because it was the majority view. He followed his own advice strictly, was demanding when administering rules, and expected conformity to them. While reforming consular procedures in Germany in 1930– 31, he established so many rules that others thought he was a zealot. He refused to give in to criticism and had the satisfaction of seeing his reforms bring major improvements.[6] Whenever he wrote a despatch or letter, Messersmith believed he had to discuss all angles of a question. In his opinion, diplomatic correspondence was intended to educate not merely inform the reader. In State Department circles his hefty despatches won him the nickname "Forty Page George." Messersmith ignored repeated suggestions to shorten his reports, claiming that to do so would force him to present an incomplete picture.[7] Such defensiveness about his work was common. Messersmith's despatches reflected an unyielding commitment to thoroughness, but they also suggested an author so short of time that his thoughts could not be compressed into concise and readable reports.

No officer in the consular service could avoid falling under the influence of its director, Wilbur J. Carr. Until Carr left Washington in 1937, he adamantly argued that trade policy was a central element of American foreign policy. The economically burdened world of the 1920s, with its postwar reparations and debts, nationalistic trade policies, and Great Crash in 1929, proved the importance of economic issues in shaping international political stability. Carr explained that internal economic conditions were a greater determinant of foreign relations than political rivalry or security. With international political tension rising after 1929, it would have been difficult to disagree with Carr.[8]

Messersmith absorbed Carr's arguments and did his best to apply them as consul general in Berlin and as minister to Austria. Like Carr, Messersmith assumed that those who focused all their attention on political matters were missing much of the picture. In 1932, in a typical example of his turgid prose, Messersmith outlined his thinking for Secretary of State Henry L. Stimson:

> While it is generally recognized that the political relations between states, with which the diplomatic mission of our Government has to concern itself, have almost entirely an economic, financial or social background, and that purely political relations in the old sense of the word no longer exist, experience has shown that the officers of the Department in the field do not all understand the necessity of their informing the Department regularly and (with) sufficient clarity and comprehensiveness of those factors concerning it which must be fully

informed in order to have the necessary background to understand the political relations in a certain country or determine our own policy.[9]

During Hitler's first months in power in 1933 Messersmith, reporting from Berlin, emphasized his economic interpretation. He believed that the anti-Jewish demonstrations and hateful propaganda distributed by Nazi organizers were part of the leadership's effort to divert the public eye from Hitler's failure to relieve economic problems.[10] If Hitler could find a way to stabilize the economy Messersmith thought the chancellor would halt some of the violent activities of his followers. Messersmith's concept of Hitler was reinforced by his acquaintanceship with several leading government and Nazi figures. This perspective caused Messersmith to believe that German political policies reflected economic and financial needs and that Berlin's attitude toward the United States was a function of economic matters. Therefore, it was logical that American policy should be aimed at the German economy.[11]

Messersmith's ability to approach German officials on a personal level complemented Washington's desire to avoid official disagreement with Berlin. The State Department did not want the embassy to make any remark that might complicate relations with Hitler, who was viewed with uncertainty. Because Roosevelt did not immediately appoint a new ambassador to Berlin, the chargé d'affaires George Gordon and Messersmith were left in control of diplomatic responsibilities. The chargé was to represent the United States before the German government, but Washington's cautious stance did not give him the freedom to lodge protests. Besides, the protests seldom mattered since the American embassy quickly learned the futility of petitioning the German government. In Germany, the Nazi party was the real source of government policy, and the United States did not have the authority to protest officially to the leadership of a political party. To have done so would have been an invitation to accuse the United States of interference in Germany's internal affairs. The State Department, for example, did not wish to protest officially against anti-Jewish laws for fear of worsening diplomatic relations and driving the Germans to even harsher anti-Jewish measures. It was left to Messersmith to circumvent the government and approach party leaders, who it was hoped would understand the damage of anti-Jewish actions to Germany's image. Washington supported this indirect approach, and in the summer of 1933, regarded it as a success. The chief of the Division of West European Affairs, J. Pierrepont Moffat, praised Messersmith for his efforts.[12]

Developments during the last six months of 1933 shattered Messersmith's confidence in German leaders. By the year's end he believed that the Germans had to be confronted directly. He wrote Undersecretary of State William Phillips that Germany's leaders appeared to be clinical psychopaths who could only be stopped by war.[13] Several developments had brought Messersmith to this drastic conclusion. Germany, in the face of international outcry, had continued its anti-Jewish policy and had threatened to rearm itself in direct violation of the Versailles treaty. During the summer of 1933 Hitler destroyed most of his political opposition to the left and center of German politics. The German government also bombarded its people with propaganda which told them Germany was surrounded by foreign enemies. The extremism of German policy erased the hopes Messersmith had had in early 1933.[14]

Messersmith realized, however, that war against Germany was impossible in the international climate of 1934. Hitler's worried European neighbors were not psychologically or militarily prepared for such action, nor was the United States, where disillusionment with involvement in World War I controlled public opinion. In 1933 Roosevelt enjoyed more freedom in foreign policy than he would two years later when Congress passed the first neutrality law. But the president was thinking only in terms of a loose commitment to European security through an arms embargo.[15]

The best strategy against Germany was a firm trade policy that refused compromise on major commercial questions. Trade policy had the advantage of not being closely restricted by a Congress concerned with American intervention in another war. Although Congress did rule on trade bills, their execution was strongly guarded by the president and the State Department. Recent German actions reinforced the belief that American trade policy might have a significant effect on Germany. To correct long-standing problems of inflation, foreign debts, and a shortage of natural resources the Berlin government had introduced a number of measures including high tariffs and restrictions on foreign business in Germany. As an additional rescue measure Berlin tried to subsidize the export of German manufactured items with "blocked marks." These marks lost fifty percent of their value when their holder exchanged them for foreign currency but retained their full value if used to purchase German exports. Furthermore, the Germans proposed a direct link between payment of their debts and the fair treatment of exports to Germany. These actions were indications of Germany's economic problems and revealed its dependence on foreign cooperation.[16]

Messersmith clearly believed American trade policy could topple Hitler's government. Some of Hitler's greatest trouble came from Nazi extremists who were convinced that other foreign economies desperately needed German exports. The myopic view governing radical thought was that "Germany is too great a country for the world to let it go to pieces and that [the U.S.] will make any kind of a bargain with [Germany] for raw materials to keep [it] going." American opposition would challenge this arrogant analysis and consequently begin a crisis within the Nazi party.[17]

During Messersmith's last months in Berlin, American policy moved in the direction he wanted. In the early spring of 1934 the State Department refused to negotiate a revision of the 1923 commercial treaty with Germany. American officials told Ambassador Hans Luther that German policy contradicted the Roosevelt administration's desire for equal treatment of exports.[18] When the president's trade adviser, George N. Peek, pressed for bilateral trade agreements with Germany, department officials tried to dissuade Peek by showing him Messersmith's letters. It is also apparent that Messersmith had highly placed allies in Washington in William Phillips and Herbert Feis, adviser to the secretary of state. Feis echoed Messersmith about Berlin's desire to establish a better credit relationship with the United States and advised against accepting German terms.[19]

If Messersmith hoped American trade policy would stop Hitler, he likewise wanted to avoid any act that would seriously damage trade with Germany. These two expectations were contradictory and showed a split purpose in American policy that was widely supported. Messersmith and the State Department opposed efforts by other government officials, particularly in the Treasury Department, to impose countervailing duties on German exports. Messersmith feared the Germans would retaliate by placing higher duties on American exports.[20] Similar instances of cautious treatment of German exports recurred during the following years as Washington sought to prevent a breakdown in negotiations. Domestic conditions, especially the depression, also acted as a restraint. With the American economy only haltingly recovering, the State Department knew it could not find domestic support for measures that might cost American exporters a major market.[21]

As Messersmith prepared to leave Berlin for Vienna, he believed that internal strife in the Nazi party was creating a need for American caution. During early 1934 Hitler was engaged in a struggle against Ernst Roehm, the chief of the Nazi stormtroopers (SA), who wanted to integrate the German army with his SA units. A victory for Roehm on the military issue would give Nazi militants more voice in the party. From Nazi sources, Messersmith learned Roehm's victory would instigate more anti-Jewish demonstrations. He warned Ambassador Dodd of the need for caution and restraint in dealing with radicals like Roehm who had such unrealistic notions about German economic and political power. An American announcement of restrictions on German exports would weaken Hitler's control and thereby throw the government into the hands of extremists more irrational than the Führer himself.[22]

When President Roosevelt promoted Messersmith to the post of minister to Austria in April 1934, he told a friend that Messersmith was needed in Vienna because Austria's relationship to Nazi Germany made it a "key spot."[23] Hitler's wish to unite his former homeland with Germany was no secret, and by early 1934 the Germans had increased their support of pro-German groups in Austria. However, in mid-1934 few in the United States or Europe expected Hitler to intervene in Austria. This false sense of security made Vienna more of a listening post than a center of diplomatic attention for the Americans. In Vienna, with its banking houses and cultural and political relations with Germany, Messersmith could receive excellent information about Berlin's domestic and foreign policies. On arriving in Vienna, he found the country shaken by recent turmoil. Its chancellor, Engelbert Dollfuss, had just dissolved

Parliament a year before, crushed a labor revolt in Vienna with government artillery, and outlawed the Social Democratic party. This turmoil was exploited by Austrian Nazis, and Messersmith quickly realized the importance of Austria to Germany and the objectives of German policy in central and southeastern Europe.[24]

Hitler's assassination of Roehm and his followers during the Night of the Long Knives (30 June to 1 July) forced Messersmith to reassess his appraisal of Hitler. That brutal night frightened Messersmith by its revelation of the malicious principles guiding Hitler. He concluded there was no effective way to stop him except by "complete removal." In the shock following the purge, Messersmith predicted a possible revolt against Hitler by the public and party faithful. Messersmith believed that the army and ambitious Nazis, like Hermann Goering, could step into the turmoil of Germany's politics and economy, restore order, and create a new government. Yet no such event occurred. Hitler's purge had strengthened his control over the nation and the party.[25]

Events in Austria in late July 1934 deepened Messersmith's fear of Hitler's power and ambition in Europe. For Messersmith, the brutal murder of Chancellor Dollfuss by Nazi assassins revealed clearly for the first time the expansionist aims of German foreign policy. Henceforth, Messersmith accurately suspected that Hitler would use subversion and eventually military force to destroy the independence of Austria and southeastern Europe in order to make Germany the most powerful nation on the Continent.[26]

Messersmith also revised his assessment of the German people and their relationship to Hitler. While not willing to claim that Hitler represented the choice and spirit of the German people, Messersmith now thought that Hitler's leadership reflected disturbing patterns in German history. Turning to the diplomatic analysis of Sir Eyre Crowe, a German specialist in the British Foreign Office before World War I, Messersmith pointed out that a belief in national superiority and a worldwide mission had dominated modern German history. Hitler's course was determined by history, and the German people had merely acted in accordance with their historical sense. Nevertheless, Messersmith did not believe Germany was set on an unalterable course. No diplomat worth his salt could submit to such a deterministic explanation of national behavior. Messersmith subsequently showed his conviction that the Germans could be forced to see their mistake and drop Hitler before he took the nation in a more disastrous direction.[27]

In the aftermath of Dollfuss's assassination, Messersmith regarded European collective security as the best means to stop Hitler. A successful defense of Austrian independence would thwart Germany's ambition in southeastern Europe and thereby end the possibility of German dominance over Europe. If Britain, France, and Italy could act jointly against Hitler, Messersmith believed they could "secure from an insecure and trembling Germany guarantees for Austrian independence."[28] Of the three powers, Britain was the most important. While French participation in collective security was vital, it could not succeed without the support of Britain which held the strongest position against Germany. Germany, Messersmith later wrote, "can never reach what she is after as long as England is strong, and she must get Central and Southeastern Europe if she is to be strong enough to dictate to London."[29]

The challenge before Messersmith was to persuade Washington of Austria's importance and then aid the administration in searching for a realistic policy to support European collective security. On the highest levels of discussion, Messersmith, President Roosevelt, and internationalists in the State Department all agreed on the desirability of American support of European security against German expansion. But Messersmith and the State Department knew there was little chance that Roosevelt could commit the United States to any arrangement for European collective security. The commencement of neutrality legislation in 1935 tied the president's hands. Roosevelt himself was unwilling to unleash criticism on himself and the New Deal by risking major initiatives in foreign policy. His fear of damage to the New Deal made him resemble his Republican predecessors of the 1920s who had similarly avoided foreign entanglement because domestic needs had higher priority.[30] Messersmith regretted the self-imposed isolation of the United States and feared isolationist policy could "unwillingly and unintentionally" make the United States, at least in part, responsible for the next war.[31]

While Messersmith realized the administration could not formally join a security arrangement, he believed that an uncompromising trade policy would have the same effect, particularly when combined with the signs of an emerging coalition of west European powers. Europe's future, he told Phillips, depended on a "united front of the Powers as now maintained and a maintenance of our attitude of no moral or material support to Germany."[32]

The "united front" which Messersmith mentioned to Phillips was the recent reaction of France, Britain, and Italy to the Dollfuss affair. Messersmith had strong confidence in Benito Mussolini, who on hearing of Dollfuss's assassination had alerted Italian troops on maneuver near the Austrian border. Although history would reveal the mistake of placing confidence in Mussolini, in late 1934 there was justification for such trust. Messersmith, as well as Phillips and Moffat, thought Mussolini's fast reaction had saved Austria from falling under German control. Mussolini's concern about German attempts to erode Italian influence in central and southeastern Europe was also well known. Germany's signature of trade treaties in 1934 with Yugoslavia and Hungary competed with the commercial protocols Austria and Hungary had signed with Italy in March 1934. In the autumn of that year Austria and Hungary consequently sent envoys to Rome to negotiate a more comprehensive arrangement.[33]

Messersmith was confident that Britain stood ready to confront Hitler. In August 1934 he wrote that London now recognized the fact that Austrian and Danubian problems were "the major factors in the threats to European peace." More significantly, it appeared Britain would act without depending on the close support of the United States.[34]

Developments during the first months of 1935 increased Messersmith's confidence in European collective security. In March Italy joined France and Britain to condemn Hitler's announcement of military conscription. A month later these three powers met at Stresa, Italy, and agreed to support Austrian independence and oppose "unilateral repudiation of treaties which may endanger the peace of Europe."[35] The Stresa Front was as close as Europe came to collective security during Messersmith's service in Vienna. Its promise was destroyed within six months, as Britain signed a naval agreement with Germany, and Italy invaded Ethiopia.

After Mussolini's invasion of Ethiopia, Washington's hope for European collective security was shattered by the announcement of the Hoare-Laval plan in late 1935. This Anglo-French proposal offered Italy control of parts of Ethiopia and signaled a shameful compromise with Italian aggression. The proposal seriously shook Roosevelt's belief in the ability of the European powers to solve their own crisis. But unlike Roosevelt and the State Department leaders, who responded to the Anglo-French appeasement by retreating, Messersmith pressed for firmer American intervention.[36]

With European collective security foundering, Messersmith believed the United States had to take new steps to reinforce it. He turned again to American trade policy and argued that a relaxation of Open Door objectives in southeastern Europe would aid the stability of nations in the Danube valley and reinforce British and French will. Particularly valuable would be American support of efforts by the Danubian nations to sign commercial agreements among themselves directed against Germany.[37] The president and State Department could consent to a system of special trade preferences in southeastern Europe without an outcry from Congress. Dropping the demand for equal treatment of American exports might not aid American business, but Messersmith was confident it would assist European security and the interest of the United States in world peace.

Messersmith first proposed such action in November 1934, while his confidence in collective security remained high. He suggested that Washington remove Austria from a list of nations with which the United States wanted to negotiate a reciprocal treaty. The Austrian government in recent months had attempted to arrange a system of preferential trade agreements with its neighbors, including Czechoslovakia and Hungary. Messersmith reminded the secretary of state that American exporters already enjoyed a favorable balance of trade with Austria. If Washington pressed for full most-favored-nation treatment, it would weaken Austria's policy of regional negotiations.[38]

The department's answer, given four months later, was not the large concession Messersmith wanted. Nevertheless, it indicated an appreciation of the political overtones of trade in southeastern Europe. The department agreed to remove Austria from the list of nations discriminating against American exports, since the "Danubian area has certain problems confronting it which might justify some sort of preferential arrangements." However, the grip of the

Open Door policy had only loosened. Although the Austrians were encouraged to pursue their negotiations, the State Department insisted Vienna offer American exporters terms similar to those extended in any preferential agreements.[39]

By 1936 Secretary of State Cordell Hull was concerned about the political implications of Germany's attempts to develop a bilateral trade system in southeastern Europe. Berlin's attempt to form a system of trade preferences was in the hands of the finance minister, Dr. Hjalmar Schacht, whose aims included the undermining of regional negotiations by Austria and Czechoslovakia. Although these two countries signed a mutual trade agreement, strong German opposition delayed its enactment. American onlookers reported Schacht was discouraging these nations from signing trade treaties with the United States or any European power opposed to Hitler. Schacht's travels laid valuable groundwork for German expansion. In 1936 Yugoslavia and Bulgaria signed trade agreements with Berlin. Under obvious German pressure, Vienna also entered an agreement with Berlin to reconcile economic and political differences between the two governments.[40]

Given these developments, Messersmith concluded the United States could not overcome such "insuperable difficulties." His recommendations for American encouragement of regional pacts against Hitler foundered on Washington's weak economic and political influence in southeastern Europe. Even if the State Department had completely followed Messersmith's recommendations, it is unlikely that American policy would have had any effect, because Germany's economic role in that troubled area was older and stronger. Austria, perhaps all southeastern Europe, was falling into Hitler's grasp and there seemed to be nothing America could do to prevent it.[41]

Messersmith had hoped Hitler's occupation of the Rhineland in March 1936 would persuade Washington to reconsider its isolation from European collective security. Instead, the incident discouraged Roosevelt and affirmed for much of the American public the wisdom of political isolation from Europe. His hopes blocked, Messersmith returned to his argument that economic pressure against Germany could topple Hitler in a domestic crisis. However, an impartial observer could only conclude that Messersmith's suggestions had become as fruitless as the futile efforts at collective security made by London and Paris.[42] The German economy had not been seriously affected by American actions since 1933, and Hitler's diplomatic victories had won him greater public support. Stronger measures than economic pressure were needed to stop the German dictator. After the Rhineland affair most British, French, and American statesmen stood intimidated before Berlin's illusion of military might.

One alternative that Messersmith insisted western Europe and the United States should explore was never thoroughly investigated — Soviet participation in European collective security. The fear of communism and an unfortunate gullibility for Nazi anti-Soviet propaganda caused many western statesmen to accept Nazi Germany as a bulwark against dreaded bolshevism. Messersmith believed these concerns caused a widespread misunderstanding and neglect of Soviet Russia's position in European power politics. The Kremlin, Messersmith argued, was interested in consolidating its domestic position rather than promoting world revolution. Of all the Soviet Union's enemies, Germany was certainly the most serious. Messersmith did not dispute the anticapitalist, authoritarian nature of the Soviet government, but Nazi Germany, he insisted, was far "more dangerous than anything we have had in Russia."[43]

Most in the Roosevelt administration could not accept Messersmith's argument. The one important exception was Roosevelt himself, who ordered Joseph Davies to Moscow in January 1937 to improve relations with Premier Joseph Stalin. However, the prevailing view among American diplomats was very hostile. While Claude Bowers, a political appointee in Spain, supported Messersmith, Breckinridge Long reflected the majority opinion of conservative Foreign Service and State Department professionals when he wondered "whether German control of Central and Southeastern Europe is as objectionable as the infiltration of Communism throughout Europe."[44] Another objection voiced by Ambassador Bullitt was the suspicion that the Soviets would be an unreliable partner in collective security, since Moscow would be likely to continue its search for a chance to improve relations with Germany. Trained Soviet specialists, like Loy Henderson and George F. Kennan, argued that the worldwide promotion of Marxist-Leninist doctrine was still very important to Soviet leaders. Kennan and others certainly did not disagree with those who claimed the Kremlin wished to strengthen its hold on the Russian people, but they insisted this policy had not diverted the Soviets from their commitment to world revolution.[45]

Messersmith's answer to these arguments contained points which still surface in debates about the Soviet Union. Unable to deny the Soviet commitment to ideology, he nonetheless reminded his critics that leftist political movements could develop without the instigation of Soviet agents. Messersmith knew it was impossible for the Soviets to have such control over world politics; a claim like this ignored the history and domestic conditions of nations. When looking into the future, he admitted the Soviet Union could become a threat to world security, but that situation was "too remote for a realistic statesman to envisage." It was more likely that the Soviets would moderate their commitment to communism and let the nation evolve into a moderate type of state capitalism.[46]

Messersmith's analysis of Soviet communism is interesting when compared with his treatment of Nazism, for in both instances he believed the regimes acted primarily from domestic considerations. However, because of Germany's economic situation and the political objectives of the Nazi state, Berlin had to alter the political balance of Europe to accomplish and protect its objectives. The dual aims of acquiring valuable natural resources and protecting the political and racial security of the German Reich meant Hitler would seek dominance over Europe. Messersmith never outlined his views on the Soviet system as thoroughly, but it is clear that he thought the class-oriented ideology of Marxism did not need to change the European balance of power to accomplish its aims. As noted, few shared this interpretation, and toward the end of the Second World War, Messersmith surrendered it, as he started to worry about the expansion of the Soviet influence into western Europe and the western hemisphere.[47]

Messersmith's appointment as assistant secretary of state for administration in the summer of 1937 should have ended a period of frustration. His years in Vienna had not been rewarding to one so alarmed about the future security of western Europe and the United States. Congressional restraint and isolationist public opinion had so reduced the administration's effectiveness in foreign policy that Messersmith's suggestions for a more active American role in Europe were scarcely plausible. Service in Washington would increase his chances for changing policy, but he soon discovered the president and State Department were inclined to negotiate with Hitler. Roosevelt's interest in a conference with Hitler and Mussolini in late 1937 horrified Messersmith, and he and Hull had to dissuade the president from the scheme.[48]

Messersmith's credibility was undoubtedly hurt by his adherence to old arguments. Despite evidence of Germany's increasing economic and political strength, he continued to believe economic pressure could change Berlin's policies. In fact, his confidence in economic coercion lasted until September 1939, when war made this argument useless. Thus, while his listeners believed much of what he said about German ambition they rejected his recommendations. Evidence for believing so faithfully in Germany's weakness simply did not exist.[49]

Messersmith found it difficult to deal with disagreement from friends and colleagues, and his dissatisfaction increased as he perceived that few realized the extreme seriousness of the German problem. Straining his health — he had a history of stomach disorder — and pressing himself eleven to twelve hours seven days a week, Messersmith often became tense and irritable. When Moffat told him that this pace was dangerous, the advice went unheeded. Sadly, his mental strain was revealed in accusations against others for undermining him. Moffat confided in his diary that Messersmith saw issues "only in black and white," and had become "very intolerant of anyone who does not see eye to eye with him."[50] A person with less prestige might have suffered exclusion, but his colleagues treated him sympathetically and tried to sift valuable information from his arguments. Nevertheless, when Roosevelt appointed him ambassador to Cuba in early 1940, many must have been relieved for their sake as well as Messersmith's. He welcomed the appointment and assumed his new post in March 1940.[51]

Messersmith's assignment in Havana began seven years of service which made him one of the most influential American ambassadors in Spanish America. From early 1940 to December 1941 Messersmith ironed out economic problems between the United States and Cuba and helped secure Cuban support of the war. Roosevelt then selected him for the embassy in Mexico City. Beginning in early 1942 Messersmith served for four years as ambassador, successfully negotiated Mexican support for the war, and searched for a solution that would grant the United States access to Mexico's valuable natural resources during the war while assuring the Mexicans economic development in the process. He ended his career as ambassador to Argentina during the last half of 1946 and early 1947. In Buenos Aires Messersmith's recommendations that Washington relax its pressure on the rightist regime of Juan Peron collided with the State Department's public criticism of that government. Turning this disagreement into a personal feud, Messersmith so upset Secretary of State George C. Marshall and his subordinates that he was forced to submit his own resignation, but only after reading in the newspaper that he had supposedly done so already. He retired from the State Department in August 1947.[52]

When war broke out in Europe in September 1939, Messersmith must have felt vindicated. Everything he had predicted about the danger of Hitler's Germany had apparently come true. Years later he recollected how Moffat entered his office and remarked that he must have been satisfied with the news of war. Messersmith replied that such a remark was very unfair and demanded that Moffat apologize. According to Messersmith, Moffat, nearly in tears, admitted he had always suspected Messersmith was right but had been unwilling to face the truth.[53] While this story has a self-serving aura, it reveals the pride with which Messersmith regarded his accomplishments. He was justly proud of having emerged as a realist. While he had had misconceptions about Hitler's strength and support, he had also foreseen the danger of Nazi Germany for Europe and the United States.

Messersmith's service in Berlin and Vienna reveals the limited ability of a respected diplomat to influence foreign policy when his nation and much of its leadership desires different objectives. American political isolation, not indifference from Roosevelt or the State Department, determined the ultimate fate of Messersmith's suggestions. From his despatches and those of others, Roosevelt knew what was happening in Europe. Indeed, the president's inclination to take some form of limited action between 1933 and 1937 coincided with Messersmith's desires, but the president had to listen to the public and most of the State Department. The dominant view in and outside of Washington was isolationist. Roosevelt, knowing the danger to his presidency of a controversial foreign policy, chose to follow the country's demands.

Messersmith's career also raises questions about the content and style of American diplomacy. In recent years historians have tried to define the professional diplomatic mind in order to see what principle or principles have guided it. Such writers have fortunately realized the continuity provided by professional diplomats.[54] This trend in scholarship is perhaps narrowly focused; too often, the professional diplomatic corps has been associated with the social and political values of an Eastern elite. While one cannot deny the latter's influence, it is important to remember that Messersmith was never part of this elite. He did not have its educational background, nor did he rise from the diplomatic ranks. As a consul, his perspective was different; instead of dealing with the issues of political representation between nations and the weight of their respective political power, Messersmith judged international relations by the influence on a nation's foreign policy of its internal economic and political system. One recent student of professional diplomacy argues that the Foreign Service, while not believing in the importance of commercial diplomacy, used the rhetoric of commercial expansion during the 1920s to win the support of the business community. While that may indeed be true, it does not exemplify Messersmith. Because of his consular training, Messersmith believed economic and commercial matters to be of crucial significance in international relations. Messersmith's example does not disprove such an interpretation; he does not speak for the entire Foreign Service. However, his case forces one to realize that no single intellectual tradition has guided modern American diplomacy and that the consular tradition, largely ignored by historians, has played a greater role than believed.[55]

Claude Bowers

Claude Bowers

1878	Born 20 November in Hamilton County, Indiana
1896	Graduated from Shortridge High School, Indianapolis
1901	Editorial writer, *Indianapolis Sentinel*
1903	Editorial writer, *Terre Haute Star*
1917	Editor, *Fort Wayne Journal Gazette*
1923	Political columnist, *New York Evening World*
1925	Published *Jefferson and Hamilton*
1928	Keynote speaker at the Democratic National Convention, Houston
1929	Published *The Tragic Era*
1931	Political columnist, *New York Journal*
1932	Published *Beveridge and the Progressive Era*
1933	Appointed ambassador to Spain
1939	Appointed ambassador to Chile
1953	Retired from diplomatic service
1954	Published *My Mission to Spain*
1958	Died 21 January in New York City

CHAPTER 8

Claude Bowers and His Mission to Spain:
The Diplomacy of a Jeffersonian Democrat

Douglas Little

At St. Jean de Luz, a French resort town just a short distance up the Biscayan coast from the Spanish border, Claude Bowers — historian, journalist, and American ambassador to Spain — watched as the war clouds gathered in early 1939. Marooned in France and thus forced to remain a spectator throughout most of the Spanish Civil War, Bowers concluded sadly that there was little hope for democracy in Europe. High in the mountains of the Sudetenland, Hitler's troops were poised for their final strike against Prague. Fifteen hundred miles to the southwest on the plains of Castile, Franco's forces, armed with German weapons, prepared to renew their assault on Madrid. On 1 March the State Department summoned Bowers to return home for consultation. Three days later, while he sailed west across the Atlantic on the Queen Mary, Spain's republican government was toppled by dissident elements of its own army, opening the door to a Franco victory later in the month. By the time Claude Bowers arrived in Washington, the Spanish Republic had ceased to exist.

Bowers, who had been stationed in Spain since 1933, regarded the outcome of the civil war as both a personal and a diplomatic tragedy. He had been sympathetic to the Spanish Republic from its very inception in 1931 and had welcomed the series of political and social reforms introduced during the following five years. A long-time admirer of Spain's left-wing republican leaders, Bowers warned American officials that a right-wing triumph would turn the clock back to the sixteenth century. He saw broader international implications as well. Deeply troubled by German and Italian military aid to Franco's rebels, Bowers viewed the Spanish Civil War as a struggle between fascist autocracy and liberal democracy and prophesied that Washington's unwillingness to resist such aggression in Spain would make wider war inevitable.

Bowers received but modest vindication upon his return to the United States. "We have made a mistake," Franklin Roosevelt told him privately in late March 1939, "you have been right all along."[1] This admission came as small comfort to Bowers, who prided himself on his political connections with the White House. Indeed, historians have long wondered why Bowers, a personal friend

129

of President Roosevelt, wielded so little influence over American policy toward Spain. Most accounts of United States diplomacy during the Spanish Civil War have emphasized that isolationist sentiment among the public, recent congressional neutrality legislation, and the State Department's desire to cooperate with the British Foreign Office in an informal system of collective security drowned out Bowers's warnings until it was too late.[2] Bowers himself has offered a more sinister interpretation in his memoirs. Charging that a "strategically placed" and "pro-Franco element" in the State Department sidetracked his own reports from St. Jean de Luz, Bowers has suggested that Roosevelt never received an accurate picture of the situation in Spain.[3]

Neither interpretation, however, offers an adequate explanation of Bowers's relative ineffectiveness. If isolationism, neutrality laws, and collective security requirements thwarted Roosevelt's desire to assist the Spanish Republic, why did not similar obstacles prevent the president from aiding Chiang Kai-shek's China after 1937? On the other hand, how could sinister forces in the State Department block Bowers's access to the White House when he carried on a private correspondence with Roosevelt throughout the Spanish Civil War? The answer to the riddle of Bowers's lack of influence has less to do with isolationism or conspiracy than with the poor state of relations between the State Department and its ambassador to Spain.

Three factors seem to have reduced Bowers's influence on American policy toward Spain in the 1930s. First, he was a political appointee rather than a career diplomat. Since the Foreign Service had recently undergone a process of professionalization, many experienced American policymakers were bound to discount Bowers as an amateur. Second, during his first three years in Madrid Bowers had come down on the wrong side of certain political and economic disputes between the United States and Spain. As a result, State Department officials concluded that he had contracted an acute case of "localitis." Finally, once the civil war erupted in 1936, Bowers was stranded in France and out of touch with developments south of the Pyrenees. Consequently, his superiors tended to rely more heavily on reports from American officials who were actually in the war zone. Ironically, Bowers's political connections, his sympathy for the Spanish Republic, and his exile at St. Jean de Luz combined to limit rather than to enhance his influence in Washington.

Born in 1878 on a farm in central Indiana, Claude Bowers later claimed to have been a Jeffersonian Democrat since the age of two. While still a schoolboy in Indianapolis, he won the state oratorical championship with a critical evaluation of Alexander Hamilton. More interested in politics than in pedagogy, Bowers shunned college in favor of journalism and for two decades served as an editorial writer for several Indiana newspapers. Having built a national reputation with his attacks on "Hamiltonians" past and present, in 1923 Bowers was hired as a political columnist by the *New York Evening World*, a partisan Democratic daily. Two years later he published *Jefferson and Hamilton*, a work which not only depicted Jefferson as a master politician and friend of the common man but also established its author as one of the leading popular historians in the United States. His credentials as a spokesman for Jeffersonian Liberalism firmly established, Bowers was invited to make the keynote address at the Democratic National Convention in Houston in 1928. With Franklin Roosevelt in the audience, Bowers delivered a stirring attack on the Republicans, whom he likened to the Federalists, and called upon all Americans to return to "the old landmarks of liberty and equality" as embodied in the Democratic party.[4]

Bowers's friendship with Roosevelt dated from 1925, when he had asked the squire from Hyde Park to review *Jefferson and Hamilton*. Roosevelt, who regarded the book as something of a revelation, saw many parallels between the 1790s and the 1920s. Both men stumped for Al Smith in the Empire State in 1928, and three years later Bowers applauded Roosevelt's reformist administration at Albany from his own new post as an editor of the *New York Journal*. A vocal supporter of the Roosevelt presidential campaign in 1932, he interpreted the outcome of the November elections as a popular mandate for a return to Jeffersonian Liberalism. Bowers received his reward in February 1933. Raymond Moley, Roosevelt's chief of staff during the interregnum, telephoned to say that the president-elect was very grateful for the "great work" Bowers had done during the campaign and wished to repay the favor by naming him ambassador to Spain. Bowers, who wanted "a foreign post where there was quiet and leisure for writing," looked forward to spreading the democratic gospel south of the Pyrenees and accepted the offer at once. "So it seems that we are going to Madrid," he remarked privately. "It is the post I wanted."[5]

Bowers was only one of several political appointments which Roosevelt made during 1933 in an effort to dispel the popular notion that most American diplomats were stuffed shirts. Persuaded that the State Department contained much deadwood, which might undermine his foreign and domestic policies, the new president was determined to weed out some of the more objectionable "career boys" and replace them with party loyalists. In short order Roosevelt named Josephus Daniels, his old chief at the Navy Department, as envoy to Mexico, Robert Bingham, a Democratic newspaper publisher from Louisville, as American representative to the Court of St. James, and William R. Dodd, a noted liberal historian at the University of Chicago, as ambassador to Nazi Germany.[6]

Although these selections were quite popular among the party faithful, the reaction at the State Department was less than enthusiastic. There had often been tension between political appointees abroad and high-ranking policymakers at home during the nineteenth century, but the growth of a State Department bureaucracy and the rise of a professional Foreign Service after 1900 exacerbated the conflict between amateur and career diplomat. Indeed, these developments hastened the emergence during the 1920s of a generation of dedicated professionals, such as Joseph Grew, who regarded diplomacy as a ather an an occupation. Usually well-to-do and Harvard-educated, this soon constituted what Grew called "a pretty good club" which charged with furthering the national interest of the United States. Self-confident junior diplomats like Hugh Gibson, who helped Grew found "the club," quite naturally bridled at the prospect of "a bunch of incompetents with political pull" meddling in the affairs of state. Bowers, Bingham, Dodd, and Daniels would all be treated like rank amateurs by the old pros.[7]

Despite his distrust of professional diplomats, Roosevelt was convinced that Secretary of State Cordell Hull needed a careerist to handle the departmental bureaucracy. As a result, the president named William Phillips, a fellow classmate at Harvard who had joined the Foreign Service in 1907, as undersecretary of state. Phillips was careful to cultivate the friendship of Hull and Roosevelt, but he shared Grew and Gibson's disdain for amateur diplomats. According to Raymond Moley, one political appointee particularly offensive to the undersecretary's sensibilities was Claude Bowers, "whose charming lack of tonishness gave Phillips an attack of horrid misgivings." The undersecretary acquiesced in the appointment only after Roosevelt himself intervened.[8]

When Bowers arrived at the State Department for his background briefings on 11 April, Phillips not surprisingly seemed "a bit stiff, very polite, and very cold." After an exchange of pleasantries with Hull, the old "professional" took Bowers over to the Division of Western European Affairs to meet John Wiley, the department's acknowledged Spanish expert. Wiley, a career diplomat who had served in Warsaw, Berlin, and most recently, Madrid, spent the afternoon educating the freshman ambassador about the sorry state of relations between Spain and the United States. Considerable tension had developed since the republican revolution of 1931. Spain had hiked its tariffs on certain American goods to prohibitive levels while simultaneously granting favored treatment to French exports. More important, in December 1932 Spain had attempted to expropriate the Spanish subsidiary of the International Telephone and Telegraph Company (ITT). The Spaniards backed down after the United States threatened to sever diplomatic relations, but Wiley expected more trouble in the near future.[9]

Although Bowers was determined to improve Spanish-American relations, he came away from his briefing convinced that the careerists did not share this desire. Troubled by "the evident wish of the bureaucratic element at the State Department to hold off from any attempt to negotiate a commercial treaty in Spain and use it as a club in the interest of the Tel. and Tel.," he sought support from Hull and Roosevelt prior to departing for Madrid. Both men assured Bowers that the tariff would not be employed as a lever solely for the benefit of ITT. "The old diplomatic method" of linking trade negotiations to political matters, they explained, was "outdated now." Roosevelt in particular was "anxious to have Spain on our side of the table" and asked Bowers on 2 May to undertake a study of the status of democracy there. In addition, the president reaffirmed his warm personal relationship with Bowers by asking him to contact the White House directly "whenever you find anything you think I should know." The freshman ambassador sailed for Spain two weeks later convinced that with Hull and Roosevelt's backing, he could engineer a rapprochement between Washington and Madrid without further trouble. Bowers, the diplomatic novice, intended to accomplish in two months what the professional diplomats had been unable to achieve in two years.[10]

Upon his arrival in Madrid, however, Bowers found that his task would not be easy. He quickly learned that Irwin Laughlin, the career foreign service officer who served as American ambassador to Spain from 1929 to 1933, had given the United States a bad reputation among Spanish democrats. "It seems our ambassadors here have been high flying monarchists for years," Bowers wrote his old friend Josephus Daniels in July 1933, "and never more so than after the advent of the republic." Indeed Laughlin, a self-styled aristocrat with conservative Republican party credentials who frequented the court of Alfonso XIII, had warned that the bloodless revolution which toppled the monarchy in April 1931 would bring bolshevism rather than democracy. Skeptical of the Spanish Republic from the start, he had concluded his stormy tenure at Madrid by boycotting several diplomatic dinners in early 1933 after the chief of protocol refused to seat him ahead of the prime minister.[11]

Much to his dismay, Bowers discovered that Laughlin's antipathy toward the republic was not unique. Almost the entire American colony in Madrid, Bowers remarked acidly, was "against democracy and republicanism and all seem monarchist[s] of the deepest dye." Moreover, he was appalled to find that "the embassy was saturated with monarchist sentiment" as well. "Practically all the career men are rabid [R]epublicans of the big money variety," Bowers complained bitterly to Daniels. He regarded the attitudes of his two "millionaire secretaries," Walter Schoellkopf and Hallett Johnson, as particularly offensive and charged that the professional diplomats were "mostly antipathetic" to the Roosevelt administration. For their part, careerists Schoellkopf and Johnson can have had little respect for an ambassador who spoke neither French nor Spanish and who stripped away the pomp and formality which had previously characterized embassy life under Laughlin.[12]

Nevertheless, Bowers was determined to erase the unfavorable impression which Laughlin and the other professionals had created by their haughty manner and monarchist sentiments. The freshman ambassador went out of his way to assure Spanish journalists and businessmen of his own democratic sympathies. Bowers quickly found kindred spirits in Prime Minister Manuel Azaña, whom he termed "a genius in government," and Foreign Minister Fernando de los Rios, a "pro-American" academic who possessed "a great admiration for our institutions." The results were electric, and by the summer of 1933 American relations with Spain were on the upswing. "By smashing some precedents," he wrote Roosevelt on 28 June, "and reversing some policies of my predecessors I have, blindly enough, made an unusual appeal to the Spanish." To prevent his subordinates from negating his own efforts, Bowers made it clear that both he and the White House were committed to a rapprochement with the Spanish Republic. One year after his arrival at Madrid, he was convinced that his personal campaign to dispel the antirepublican reputation of the United States in Spain had been a success. "I was shocked and indignant over the fact that everyone here appeared to be ardent monarchists, bitterly prejudiced against the present regime," Bowers observed in June 1934. "By making my position very plain and very emphatic I have heard none of this sort of thing for months." The amateur envoy, he managed to persuade himself, had prevailed over the professional diplomats.[13]

This victory proved to be rather short-lived. Bowers might force his own staff to shape up, but he could exercise no such influence over the State Department bureaucracy. Bowers's amateur status had made him suspect among the seasoned professionals in Washington from the start, and his tendency to side with Spain on commercial and political matters did nothing to relieve those suspicions. Well aware that mutual charges of discrimination had bedeviled Spanish-American commercial relations for two years, Bowers nevertheless arrived in Madrid in 1933 convinced that the liberal trading principles espoused by Roosevelt and Hull would make it relatively easy to resolve these disputes. Indeed, he soon noted that the Spaniards were quite receptive to the possibility of a general lowering of trade barriers. "I find the people here eager for commercial understandings with us," he advised the White House on 28 June 1933, "and with the atmosphere friendly, [I] think that something can be accomplished when the Administration is ready to move in that direction." Roosevelt agreed that "it is just as much our diplomatic duty to encourage a nation to sell to us as it is to encourage a nation to buy from us" and asked Bowers two weeks later to "search for individual commodities which Spain could sell here."[14]

The State Department, however, was not nearly as enthusiastic as the White House. To be sure, Secretary of State Hull was an ardent apostle of commercial expansion who advocated the removal of tariff barriers as the surest and the swiftest way to guarantee world peace and prosperity, but he questioned whether republican Spain shared his goals. Grumbling that "Spain, of course, is a very high tariff country," Hull refused to commence commercial negotiations until Madrid suspended its discriminatory policies and extended most-favored-nation treatment to the United States. Most of the careerists, including Phillips and Wiley, took the same position and brusquely dismissed repeated suggestions by the Spanish Embassy that trade talks begin at once.[15]

Convinced that Spain was "deeply interested in a treaty," Bowers quickly grew impatient with the State Department's go-slow tactics. "I do not believe," he advised Washington on 19 July, "that we will gain anything by appearing indifferent to, or contemptuous of, this country commercially." Angered by what he regarded as sabotage by "protection Republicans holding over from the late regime," Bowers vented his frustration privately to Josephus Daniels. "I am afraid that there are forces in the State Department subordinate to Hull," he wrote on 26 July, "who are bending every effort to continue the policies in which they have been trained in the last twelve years." Bowers's only hope was that Hull would correct this "intolerable" situation when he returned from the World Economic Conference in London later that summer. The secretary of state, however, dispelled any doubts about where he stood on the matter when he confirmed in September 1933 that commercial negotiations with Spain would not commence until the discriminations against American commerce ceased.[16]

For the next six months, Bowers peppered Washington with warnings that unless the United States demonstrated "a generous disposition" in handling "basic Spanish products" such as grapes and wine, there might be "a flare-up."[17] The State Department's reaction was predictable. Convinced that the freshman ambassador was "putting the cart before the horse" in advocating unilateral American concessions, Undersecretary Phillips drafted instructions in January 1934 "designed primarily to keep Bowers and the Department walking hand in hand." Since Spanish trade represented only "one small block in the total American export picture," he told Bowers on 13 January, "we cannot extend gratuitous favors to Spain and thus give other countries, . . . who do not discriminate against us, ground for complaint."[18]

Bowers interpreted this message as further evidence of the "deep hostility" of the careerists toward Spain. "The idiotic notion of the 'Deep Voices' among the subordinates of the Department" that American interests could best be served "by treating Spain with contempt," he complained bitterly on 14 January, was undermining his own efforts to improve relations between the two nations. "I have made friends here and Spain is anxious to straighten out all our commercial tangles," Bowers lamented, "but it looks as though the old regime still runs things in Washington."[19] The frustration was mutual. Pierrepont Moffat, a career foreign service officer who had risen meteorically from second secretary in Warsaw to chief of the Division of Western European Affairs in little more than a decade, believed that Bowers's pro-Spanish outlook had affected his work at Madrid adversely. "As is the case with so many new Ambassadors," Moffat remarked with more than a trace of irritation on 12 January 1934, "he seems to regard his role as primarily that of the Ambassador of rather than to Spain and gives all the Spanish arguments without assuring us that he presses our case in Spain with anything like the same vigor."[20]

The White House, however, continued to be more receptive to Bowers's views than the State Department. Troubled by his old friend's forecast of "bad weather" for American interests in Spain, Roosevelt asked Undersecretary Phillips for an update on the status of Spanish-American commercial relations in early 1934. Upon learning that there had been little progress, the White House encouraged the Export-Import Bank to approve a $675 thousand loan for the Spanish Republic and authorized the Tariff Commission to expand Spain's share of the American wine market. These actions, plus the passage of the Reciprocal Trade Agreements Act and Madrid's pledge to suspend its discriminations against American exports indefinitely later that summer, opened the door to serious commercial negotiations between Spain and the United States in September 1934.[21] Bowers quite understandably regarded the start of these talks as a personal victory and made plans to return home sometime during 1935 to help defend the proposed treaty on Capitol Hill. "The entire atmosphere of Spanish-American relations has been changed since I came," he wrote Daniels with considerable satisfaction on 11 December 1934. "If it all works out in the end it will justify my own theory that good diplomacy is just a spirit of justice and sympathy and that a spirit of good will goes farther than trickery, slyness, or a big stick."[22]

Unfortunately, by the time Bowers arrived in Washington in June 1935, the commercial talks were deadlocked once again. Despite their promise to treat the United States equitably, the Spaniards had recently reimposed a discriminatory import quota on American automobiles. The State Department refused to proceed further until Madrid raised the American figure from five hundred to five thousand motor cars. Bowers spent two weeks in Washington arguing for a more realistic quota of two thousand automobiles. He insisted that the United States "was asking too much considering the great adverse trade balance of Spain," but the State Department remained adamant and Bowers returned to Madrid in mid-July convinced that Hull was pursuing an "absolutely destructive" course which risked "ruining American export trade with Spain" entirely.[23]

Much to his dismay, Bowers watched Spanish-American commercial relations deteriorate gradually during the next twelve months. Fifteen years of trade deficits had reduced Spain's supply of foreign exchange and created a payments backlog of nearly $100 million. As a result, in December 1935 the Spanish government concluded a pair of clearing agreements designed to liquidate exchange arrears with Great Britain and France, Spain's two most important trading partners. Hull angrily charged that such preferential treatment for British and French exporters was "directly contrary to the premises upon which our whole program is based." Bowers defended Madrid's actions, pointing out on 8 January 1936 that "Spain was forced to conclude exchange agreements with France and England to save her two best markets." The secretary, however, was not impressed with this line of reasoning and the trade talks remained stalemated.[24]

Despite this setback, Bowers still hoped that a commercial treaty would be forthcoming. Throughout the spring of 1936 he assured Hull that the exchange imbroglio would be cleared up satisfactorily and urged the State Department to approve an $80 million currency stabilization loan for Spain.[25] But Bowers's appeals fell on deaf ears, for the White House was by this time more concerned with election-year politics than with Spanish commercial policy, and the State Department adamantly refused even to consider further concessions to Spain.

Hull warned the Spanish negotiators that since the success of his reciprocal trade policy had "tremendous bearing . . . on both the business and the peace situation of the world," he "could not permit the fundamentals of our trade agreements program to be discredited or impaired by making vital exceptions to each country calling for the same." Bowers's pro-Spanish sympathies notwithstanding, the two nations could not compose their commercial differences and the proposed treaty was never signed.[26]

Commercial policy was not the only area where Claude Bowers crossed swords with the State Department. Identifying republican Spain's quest for social reform with his own brand of Jeffersonian Liberalism, he soon found himself at odds with the more conservative careerists in Washington who suspected that the Spanish Republic was a breeding ground for bolshevism. As early as April 1931 Irwin Laughlin had warned that there were "widespread Bolshevistic influences" at work in Spain, and the strikes and riots which erupted during the next two years seemed to confirm his charges. By 1933 the State Department worried that communism might spread to politically unstable nations like Cuba or Spain. Even as Bowers journeyed to his post in Madrid, the consul at Malaga warned Washington that "the most probable political development is that the Socialists will continue their sovietization of Spain until it provokes a spontaneous rising of all the non-Leninist classes."[27]

Bowers swiftly set about reversing this unfavorable verdict. After three weeks of careful observation, he gave democracy in Spain a clean bill of health. Despite newspaper accounts to the contrary, Bowers assured the White House on 28 June that there was "not the slightest possibility of either a communistic or fascist dictatorship." Indeed, his favorable assessment of the Azaña regime squares well with most recent scholarship, which has concluded that Spain's republican reformers more closely resembled New Deal Liberals than newsreel Leninists. "There are extreme parties and elements but nothing extreme has been done from our American point of view," Bowers wrote Daniels on 3 July. "They have confiscated the surplus land of the great land hogs, but that is essential."[28]

The collapse of the Azaña government two months later and the victory of a conservative republican coalition at the polls in November 1933 worried Bowers. Arguing that the recent elections indicated "nothing like a restoration of the monarchy," he told Roosevelt that the new prime minister, Alejandro Lerroux, was "a typical American politican[!]" But when Lerroux was forced to resign in the spring of 1934, Bowers began to suspect that certain "reactionaries" were bent on "knocking the [Spanish] Constitution into a cocked hat."[29] His worst fears were confirmed when the Confederación Española de Derechas Autónomas (CEDA), a right-wing clerical party, persuaded Ricardo Samper, Lerroux's successor, to halt most republican reform programs. By the late summer of 1934 Bowers was convinced that Samper, who possessed "the brain of a frog," would step down soon, permitting CEDA leader José María Gil

Robles to organize a government composed of "reactionaries" when parliament reconvened in October. "Just what will happen then," Bowers warned Roosevelt, "is on the lap of the gods."[30]

Samper resigned on 1 October and a trio of CEDA ministers entered the new cabinet two days later, sparking a major revolutionary upheaval. Persuaded that Gil Robles intended to destroy the Spanish left just as his clerical counterpart in Vienna, Engelbert Dollfuss, had suppressed the Austrian Social Democrats the previous February, Spain's Socialist party called a general strike for 6 October. Within hours, mobs of workmen and their left-wing leaders had seized control in Catalonia and the Asturias. Terming the CEDA's grab for power "incredibly provocative," Bowers was sympathetic to the insurrection. "I am thoroughly convinced myself," he remarked privately, "that the Left Republicans are right in their position that the domination of the [Gil] Robles party . . . means the speedy destruction of the republic." When the army succeeded by 8 October in crushing the uprising everywhere except in the Asturian mining towns, Bowers concluded sadly that political power would now be concentrated in the hands of "the Rightwing republicans who are not likely to make any very drastic reforms in the educational or social system of Spain."[31]

The State Department, however, was not nearly so distressed by this outcome. As early as September 1933 Hull had warned Bowers that better relations between Madrid and Washington were impossible unless the republican regime restored stability and guaranteed that Americans and their property would be "adequately protected" in Spain. Not surprisingly, policymakers like Pierrepont Moffat welcomed the swing to the right in early 1934 and worried only that Lerroux and Samper's efforts to steer a more moderate course might be thwarted by "a revolution from the Left side." Unlike Bowers, Moffat saw no justification for the October uprising, was relieved that "the backbone of the revolutionary movement had been broken," and anticipated "a new Government more to the Right with a strong military tinge." Indeed, when Bowers suggested in March 1935 that the CEDA had used the abortive revolt to smear Manuel Azaña with "a fusillade of charges and abuse comparable with nothing I have ever seen or heard in American history," an anonymous commentator offered the following marginal note which probably captured the entire department's skeptical reaction to Bowers's brand of political reporting: "From the author of the Tragic Era this is a 'Tall' statement."[32]

Bowers was nonetheless openly delighted when the corrupt and repressive government dominated by the CEDA collapsed in November 1935. Convinced that Gil Robles "was not a real republican and less of a democrat," he believed that "if honest elections were called today, Azaña would return to power." Frankly pleased by the emergence of a Popular Front coalition in Spain embracing both moderate liberals and militant leftists, Bowers attributed rumors of "a proletarian revolution . . . as bloody as that of Russia" to some "thoroughly alarmed" right-wing imaginations. When, as expected, the Popular Front won a narrow triumph at the polls on 16 February, he was thrilled.

"Left electoral victory conceded," Bowers cabled Washington the next day, "Azaña's return to power probable." Despite "exaggerated reports of disorder in Spain in the foreign press," he informed Hull on 24 February that the country was "tranquil" and the prospects for stable government were good.[33]

Most American officials, however, harbored deep suspicions about Azaña's Popular Front coalition because it closely resembled the "united front" strategy advocated by the Communist International.[34] In the wake of the left-wing victory in Spain, Undersecretary Phillips noted that even Spanish diplomats in Washington feared "communistic tendencies." Although the embassy at Madrid discounted the notion that the recent elections marked the start of "the Kerensky period in Spain," the State Department soon had reason to conclude otherwise.[35] In mid-April reports began to arrive from American military observers stationed south of the Pyrenees that the "Russian Komintern" was behind "the communistic movement which is taking place in Spain."[36] A later despatch from William Bullitt, the American ambassador to Russia, seemed to confirm the fears of the military experts. Bullitt's report, which found its way to the desks of both Roosevelt and Hull, dismissed Moscow's united front pronouncements as "the tactics of the Trojan horse." The Soviets were prepared "to take advantage of any opportunity which appears," and Bullitt cited the Spanish Republic as an example. "Twenty young Spaniards trained in Moscow in the technique of the Bolshevik revolution," he remarked, "left Moscow yesterday for Spain."[37]

Bowers himself was troubled by the wave of disorders which swept Spain that spring and worried that the Popular Front regime might let things "get out of hand." By mid-May, however, he reported confidently that the Spanish Government was "in a strong position" to prevent "any serious revolutionary trouble."[38] Nevertheless, Undersecretary Phillips, who conferred with Bullitt on 2 June, held out no such hope. Disturbed to learn that Moscow had "recently sent out a large number of Soviet agents supplied with ample funds to Spain," Phillips noted that the Kremlin thought that "in the course of three months Spain may become communistic."[39] Not surprisingly, after the Spanish Civil War erupted on 18 July 1936, Bowers would heap praise on Azaña as "the most enlightened and constructive statesman Spain has produced in fifty years," while Phillips would express grave concern over "what amounts to a communistic government" at Madrid.[40]

In the wake of Franco's uprising, the State Department and its ambassador to Spain were clearly marching out of step. Bowers angrily branded predictions that the Popular Front regime would succumb to communism "outrageous propaganda" and embraced the republican cause whole-heartedly. "Of course my sympathy is with the Government," he told Roosevelt in August. "The rebels are of the same element as that opposing your administration."[41] Needless to say, other American officials were quite familiar with Bowers's sentiments and tended consequently to discount his reports. Hallett Johnson, the career foreign service officer who served as counselor to the embassy at Madrid, complained in his memoirs that "political appointee" Bowers "was impregnated with such a strong bias in favor of the [Spanish] Republicans" that there was "an inevitable distortion" in some of his reports. Cordell Hull was not happy about this situation either. "Bowers, being himself a liberal," he grumbled in 1946, "promptly took sides in the Civil War." Despite Bowers's belief that the United States should act "in harmony with certain of the vital interests of the liberal forces . . . in Spain," Hull had professed "an impersonal attitude toward both sides to the conflict" and had pressed for a policy of strict nonintervention.[42]

By the outbreak of the civil war, then, Bowers's nonprofessional outlook, his pro-Spanish attitude during the commercial talks, and his avowed sympathy for Azaña and the republican cause severely limited his influence in Washington. He could still write Roosevelt freely, but with the president increasingly preoccupied with the upcoming November elections, the State Department rather than the White House made the crucial decisions regarding Spain.[43] Whatever influence Bowers might have retained with Hull and his aides was eroded by circumstances beyond his control. For while the State Department pondered what course to follow during the Spanish Civil War, Claude Bowers was marooned in France.

During the first week of July 1936 Bowers made his annual trek to San Sebastian on the Biscayan coast to escape the hot Castilian summer. A fortnight later the Spanish army rose against the republic, making it impossible for him to return to Madrid by train. The State Department hoped to make the best out of a bad situation and instructed Bowers to board the Coast Guard Cutter *Cayuga* on 20 July to supervise the evacuation of American citizens from northern Spain. For the next ten days he cruised along the coast in his "floating embassy," putting ashore at Bilbao, Gijón, and La Coruña to observe the fighting.[44] Bowers believed that this voyage provided him with first-hand information about the course of the civil war, but as early as 26 July the State Department received a report that he was in fact "completely out of touch with the situation throughout Spain." This being the case, Washington did not object when in early August, with Franco's forces threatening to seal off the border between France and Spain, Bowers decided to disembark at the French resort town of St. Jean de Luz, where he proceeded to establish an embassy-in-exile. Although he did not know it at the time, Bowers would never again set foot in Spain.[45]

Shortly after Bowers arrived in France, all the major European powers agreed to adopt policies of nonintervention with regard to the Spanish Civil War in an effort to localize the conflict. Unwilling to become formally involved in the affairs of Europe, the United States chose instead to announce its own "moral embargo" on arms sales to Spain on 11 August. In theory, these policies of nonintervention should have prevented any foreign assistance for either side in the civil strife, but in practice Germany and Italy supplied the rebels with increasing amounts of war matériel on the grounds that Franco was engaged in a death struggle with bolshevism. The Soviet Union, however, actually withheld military aid from the Spanish Republic until October 1936, at which time the Kremlin denounced the nonintervention program as a farce and began to ship weapons to the republicans.[46]

Nevertheless, American observers in Spain almost immediately interpreted the civil war as a nationalist backlash against international communism, and with Bowers isolated at St. Jean de Luz, such grim reports from the war zone carried considerable weight. Eric Wendelin, who served as chargé d'affaires at Madrid in Bowers's absence, warned on 22 July that the streets of the Spanish capital were no longer safe because "Communist and Socialist youths" were committing "acts of depredation." Two days later, Hallett Johnson reported that as conditions in San Sebastián deteriorated, many middle-class Spaniards feared "personal violence from Communists or other Left Extremists."[47] When the left-wing government in Barcelona authorized the seizure of subsidiaries belonging to ITT, General Motors, and Ford in early August, the State Department delivered a stiff protest and privately advised reporters that these confiscations constituted the most serious threat to American property abroad "since the Russian revolution of 1917."[48] American officials were disturbed but not surprised a month later when a pair of Communists entered a new Popular Front cabinet at Madrid headed by left-wing Socialist Francisco Largo Caballero.[49]

These frightening accounts of the situation in the republican zone contrasted sharply with the picture which was emerging of Franco's Spain. Merle Cochran, a Treasury Department official who had been stranded in the rebel zone since late July, cabled Washington on 7 August that the insurgents had widespread support among "respectable citizens [who] considered situation unbearable and were willing to risk everything in effort to overthrow Communist Government."[50] Three days later Military Attaché Stephen Fuqua confirmed that the "primary object" of Franco's uprising was to prevent "the soviet revolutionary movement" from converting Spain into a "socialist or communist state."[51] After Bilbao fell to the rebels in September, William Chapman, the American consul there, told Hull frankly that "in the interest of humanity" he hoped Franco would "win and beat out of Spain completely the deadly spirit of anarchy now so powerful an enemy of humanity on the side of the so-called government."[52]

Bowers did what he could from his embassy-in-exile to counteract the notion that the Spanish Civil War constituted a struggle between communism and nationalism. He warned Hull on 8 August that "too many Americans here have been expressing open partiality for the rebels." Indeed, within days he had "to brush aside" Hallett Johnson "because of his hysteria and blatant advocacy of the rebel cause."[53] Moreover, Bowers vehemently denied that the Popular Front was "communistic." The preponderant power in the Spanish government, he assured Hull on 11 August, was held by the "moderate Republican" and "evolutionary" Socialist parties, "neither of which has any sympathy with communism." Two weeks later Bowers told Roosevelt that the widespread misconceptions about the true nature of the republican cause merely reflected the prorebel sympathies of most foreign diplomats, whom he termed "weak sisters, bridge and golf players, snobs, enemies of democracy, toadies to rank and fortune."[54]

As evidence of Italian and German violations of the nonintervention pact mounted, Bowers denounced recurrent reports of communist subversion in republican Spain as fascist propaganda. "More and more," he wrote Hull on 23 September, "the controversy is taking the form of an international fascist conspiracy to destroy democracy in Spain under the pretext of saving it from communism."[55] Nine weeks later Bowers termed the Spanish Republic's decision to accept Soviet war matériel a desperate response to "two months of flagrant violations of the nonintervention pact by Germany, Italy, and Portugal" and denied that Russian military aid was a sign that republican Spain was about to succumb to communism. "Just as a drowning man does not scorn the rescuer who pulls him from the water because of his religion," he told Hull on 20 November, "the [Spanish] Government did not refuse the support of Russia because it is Communistic."[56] Bowers warned the White House as well that most American journalists had misinterpreted Soviet aid to the Popular Front regime. "Make no mistake about it—this is not a fascist war on communism, it is a fascist war on democracy in Europe," he wrote Roosevelt a week before Christmas. "Everyone who believes in democracy here is a 'red' just as everyone who believed in democracy in America in the days of Jefferson was a 'Jacobin'."[57]

Yet ironically, despite his growing conviction that the nonintervention pact was merely "an excuse for selling nothing to the constitutional government of Spain" while "supplies for the rebels come in by the ship load,"[58] Bowers did not at this time urge either the White House or the State Department to rescind the American prohibition of arms sales to both sides in the civil war. He had actually welcomed the August 1936 moral embargo out of the "firm conviction" that the United States "must not become involved by any kind of meddling with the domestic quarrel of Spain."[59] Bowers advised Hull on 23 September that "I think we should continue our policy without deviation" and three months later praised the "wisdom of the Department in taking a position of absolute neutrality and non-interference in this wretched war."[60] Even as the Roosevelt administration prepared to transform the moral embargo into legal doctrine by act of Congress on 8 January 1937, Bowers raised no objections. In fact, he reported on 12 January that the Spanish Embargo Act had yielded "gratifying" results in Spain, where both the republicans and the rebels were praising the United States because "we alone among the nations had been scrupulously neutral."[61]

These views, however, reflected neither a loss of faith in the republican cause nor an abject acceptance of existing policy, but rather the conviction that the Spanish Republic could suppress Franco's uprising handily if only the great powers would follow the American example and enforce the nonintervention accord impartially. The right-wing rebellion "would have failed without the assistance of foreign troops," Bowers advised Washington in October 1936. Indeed, most historical accounts of the Spanish Civil War have substantiated his claim, first expressed on 10 December 1936, that "Franco cannot possibly win without open military support on a large scale from Hitler and Mussolini."[62] As late as April 1937 Bowers remained convinced that "unless Italy or Germany or both run amuck and send in a very large army, with the consent of Europe," the republic would enjoy "ultimate success."[63]

Only after the German terror bombings of Barcelona and Guernica that same April, and only when London and Paris made it clear a month later that they had no intention of enforcing the nonintervention pact against Berlin and Rome, did Bowers begin to doubt the wisdom of what he came to call the "hypocritical position" of the United States. "We know damn well that Italy and Germany are at war with Spain — but we sell them arms and ammunition," he noted sadly in his diary on 24 June. "And we too set aside international law by refusing to sell to the legal government of Spain [weapons] with which to defend itself."[64] One year after the start of the Spanish Civil War, Bowers warned Washington that the nonintervention policy was increasing rather than decreasing the danger of a general conflagration. "My own impression," he prophesied on 20 July 1937, "is that with every surrender, beginning long ago with China, followed by Abyssinia and then Spain, the Fascist powers, with vanity inflamed, will turn without delay to some other country — such as Czechoslovakia — and that with every surrender the prospects of a European war grow darker."[65]

Not until mid-1938, however, did Bowers finally ask Hull to rescind the American embargo. By then the war had turned sharply against the republicans, largely, as Bowers pointed out, because the rebels were "backed with the latest mechanical instruments of destruction" from Germany and Italy. Convinced that Berlin and Rome only understood "the language of force," he told Hull on 10 June that the best way to end fascist aggression in Europe was "to grant the Spanish Government the right to buy planes and guns necessary for the protection of its people."[66] But by then it was too late. In the wake of Hitler's recent occupation of Austria a wider war seemed a real possibility. And with the isolationist chorus on Main Street and on Capitol Hill mounting, neither Roosevelt nor Hull was prepared to take the initiative required to repeal the legislation which blocked arms sales to republican Spain.[67]

Yet even if Bowers had taken issue with the moral embargo in August 1936, it is doubtful that he could have altered the course of American diplomacy. Isolated across the French border and known to be sympathetic to the republican cause, "Admiral Bowers" was largely ignored by the State Department, which relied more heavily on the "magnificent" reports of officials, like Eric Wendelin, who had "distinguished themselves" in the war zone. "Bowers has been a great trial to us," John Hickerson, the career diplomat who served as assistant chief of the Division of Western European Affairs, complained in October 1936. "One can't tell a political Ambassador that he is out of things and doesn't really count, but that has been about the size of it since the first days of August."[68] This view of Bowers as something of a nuisance was not unique. Herbert Feis, the State Department's Economic Adviser, recalled long afterwards that "Roosevelt and Hull favored his absence from Madrid since it made it easier for them to sustain a policy of detachment."[69] Indeed, when in March 1938 the White House briefly considered stationing Bowers in Barcelona, Pierrepont Moffat, the new chief of the Division of European Affairs, dissuaded Roosevelt by pointing out that such action "would be construed under present conditions as a move to bolster up the Loyalist Government despite our policy of . . . non-intervention."[70]

Once it became obvious in early 1939 that a Franco victory was inevitable, the State Department decided to order Bowers to Washington for consultation. "Bowers . . . has been so partisan and so hostile to the insurgents," Moffat observed on 27 February, "that any possibility of using him in the event of their victory has long since been discarded by everyone from the President down." But because Roosevelt and Hull were "afraid of Bowers['s] trenchant pen," they hinted on 1 March that he would receive another diplomatic post. Moffat, who found the ambassador's "intense partisanship in favor of the Loyalists" quite unprofessional, worried that Bowers would try to use his influence in Washington to thwart plans to recognize Franco's Spain swiftly.[71]

Bowers was well aware of what was afoot and arrived in New York in mid-March "breathing fire and brimstone against the recognition of Franco." He hurried to Washington, where he urged the White House and the State Department not to establish formal relations with the new regime until it pledged to respect American interests, guaranteed there would be no reprisals or executions, and released all republican political prisoners. As late as 29 March Roosevelt was "in no hurry" to extend recognition, but with the fall of Madrid it was no longer possible "to ignore facts." On 1 April the United States recognized Franco's Spain. Six weeks later Claude Bowers was appointed American ambassador to Chile. He served ably in Santiago for fourteen years, preaching Jeffersonian Liberalism, writing his memoirs, but neither forgiving nor forgetting what he regarded as American complicity in the death of democracy in Spain.[72]

Claude Bowers always suspected that he had fallen victim to the same "Fascist clique in the [State] Department" which had given fellow historian and Jeffersonian Democrat William Dodd such a "dirty deal" as ambassador to Nazi Germany.[73] An outspoken critic of Hitler's regime who advocated a tough stand against international fascism, Dodd, like Bowers, had frequently tangled with such high-ranking American officials as Pierrepont Moffat, had taken his case directly to Roosevelt, and had subsequently been summoned home because of his partisan views.[74] To be sure, the clash between the liberal principles espoused by these two Democratic diplomats and the conservative values championed by much of the State Department bureaucracy explains in part their inability to rouse Washington to the danger which unrestrained fascism in Europe constituted for world peace. The reasons for Bowers's lack of influence during the Spanish Civil War are considerably more complex, and they reveal much, not only about his own character, but also about the limitations of American foreign policy in the 1930s.

As a political appointee, Bowers was suspect among the professionals at the State Department from the start. The Democratic party connections which ensured him access to the White House merely strengthened the conviction on the other side of Executive Avenue that the ambassador to Spain was a rank amateur more interested in politics than in policy. Consequently, the self-confident, and at times, self-righteous careerists routinely dismissed the warnings of Bowers and other diplomatic novices as either baseless or biased. This virtually guaranteed that the course of American relations with Europe would be shaped decisively by a closely-knit group of professional diplomats who hoped to appease rather than to oppose Hitler and Mussolini.

Bowers's conflict with the State Department bureaucracy was compounded by his abiding affection for the Spanish Republic. Convinced that the republican reform program in Spain combined the best aspects of Jeffersonian Democracy and New Deal Liberalism, Bowers appreciated the enormous social and economic problems facing the Madrid government. As a result, he urged his superiors to make important concessions to Spain on commercial policy and pressed them not to mistake recurrent disorders south of the Pyrenees for communist subversion. Hull and his aides, however, believed that Spanish autarky jeopardized the entire reciprocal trade plan to restore world peace through world prosperity and that Spain's Popular Front regime was little more than a stalking horse for the Kremlin. Persuaded that Bowers's republican sympathies had limited his effectiveness as a commercial negotiator and political reporter, the State Department openly questioned the reliability of his advice once the civil war erupted.

If reciprocal trade disputes and a fear of bolshevism bedeviled American relations with Spain after 1933, by the eve of World War II these same problems complicated matters with Great Britain and the Soviet Union as well. The British system of imperial preference, which curtailed American commerce, and the Soviet program of world revolution, which challenged American values, helped prevent the emergence of a grand alliance against fascism until Hitler's shadow stretched from the streets of Madrid to the gates of Moscow. Claude Bowers had been among the first to warn that the United States could no longer afford to embrace isolationism in an era of global conflict. "The time has come," he wrote Roosevelt on 20 February 1938, "when in all democratic countries everyone will have to stand up and be counted for fascism or against it."[75] But a cruel twist of fate had left Bowers himself isolated on the periphery of the Spanish Civil War, creating the impression among many American policymakers that he was completely out of touch with events both in Barcelona and in Berlin. And since Bowers found little fault with American policy toward Spain until June 1938, it was all too easy to dismiss his reports as the bitter lamentations of a sore loser rather than the sober observations of a prophet scorned.

Loy W. Henderson

Loy W. Henderson

1892	Born 28 June in Rogers, Arkansas
1915	Northwestern University, A.B.
1919–21	Member of the American Red Cross Commission to Western Russia, the Baltic states, and Germany
1922	Vice-consul in Dublin and Queenstown, Ireland
1924	Appointed foreign service officer in the Division of Eastern European Affairs of the State Department
1927	Third secretary at Riga, Korno, and Tallinn in the Baltic states
1930	Division of Eastern European Affairs in Washington
1934	Second secretary of the embassy in Moscow
1936	First secretary of the embassy in Moscow
1938	Assistant chief of the Division of European Affairs of the State Department
1942	Foreign service inspector to the embassy in Moscow and Kuibyshev
1943	Assistant chief of the Division of European Affairs of the State Department
1943	Minister to Iraq
1945	Director of the Office of Near Eastern and African Affairs of the State Department
1948	Ambassador to India and minister to Nepal
1951	Ambassador to Iran
1954	Distinguished Service Award
1955	Deputy undersecretary of state for Administration
1958	Presidential Award for Distinguished Federal Civil Service
1961	Retired from diplomatic service

CHAPTER 9

Loy W. Henderson and Soviet-American Relations: The Diplomacy of a Professional

Thomas R. Maddux

The Soviet Union had a potentially significant role in America's response to the increasing likelihood of war in Europe during the thirties. As Washington maneuvered to ward off the danger of war, the degree to which the Soviet Union would cooperate with the Western democracies became a central question. After the outbreak of war in 1939, the Kremlin's stance toward Nazi expansion became an even more crucial concern for American policymakers. Disagreement between President Franklin D. Roosevelt and the State Department concerning Joseph Stalin's potential role in the search for peace and security persistently troubled Washington's calculations. Although severely restrained by isolationist sentiment in Congress and the general public, Roosevelt always hoped for limited Soviet-American cooperation against Hitler and made several efforts to promote this objective. The State Department, however, usually resisted the president's suggestions, arguing that Stalin was unreliable.

The American embassy in Moscow had a significant influence on Washington's perspectives on Soviet-American relations. A few officials such as Ambassador Joseph E. Davies urged Roosevelt to cooperate with Stalin. But most professional diplomats such as Loy W. Henderson strongly endorsed the State Department's reservations concerning Soviet diplomacy. As a junior foreign service officer who specialized in Soviet affairs, Henderson never expected close cooperation from the Kremlin because of conflicting Soviet-American perspectives, principles, and objectives. Henderson reached this conclusion as a result of his training, his assessment of the ambiguities in Stalin's diplomacy during the thirties, and his experience with the Soviet totalitarian system and its massive purge in the thirties. When Henderson returned to Washington as assistant chief of the Division of European Affairs in charge of relations with Moscow, he offered Roosevelt a realistic perspective on the Soviet Union which, regrettably, the president often ignored. Henderson's doubts about the reliability of the Kremlin beyond anything but limited, expedient cooperation would have strengthened Roosevelt's perspective on Soviet-American relations after 1939. On the other hand, closer contact between the president and Russian specialists like Henderson would have enhanced the professional diplomats' perspectives by broadening their understanding of the totalitarian challenges to the United States and the need for flexibility in relations with Moscow.

Loy Henderson came to Moscow in 1934 as a second secretary with a critical perspective on the Soviet Union, but he had the capacity to change his views somewhat. As a member of the Red Cross relief mission to the Baltic states in 1919 and 1920, Henderson observed the strife and turmoil of the civil war in Russia and became convinced that Soviet Russia was a threat to the peace and stability of Europe. This view was strengthened by his early training in the new Division of Eastern European Affairs which, under the direction of Robert F. Kelley, had responsibility for the Soviet Union and Eastern Europe. Kelley had a significant influence on young officers like Henderson, George Kennan, and Charles Bohlen. He impressed upon them the importance of taking a cautious, objective approach with as much factual verification as possible in the evaluation of Soviet policies. Yet Kennan later remarked that Kelley took "a sharply critical view of Soviet policies and methods," primarily because he believed, as he warned Secretary of State Cordell Hull, that the "Communist leaders in Russia are unwilling to abandon their revolutionary aims with respect to the United States."[1]

Seven years of service in Kelley's division turned Henderson into a cautious officer who rejected Moscow's explanations of its intentions and actions. Henderson studied a number of topics which either demonstrated contradictions between the Kremlin's actions and public explanations or cast serious doubt on Stalin's willingness to respect the sovereignty of other nations. Upon his arrival in the division, Henderson reviewed its files, such as the "Russian Policy Book," and books on Eastern Europe, the Baltic states, and the Soviet Union. When Kelley asked the young officer to research the connections between the Communist International and the American Communist Party, Henderson turned to communist publications, reports from the Riga legation, and information from police and military intelligence sources. Henderson also analyzed the various meetings of the Comintern, the nature of Soviet policies with respect to Russian workers and foreign labor unions, and all of the published treaties of the Soviet Union to find out if Moscow lived up to its commitments. Henderson reached the conclusion that the Kremlin was unreliable. Despite disagreement among Soviet leaders on tactics, Henderson noted a consensus in the twenties on keeping the European states divided in order to promote chaos and revolution leading to the ultimate objective of a communist world.[2]

Henderson also helped Kelley establish a special training program for Russian specialists in 1927 which involved intensive training in Russian history, culture, and language in the Baltic states, Berlin, and Paris. Henderson wanted to participate in the program, but the State Department decided that only unclassified officers, such as George Kennan and Charles Bohlen, would be eligible. Consequently, Henderson acquired a research oriented background on Tsarist Russia, whereas Kennan, under the influence of Russian emigré teachers and Russian culture, obtained a somewhat romantic perspective on the Russian empire.[3]

Henderson's service in the Russian section of the Riga legation from 1927 until 1930 sharpened his perspective on Soviet policies. The Russian section had been expanded in 1922 into the chief observation post on the Soviet Union. The proximity of Riga to the Soviet border and the close attention devoted to Soviet affairs by Latvian observers made the section a most valuable source of information on and interpretation of Soviet affairs. After working on the organization of the legation, Henderson worked in the Russian section and took Russian language lessons. His research-oriented reports focused on Stalin's struggle to establish absolute control, the history of Soviet agriculture since 1917 as well as the current collectivization program, and assessments on how Soviet leaders hoped to accomplish their avowed aim of world revolution. For three months he directed the section's production of thirty despatches on Soviet problems and received praise from Louis Sussdorf, the head of the legation, who referred to Henderson as a "tower of strength" with the "power to inspire, develop, and utilize his subordinates." According to Sussdorf and David B. Macgowan, head of the Russian section, they had never encountered a better junior officer than Henderson.[4] The Riga environment also influenced Henderson and other officers. "To live in Riga," George Kennan recollected, "was thus in many respects to live in Tsarist Russia—it was, in fact, almost the only place where one could still live in Tsarist Russia." Henderson, however, who had spent almost two years in the Baltics with the American Red Cross, remembered the experience differently, emphasizing the Western orientation of the Latvians and Baltic German aristocracy and their rejection of both Tsarist and Soviet Russia. "There were numbers of refugees from Russia in Riga," Henderson recalled, "but those with whom I became acquainted were not yearning for dear old Tsarist Russia."[5]

Henderson approached Moscow in 1934 with a good amount of wariness concerning Soviet policy and the new Soviet-American relationship; but he was not as inflexibly hostile and rigid in his perspective as Daniel Yergin and Martin Weil have suggested. Yergin, for example, has argued that Henderson and other officers developed a set of Riga axioms that stressed the role of Marxist-Leninist ideology in shaping Soviet policy in the direction of expansion and world domination. Daniel Harrington, however, has persuasively challenged Yergin's Riga axioms with respect to Kennan and Bohlen. Neither officer advocated this perspective in the thirties or afterwards because they recognized the influence of traditional national interests and security as crucial factors molding

Stalin's diplomacy. Yergin, moreover, ignored the likelihood that these officers would in the thirties modify their views by increasingly emphasizing the primacy of national interest over ideology in Stalin's calculations.[6]

At first glance Henderson comes close to fitting Yergin's Riga axioms. Before Washington's recognition of the Soviet Union in 1933, Henderson believed that the Kremlin remained committed to overthrowing noncommunist governments. On the voyage to Moscow in February 1934, Henderson thought about and tried to believe in the possibility of friendly Soviet-American relations. Nagging doubts, however, persisted in the young officer's reflections, particularly about Stalin's willingness to end Soviet interference in American affairs.[7] Later in 1936 in his first comprehensive assessment of Soviet objectives, Henderson concluded that world communism remained the ultimate Soviet ambition, "although this objective might be somewhat dimmer than it was a few years ago, and although the possibility persists that the Soviet leaders might eventually become so engrossed in the accomplishment of their more immediate objectives that they will lose sight of it altogether." Yet Henderson recognized that the Kremlin's desire to control revolutionary forces reflected not only the desire to use them for Soviet ends but also "its fear that if it loses all guidance over those forces they are likely to develop into implacable foes of the Soviet Union and the Soviet system."[8] Furthermore, Henderson considered defense against Japan and Germany as the most immediate concern of Stalin's diplomacy.

Henderson applied this perspective to Stalin's involvement in the Spanish Civil War in 1936. The Soviet desire to check the spread of fascism as well as retain influence over the revolutionary forces prompted the Kremlin to aid the Spanish government. Yet at the same time Stalin purged Trotskyites and other radical supporters of the Spanish republican side. The Kremlin also resisted the creation of a communist regime in order to avoid alienating British, French, and American opinion. "It is no more than a logical consequence of the course of Soviet policy during the last few years," Henderson informed Washington, "that the Russian Bolsheviks should now suddenly find themselves applying the brakes to one of the first serious attempts to establish communism anywhere outside of the Soviet Union. . . . The Communist International and the parties subservient to it have for years represented an instrument of the Kremlin," the first secretary continued, and "this instrument has been wielded, in the interests of Soviet foreign policy."[9]

By 1938 Henderson put more emphasis on power politics, and ideology began to disappear from his assessments. Henderson informed Washington in 1938 that he and the other secretaries in the embassy believed that Stalin was following a course of realpolitik and increasingly using the Comintern as an instrument in this policy. When Henderson reviewed the guiding principles of Soviet policy in July 1939, he emphasized power politics and dropped ideology from its prominent place in his analysis. Security and hegemony over Eastern

Europe stood out as the most important Soviet concerns as Stalin maneuvered with the Western powers and Germany before the outbreak of war. Yet Henderson remained alert for signs of continuing Soviet support for revolutionary activity, most notably in the Moscow press, and expected that Stalin would try to encourage a Nazi conflict with the Western powers.[10]

Stalin's nonaggression pact with Hitler in 1939 presented the greatest challenge to Henderson's lingering suspicions concerning Soviet intentions. The pact prompted Henderson to reconsider his beliefs, for it looked as if Stalin was "really fulfilling Trotsky's prophecies in deserting the world revolutionary movement."[11] As he recollected in his memoirs, Stalin, in order to avoid war with Germany and gain territory, may have "decided to junk the Communist International and what it stood for." Within two weeks Henderson recovered from his uncertainty. Based on Soviet policy lines, the positions taken by communist parties, and the tone of the Soviet press, Henderson considered the pact as "merely a change in tactics" to strengthen the Soviet Union and weaken the forces opposed to communism.[12]

Henderson's reluctance to shed his belief that Stalin remained interested in world communism kept him close to Yergin's Riga axioms. Yet this Russian specialist shifted his views in the thirties and included considerations of security and national interest along with Marxist-Leninist ideology as crucial molding factors in Soviet diplomacy. Henderson's suspicions helped him to understand the ambiguities in Stalin's diplomacy. Although he may have overestimated the importance of Soviet press and communist party maneuvers, Henderson recognized that ideology influenced Stalin's perspective, no matter how he twisted it and used it to his own ends.

The new Soviet-American relationship that Henderson participated in was managed by President Roosevelt, the State Department, and Ambassador William C. Bullitt. After the recognition of the Soviet Union in November 1933, President Roosevelt and Bullitt hoped to expand successful trade relations and informal cooperation with respect to European problems and Japan in the Far East. The State Department, however, persistently resisted any significant diplomatic cooperation with the Kremlin. The surge of isolationist sentiment in the United States further undermined Roosevelt's ideas concerning American support for Western cooperation with Stalin against Hitler. When Stalin's expectations of substantial American assistance against Japan were dashed, he lost interest in the agreements made with Roosevelt at the time of recognition, most importantly the interim accord on the issue of Russian debts and an agreement on noninterference in the domestic affairs of each other. Bullitt's failure to resolve the debt issue and Stalin's violation of the accord on noninterference at the Comintern conference in 1935 bolstered the State Department's view that the Soviet Union was unreliable and unfit to be an ally of the United States. The friction in Soviet-American relations by 1935 turned the news media against any significant interaction with the Kremlin. Consequently, the beginning of formal Soviet-American relations gave way rather quickly to estrangement.[13]

Henderson and other officers in the Moscow embassy indirectly contributed to the estrangement by reinforcing the State Department's objections to cooperation with the Kremlin. As second secretary of the embassy, Henderson busied himself with the establishment of the embassy and reports on Soviet affairs and had little influence on issues such as debts and noninterference. Yet Henderson's assessments of Stalin's diplomacy and his domestic policies, most notably the massive purge, provided ample confirmation of Secretary Hull's and other Washington officials' reservations about demarches to Stalin as Hitler moved to expand in Europe. Roosevelt, who lacked the time and interest to peruse the reports from the Moscow embassy, would have considerably improved his limited understanding of Stalin and the Soviet Union if he had looked at Henderson's evaluations. Instead, the president relied on the opinions of his ambassadors who were usually either too optimistic or pessimistic on Soviet affairs.

Henderson's appraisal of Soviet foreign policy was shaped by his training, by his suspicions concerning ultimate Soviet objectives, and by the ambiguity in Stalin's diplomatic maneuvers. Kelley's training prompted Henderson to look objectively and skeptically at the Soviet Union's rhetoric and proposals concerning collective security against fascist expansion in Europe. Stalin, moreover, projected an ambiguous image to officials in the Moscow embassy. Stalin made overtures to France, Great Britain, and the United States, but at the same time he made approaches to Hitler. Thus, the Kremlin seemed to respond to diplomatic problems with an opportunistic approach designed to avoid war or exploit it from the sidelines.[14] This perspective on Soviet diplomacy reinforced Henderson's suspicion that Stalin hoped to promote conflict between Germany and the Western powers and between Japan and the United States and profit from it through territorial expansion.

Stalin's diplomatic reorientation toward cooperation with the Western powers, culminating in the Soviet Union's entrance into the League of Nations in 1934 and negotiation of mutual assistance pacts with France and Czechoslovakia in 1935, posed the most significant challenge to Henderson and other officers. Ambassador William Bullitt and John Wiley, the first secretary, believed that Moscow would continue to maneuver to keep Europe divided until the Soviet Union was strong enough to spread communism. Henderson agreed with this view and pointed out that the Franco-Soviet rapprochement seemed to bring a "greater measure of mutual distrust than of mutual confidence" between the two powers.[15] The second secretary also questioned the Kremlin's reorientation because of suspicions about a Nazi-Soviet rapprochement. Earlier in the twenties Henderson had watched Soviet-German relations. He followed rumors on this subject very closely and despite Nazi-Soviet public hostility did not rule out the possibility of an agreement. The Kremlin "is endeavoring to work out formulas whereby, upon short notice, it might . . . come to at least a temporary understanding with Germany," Henderson warned Kelley in Washington.[16]

The multiple facets of Stalin's maneuvers were accurately presented by Henderson, but his stance on the Soviet-French detente was too negative. Admittedly both Paris and Moscow used the mutual assistance pact as a bargaining point in new, conciliatory approaches to Hitler. But the pact had potential value as a counter to Hitler and a check to improvement in Nazi-Soviet relations. A more favorable response by the Western powers to Stalin's overtures might have encouraged him to move further away from Hitler and made it more difficult for the Kremlin to cooperate with Nazi expansion as it did after 1939.

Henderson's suspicions about Stalin's intentions did not directly reach President Roosevelt who tried to improve relations with Moscow in 1937 and 1938. Faced with Japan's thrust into China and Nazi moves in Europe, Roosevelt prudently endeavored to remove some of the obstacles to Soviet-American cooperation. The White House shifted personnel, including the removal of Robert Kelley and abolishment of the Division of Eastern European Affairs, and discussed cooperation with the top echelon of the State Department. Roosevelt also sent Joseph Davies as the new ambassador to Moscow on a brief mission to find out which side Moscow would support in a war between the western democratic powers and the fascist powers. The president also asked Davies to evaluate the Kremlin's industrial and military strength as well as its policy in the Far East. Consequently, Davies let Henderson, who as first secretary had directed the embassy since Bullitt's departure in June 1936, continue this function while the ambassador spent much of his time traveling in western Russia and Europe.[17]

Davies was impressed with the Kremlin's strength and determination to check Germany and Japan and influenced Roosevelt's secret approach to the Kremlin. With only the support of the military attaché, Philip R. Faymonville, the ambassador recommended Soviet-American cooperation and believed that Moscow would cooperate with the Western powers against German expansion in the Czechoslovakian crisis of 1938.[18] When tension flared with Japan over the *Panay* crisis in December 1937, Roosevelt made secret approaches to Great Britain and the Soviet Union concerning cooperation against Japan. The president had Davies approach the Kremlin concerning a liaison to exchange data on the Far Eastern situation, but when Stalin made a favorable response in June 1938, Roosevelt backed away. The reservations of the State Department, the strength of isolationist sentiment, and the news media's growing criticism of Stalin's bloody totalitarianism forced the wary president to retreat.[19]

Henderson's disagreement with Davies's assessments bolstered the State Department's resistance to Roosevelt. When Germany and Italy moved to challenge the status quo in Europe, Henderson stressed Stalin's desire to avoid direct involvement in war. The Kremlin would continue to advocate a program of collective security, the first secretary advised the State Department, but would not rely very much on its success.[20] By the spring of 1937 Henderson and his staff noted a general withdrawal of the Soviet Union toward isolation, signaled by an antiforeign campaign, articles in the press criticizing fascists and capitalists, and a purge of the Soviet foreign office.[21] Shortly before his departure from the Soviet Union in March 1938, Henderson directed a review of Soviet policy that emphasized increasing irritation in Franco-Soviet relations and indications that Moscow was reconsidering its opposition to the fascist powers, although the first secretary doubted that Moscow would sever its ties with the Comintern and form a combination with Hitler.[22]

Henderson's doubts concerning Soviet-American cooperation and Stalin's intentions were substantially reinforced by his assessment of Soviet domestic affairs. From the perspective of Henderson and the junior officers, the increased strength of the Soviet Union from its industrial expansion was more than offset by the disruptive impact of the purge which took its deadly toll on the Red Army, the Soviet foreign office, and every other Soviet institution.[23]

The differing interpretations of Davies and Henderson also carried over into Soviet domestic developments. They disagreed considerably, for example, over the importance of capitalistic methods in Soviet industrialization. Davies, who delighted in finding examples of private enterprise, such as flower and perfume shops on a street near the embassy, predicted an almost irresistible movement toward capitalism in his reports to Roosevelt and Hull. Henderson agreed that Stalin was using capitalistic practices, but he warned the ambassador about reading too much into this: "I don't believe that Stalin or the leaders around him have any intention to permit the Soviet Union to develop into a capitalistic economy."[24]

Davies and Henderson continued to disagree over the impact of Stalin's purge. Starting with public trials of Bolshevik leaders, Stalin moved to decimate not only the leadership of all important Soviet institutions and bureaucracies but also the mass population of workers and peasants. At the first trial of Grigori Zinoviev and Lev Kamenev, two veteran Bolshevik leaders, Henderson daily watched the sessions and accurately grasped the central issues. The profuse confessions of the defendants did not fool the first secretary, who described the trial as a circus with the "director putting a group of well-trained seals through a series of difficult acts."[25] Although Davies partially accepted the charge of conspiracy against Stalin and the confessions at the second trial in January 1937, Henderson did not change his original assessment that the trials were a farce and political in nature. As he confided privately to Kelley, "the dictatorship is doing its best to discredit" former leaders, and "old grudges are being paid off."[26] When Davies and Faymonville tried to minimize the impact of the purge of the army which started with a secret trial and execution of military leaders in June 1937, Henderson rejected this approach, arguing that the "morale and self-confidence of the armed forces" would not "recover for some time."[27]

The purge intensified Henderson's view of the Soviet system as a brutal totalitarian regime. As the terror and fear spread in 1937, Henderson and other officers watched Soviet leaders and their few personal acquaintances disappear into the ever spreading wave of arrests and trials. Officials in the Moscow embassy also found themselves increasingly isolated by the antiforeign campaign with its clear implication that any contact with foreigners would lead to arrest and imprisonment in a labor camp. Henderson understood the contradictory impact of the purge. The Soviet Union functioned through the "existence of a complicated and delicately-wrought system of social control, the brain center of which in Moscow shoots off numerous nerve branches into every human activity and into every town and village," the first secretary summed up his insight into Stalin's system. If the Kremlin lost control or the system broke down, he expected it to collapse; but the purge indicated that Stalin would keep control and intensify it even at the expense of weakening the Soviet Union.[28] The experience of watching and living through the purge made it impossible for Henderson and other officers to ever forget the horrors of Stalinism or to believe in the possibility of friendly relations with the master of the Kremlin.

In the spring of 1938 Henderson left Moscow for Washington and in October became assistant chief of the new Division of European Affairs of the State Department. Henderson's experience in Moscow and his perspective on Stalin's diplomacy continued to influence his recommendation of a cautious American policy of neither breaking relations in the face of Soviet expansion nor of expecting close cooperation when Hitler turned on Stalin in 1941. President Roosevelt followed Henderson's advice until the likelihood of Nazi-Soviet conflict prompted the White House to approve a more conciliatory stance toward Stalin than Henderson endorsed. Roosevelt, however, never directly discussed Soviet affairs with Henderson and thus failed again to broaden his shallow understanding of Stalin and the Soviet Union.

Stalin's maneuvers in the spring and summer of 1939, culminating in the nonaggression pact with Hitler, reaffirmed Henderson's emphasis on opportunistic power politics as the polestar of current Soviet policy. Although uncertain as to whether Stalin would make an alliance with the Western powers or come to an agreement with Hitler, Henderson did predict in July that the Kremlin would make an agreement "only on a basis which will give it what amounts to hegemony over Eastern Europe."[29] Although somewhat "surprised and shocked at the cold-blooded manner" in which Hitler and Stalin divided up Eastern Europe, Henderson found confirmation of his belief that Stalin hoped to avoid direct involvement in war while profiting from it. The Kremlin's promise of neutrality enabled Hitler to move on Poland while Moscow regained former Russian territory and moved toward a sphere of influence in Eastern Europe.[30]

When Moscow moved to dominate the Baltic states and Finland, Henderson recommended a cautious policy of nonrecognition which Roosevelt and Secretary Hull tried to follow. They hoped that Stalin would stay on the sidelines and neither join Hitler in an assault on the Western powers nor improve Soviet relations with Japan. Thus, when Stalin invaded Finland in December 1939, they resisted public demands for aid to Finland and pressure from officials for a break in relations with Moscow. "Since I am not surprised at what has taken place," Henderson confided to a friend, "I am not engulfed in this feeling of hysteria."[31]

Yet Henderson welcomed the impact of the winter war on American opinion concerning the Soviet Union. "For the first time in many years the American people are really commencing to understand something about the Soviet Union," he wrote, "and the result has been extremely helpful and cleansing." Henderson made a similar assessment at the end of the Soviet-Finnish war to Ambassador Laurence Steinhardt in Moscow: "Many people have taken off their rose-colored glasses when they view the Soviet Union and it is easier to make people understand what the conditions really are than it was formerly."[32]

Henderson also appreciated the White House and State Department's support for a firm rejection of many Soviet complaints in the spring of 1940. Henderson and other officials pointed to Soviet cooperation with Hitler, which they expected to continue with Stalin nibbling from the sidelines, as the main obstacle to any improvement in relations. When the Kremlin completed its takeover of the Baltic states in July 1940, Henderson recommended that Washington freeze Baltic assets in the United States and continue recognition of the Baltic representatives in Washington. "Our failure to recognize Soviet conquests just now, although not pleasant to the Soviet Government," he advised the Division of European Affairs, "may possibly place another card in our hands when, if ever, a conference regarding the future of Europe takes place."[33]

Roosevelt and Undersecretary of State Sumner Welles, however, soon moved away from Henderson's firm rejection of Soviet complaints. Hitler's conquest of France and Japan's initial moves into Indochina reinforced the importance of keeping Stalin away from Berlin and Tokyo. According to Henderson, Welles and other officials wanted to get "on a friendly basis with the Soviet Union so that we can be able more frankly to discuss with the Soviet Union matters relating to Germany . . . and to Japan." Washington hoped, Henderson informed Ambassador Steinhardt, that a few concessions to Stalin might prevent him from "entering into certain commitments with Japan and Germany which would result in the strengthening of the latter two countries and in rendering more difficult the carrying out of our policies." Henderson and Steinhardt disliked the new tone and framework which Welles established in his talks with the Soviet Ambassador Constantin A. Oumansky. "I must tell you frankly that I personally have some grave doubts that our policy of so-called appeasement will get us any place," Henderson confided to Steinhardt, but "as long as that is our policy I am endeavoring loyally to cooperate in carrying it out and sincerely hope that my misgivings are without basis."[34]

Welles never made any significant concessions to Oumansky, but Henderson was troubled by his failure to follow a quid pro quo approach. When the undersecretary recommended a removal of the moral embargo from the Soviet-Finnish war, Henderson and the Division of European Affairs tried to rein him in with a critical warning from Ambassador Steinhardt. Welles and Roosevelt, however, pushed ahead with this symbolic concession probably because of confidential information concerning Nazi military preparations to attack the Soviet Union. When Welles spurned further concessions to Moscow, Henderson welcomed the latest twist in Washington's policies: "I doubt that we shall be willing to sacrifice important points in principle or any important American interests in order to create merely an 'atmosphere'."[35]

As the Nazi attack on the Soviet Union approached in June, Henderson and the Division of European Affairs prepared guidelines on how the United States should respond to the imminent war. Washington should "make no approaches to the Kremlin," advised the division. Any demarches from Moscow should be handled "with reserve" in order to make sure that the Kremlin was "not engaging merely in maneuvers for the purpose of obtaining unilaterally concessions and advantages for itself." Henderson and the division opposed any concessions "for the sake 'of improving the atmosphere of Soviet-American relations'." Finally, Washington should demand strict reciprocity and make "no sacrifices in principles in order to improve relations."[36]

On 21 June Henderson helped refine the State Department's guidelines. If Stalin requested assistance against a German invasion, he recommended that Washington "relax restrictions on exports to the Soviet Union" and provide military supplies "which we could afford to spare." Washington, however, should "make no commitment" that would prevent a refusal "to recognize a refugee Soviet Government . . . in case the Soviet Union should be defeated." He also strongly advised that "we should steadfastly adhere to the line" that Soviet resistance to Germany "does not mean that it is defending, struggling for, or adhering to, the principles in international relations which we are supporting."[37]

Henderson's recommendations represented a realistic response to the situation in June 1941. He favored material aid to Moscow despite his perceptive awareness of the different interests and outlooks of Moscow and Washington. Henderson also recognized the persuasive objections to recognition of Stalin's expansion since 1939; it would have little effect on Soviet resistance to Hitler and would seriously upset American opinion. Yet the assistant chief underestimated somewhat the strategic benefits in Europe and the Far East that Washington would gain from Soviet resistance to Hitler. The longer the Red army held off the German forces the more time the United States would have to rearm Great Britain and complete its own military buildup. If Hitler failed to knock off the Soviet Union quickly, Japan might also hesitate to expand into Siberia or Southeast Asia. The most serious weakness in Henderson's assessment emerged in his references to a refugee Soviet government. Since Henderson like most officials expected Hitler to defeat the Soviet Union, there was little reason to bargain with Moscow over any American aid and even less cause to worry in 1941 about how to limit Soviet expansion in central Europe at the expense of a defeated Germany.

Neither intimate relations with Soviet officials nor President Roosevelt's approach toward Stalin after 1941 aroused much enthusiasm from Henderson. Although he supported the White House move to extend Lend-Lease aid to Moscow, Henderson was troubled by Roosevelt's failure to follow a firm quid pro quo approach in dealings with the Kremlin and his tendency to brush aside the different interests and perspectives of Moscow and Washington.[38] Henderson's refusal to endorse unilateral concessions to Moscow prompted the Soviet ambassador Maxim Litvinov to urge Undersecretary Welles and other contacts with Roosevelt to move Henderson out of his influential position on Soviet affairs. After a brief inspection tour of the Moscow embassy, Henderson was sent away as minister to Iraq.[39] Henderson returned in 1945 to direct the Office of Near Eastern and African Affairs from which he opposed Soviet expansion and endorsed the Cold War strategy of containment. His distinguished career included service as ambassador to India in 1948, ambassador to Iran in 1951, and deputy undersecretary of state from 1955 until his retirement in 1961.

Despite some disagreements on policy issues, Henderson impressed both his superiors and his subordinates with his understanding of Soviet policy and his devotion to duty. Kennan, for example, found Henderson a man of "deep seriousness and impressive sincerity" with an "unbending consciousness." To Charles Bohlen, who replaced Henderson in 1943 at the Russian desk, he was "a man of the highest character, absolutely incorruptible, he always spoke his mind, a practice that did not make him popular." From his post in the Baltics, Arthur Bliss Lane endorsed Henderson as "one of the finest officers in the Service" for whom "I have . . . only the highest admiration . . . and affection." Even Joseph Davies strongly praised his first secretary's management of the Moscow embassy and maintained friendly personal relations with Henderson afterwards.[40]

Henderson and other officers in the Moscow embassy could do very little to prevent another world war. The Soviet Union had potential as a source of cooperation against Nazi Germany in the thirties, but President Roosevelt could not surmount either isolationist objections to any significant American involvement in European affairs or the State Department's resistance to any political ties with Moscow. Henderson certainly strengthened the stance of the State Department with his reading of the ambiguities in Stalin's diplomacy and his doubts about the reliability of the Kremlin beyond anything but limited, expedient cooperation. Stalin's totalitarian system with its massive purge also strengthened Henderson's persuasive rejection of Ambassador Davies's notion that friendly relations were possible with the Kremlin.

Yet Henderson did prepare for another conflict, and unfortunately, he and the other Soviet specialists never worked very closely with President Roosevelt. They would have complemented each other well. The president's realistic assessment of the challenges the United States faced in the thirties might have broadened the perspective of the officers in the Moscow embassy so that they could support expedient collaboration with the Kremlin by France or the United States. On the other hand, Henderson could have immensely enriched Roosevelt's superficial understanding of Stalin and the Soviet system. Henderson's recommendation of only limited cooperation with Stalin and quid pro quo tactics would not necessarily have led to a different situation in 1945 but it would have minimized the illusions that Roosevelt tended to create about post-war relations with Moscow and the ensuing disillusionment that contributed to the origins of the Cold War.

Joseph P. Kennedy

Joseph P. Kennedy

1888	Born 6 September in Boston, Massachusetts
1912	Graduated from Harvard University
1912	Entered banking, Columbia Trust Co.
1914	President of Columbia Trust Co.
1914	Married Rose Fitzgerald
1917	Appointed to Bethlehem Steel at Forge River Shipyards, Quincy, Massachusetts
1919	Motion picture production; acquired franchise for Universal Pictures
1926	Bought Film Booking Offices (FBO); merged FBO, Keith-Albee-Orpheum (KAO), and Pathé film companies
1928	Bought Radio Keith (RKO) which succeeded FBO and KAO
1930s	Wall Street
1932	Campaigned for Roosevelt; served on Finance Committee
1932	Bought an interest in Somerset Importers and received the franchise for Haig and Haig (among others)
1934	Wall Street
1934	Chairman of the Securities and Exchange Commission
1936	Chairman of the Maritime Commission
1938–40	Ambassador to the Court of St. James's
1940s	Private business; speculated in real estate; emerged as a philanthropist
1945	Purchased Chicago's Merchandise Mart
1946	Served on Second Hoover Commission
1955	Served briefly as a member of the CIA Watchdog Committee
1961	Suffered a stroke which left him incapacitated
1969	Died 18 November in Hyannis Port, Massachusetts

CHAPTER 10

Joseph P. Kennedy and British Appeasement: The Diplomacy of a Boston Irishman

Jane Karoline Vieth

Joseph P. Kennedy — the name brings to mind a freckle-faced, red-haired Irish Catholic, the father of nine children who was rumored to have nine million dollars, a devoted New Dealer, a Wall Street manipulator, a dabbler in the motion picture industry, a sharp, shrewd, ambitious man. He began his governmental career in 1934 as Franklin D. Roosevelt's appointee to the chairmanship of the Securities and Exchange Commission and received in 1936 the chairmanship of the Maritime Commission. Then, in December 1937, Roosevelt appointed him ambassador to the Court of St. James's. Kennedy began his diplomatic career with Roosevelt's blessing and the goodwill of the British. And yet, after two and one-half years of service, his career ended in utter failure. Kennedy was assailed by a throng of critics in both countries who threw a host of unflattering epithets at him — Nazi sympathizer, turncoat, Roosevelt hater, reactionary, "Fifth Columnist," "Uncle Shylock," and "Wet blanket... defeatist."[1]

The diplomatic background to World War II continues to be controversial and dominated by the orthodox school which accepts Winston Churchill's thesis that World War II was an unnecessary war. It further argues that the appeasement policy developed by Neville Chamberlain and defended by diplomats like Joseph Kennedy was an inept policy of an inept government. The war could have been prevented if only Chamberlain's appeasement policy had been abandoned in favor of Churchill's Grand Alliance whose foundation would be Anglo-American cooperation. Had this been done, Hitler could have been stopped in 1936 during the reoccupation of the Rhineland, or at the latest in 1938 before Munich. Because the appeasement policy has been derided, so too have been its advocates. The biographies and historical analyses of Kennedy have tended to judge him, on the basis of orthodox assumptions, as a diplomatic failure.[2]

Another interpretation of diplomatic history offers a revision of the orthodox school and has been influenced by the scholarship of Donald Watt. He argues that appeasement may well have been the only policy possible, politically, militarily, and imperially, for Britain in 1937 and 1938. Consequently, he takes a more sympathetic view of Chamberlain and his diplomacy.[3]

Those advocating appeasement, like Kennedy, were not necessarily inept or wrong. In fact, in some ways Kennedy's advocacy of appeasement and his analysis of Anglo-American relations were correct. Nor was his ambassadorship entirely one of failure; he had some diplomatic success — as a well-informed reporter and an able negotiator. Where he failed, it was partially because of his own limitations and his inability to understand the implications of international events and partially because his diplomacy was a reflection of the indifferently formulated, vague, confused state of American foreign policy in the 1930s.

In order to evaluate Kennedy's role as ambassador to the Court of St. James's, this study will describe his attitudes toward American foreign policy before the outbreak of war and after the war began, explain why he held those views, and evaluate their impact on his controversial performance as ambassador. In order to appreciate Kennedy's position, one must also understand the diplomatic problems that faced the United States and Great Britain in the interwar years and the political philosophies and personalities of the statesmen, especially Franklin Roosevelt, Neville Chamberlain, and Winston Churchill, with whom Kennedy worked.

From behind their broad ocean moats, Americans in the 1930s regarded international events with a marked indifference. Soured by the Great War of 1917–18 and the vindictive Versailles treaty which produced only a sullen truce, they demanded that American foreign policy guarantee their isolation from international difficulties — the collapse of the League of Nations, the Spanish Civil War, and Chamberlain's ill-fated attempt at appeasement.[4]

The dogged public and congressional adherence to isolationism forced even a staunch internationalist and big Navy man like Franklin Roosevelt to trim sail. His Wilsonian credentials were very much in order. As Wilson's devoted assistant secretary of the navy, he had traveled extensively, especially in Western Europe, and was experienced in foreign affairs. Raised in the active diplomatic tradition of his cousin Theodore Roosevelt, and in the big navy tradition of Admiral Alfred T. Mahan, Franklin Roosevelt's approach to foreign affairs was a mixture of Mahan's realism and Wilson's idealism, coupled with a certain chariness toward conventional European diplomacy. After the war he remained true to the Wilsonian tradition by becoming an avid campaigner for American entry into the League of Nations, and as the Democrats' vice-presidential candidate in 1920 he defended the "internationalist" platform of his party. However, as president, Roosevelt's internationalism made him suspect. Throughout his first administration, the priority given to domestic legislation and the prevailing isolationist mood of the country, which was reflected in Congress, forced Roosevelt to moderate his public statements on foreign policy. He repeatedly spoke of keeping America uncommitted and echoed the rhetoric of isolationism. Only in private did he dare mention America's need to throw its weight behind the efforts for peace. Although Roosevelt remained sensitive to isolationist opinion throughout his second administration, he began to grope for some means of checking the expansion of fascist powers.[5]

Roosevelt was something of a dilettante in foreign policy, sometimes more successful than the professional — brilliant, creative, adventuresome, and flexible. Because of his openness, an ambassador in a key European capital like London could exert considerable influence on his views. He was distrustful of the diplomatic corps and sarcastically referred to its members as professional perfectionists. All of his ambassadors could report directly to him, but he paid closest attention to reports submitted by his own hand-picked men; therefore, Kennedy was bound to inspire more trust and confidence, at least initially, than the supposedly apolitical career diplomats.[6] His status in the Democratic party and his ready access to Roosevelt gave him a large degree of freedom and a unique opportunity to influence foreign policy.

A bemused Roosevelt had several reasons for selecting Kennedy. He relished breaking diplomatic tradition by appointing an Irish Catholic saloon keeper's son from East Boston to a post normally reserved for distinguished "blue-blooded" Brahmins. He also chose Kennedy as a reward for his generous contributions of time and money to Roosevelt and the party. Kennedy was "an able fellow" who had cultivated the acquaintance of many of the leading British economic and political figures whom he had met on his 1935 tour, and he had been an effective negotiator as the chairman of both the Securities and Exchange Commission and the Maritime Commission. He held a commonplace opinion of the English whom he viewed not as cultivated gentlemen but as a nation of shopkeepers. Therefore, the president reasoned, Kennedy would be less susceptible than a Boston Brahmin to British charm.[7] Roosevelt could use Kennedy as a trustworthy eavesdropper, a candid reporter, a spokesman, as his eyes and ears.

For his part, Kennedy, though lacking any experience in foreign policy, considered the new post a welcome challenge. He hoped that if he performed creditably in London, he might be appointed the secretary of the treasury, a position for which he felt eminently qualified. He relished the distinction of being the first Irish Catholic to hold a post normally reserved for Anglo Saxon Protestants. For the rest of his life he would be referred to as "the Ambassador." He further revealed his feelings to a friend, "I've got nine children and the only thing I can leave them that will mean anything is my good name and reputation."[8] That legacy seemed safe enough as he sailed for England in February 1938.

The art of diplomacy was a novel experience, an art in which Kennedy had little training or background. With great fanfare he entered a world in which men moved with circumspection and discretion, a world in which men often spoke more with the intention to conceal than to convey, a world in which words were chosen for subtlety and connotation, not clarity and precision. As ambassador, Kennedy could no longer afford to express his personal opinions except in complete privacy; he was simply the spokesman of those in Washington who had the power and made the decisions.[9]

Kennedy, however, found it difficult to be bound by the conventional rules of diplomacy. In his previous government posts he had enjoyed a tremendous amount of independence, considerable prestige as an executive, and direct access to the president. Now he was a subordinate official whose job it was to gather and report information back to Washington. It would be others, not he, who would process and analyze the data. And regardless of his personal relationship with Roosevelt, he was still under the direct jurisdiction of the secretary of state.[10]

Kennedy had very definite views about his duties as ambassador. He intended to be a working diplomat who would represent the attitudes of the average American. One adviser at the London embassy told him how efficiently the embassy was run and intimated that Kennedy could let the professional staff conduct the business of diplomacy while he devoted himself to social and ceremonial functions and to pursuing "contacts." Kennedy had other ideas. The staff would continue to handle routine matters, but he must be kept well informed, and if any matter of importance arose, Kennedy himself would handle it.[11] His fierce Irish pride would not allow him merely to accept the title and not perform the duties.

One significant contribution Kennedy made was to insist that all reports be approved by him before they were forwarded to Washington. If he came across anything dubious, he simply called "Neville" and asked for the facts. Kennedy introduced this procedure when he realized that junior attachés were passing on to Washington cocktail circuit rumors and luncheon table gossip; poor sources of information for American foreign policy. The smooth running of the embassy staff and Kennedy's procedural reforms testify to his skill as an administrator.[12]

Kennedy was deeply affected by his personal and professional relationships and maintained an excellent rapport with British officialdom and with likeminded businessmen, bankers, and financiers. He was thus able to observe British attitudes and intentions and to keep Roosevelt well-informed. His closest friends in London were the "archcapitulators": Montagu Norman, head of the Bank of England; Sir Horace Wilson, Chamberlain's eminence grise and chief industrial adviser; Sir John Simon, chancellor of the exchequer; and Chamberlain himself.[13] Kennedy also developed a good relationship with Lord Halifax, the foreign secretary, and Sir Samuel Hoare, secretary of state for Home Affairs until 1939, then Lord Privy Seal through 1940.

During the spring of 1938, the newcomer joined the weekend guests at Cliveden, the country estate of the Astors, and established a similarly person-able and confidential relationship with the Cliveden Set. The Set, reputedly the purveyors of appeasement, was considered by critics to be a "second Foreign

Office" and was composed not of a formal clique, but of a hodge-podge collection of politicians, editors, Oxford dons, and writers united under the roof of Lord and Lady Astor.[14]

The Tory Prime Minister, Neville Chamberlain, also considered to be an intimate of the Set and regarded by his critics as austere, overly-sensitive, and self-righteous, was one of the most important Englishmen with whom Kennedy cultivated and maintained a strong friendship. Although some politicians, like Churchill, might have described Chamberlain as a "town clerk looking at the situation in Europe through the wrong end of a municipal drain pipe," Kennedy found in him an intimate friend and a pleasant, sympathetic personality. In fact, Kennedy was one of the few people given the privilege of first name informality by the gracious but diffident prime minister. His close relationship with Chamberlain, who kept him better informed than official routine required, enabled Kennedy to establish a very effective channel of communication between London and Washington. It also had a considerable impact on Kennedy's views on Anglo-American relations. Although it is unclear precisely who influenced whom, or to what extent Britain's political and social elite gave Kennedy his political education, there was enough similarity in their attitudes to cause Roosevelt to sputter angrily during the Munich crisis, "Who would have thought that the English could take into camp a red-headed Irishman?"[15]

Historians still have difficulty determining how much of Chamberlain's comradeship with Kennedy was politically motivated. Throughout the spring and summer of 1938, after the Anschluss, Chamberlain sought to entice Roosevelt into approving and supporting his appeasement policy. Friendship with Kennedy could serve this end. The similarities in their backgrounds and their complementary political philosophies also explain their friendship. Kennedy, the Wall Street manipulator who saw "the world through the bars of the dollar mark," must have been impressed, even awed, by this Birmingham businessman, a relic of the Victorian age who was "masterful but magnanimous, dogged, but a first-class loser, a leader who fought better, and only for causes, not himself." Both men were self-proclaimed "realists." Kennedy admired Chamberlain's "realistic" style, his attempt to consider all the salient facts in formulating policy and his well-intentioned plan of removing the causes of war by approaching the dictators and discussing their grievances. Both men were dedicated to avoiding war and to preserving capitalism. In fact, as one historian points out, Chamberlain's theme was that changes in the status of Europe not be carried out by force or the threat of force. The highly principled Victorian was thoroughly repelled by war because it "wins nothing, cures nothing, ends nothing." "In war," his biographer quoted him as saying, "there are no winners, but all are losers."[16]

Kennedy applauded and supported Chamberlain's views. His abhorrence of war was partly personal. "I have four boys," said an emotional Kennedy, "and I don't want them to be killed in a foreign war." Yet he also hated war because it was "irrational and debasing." "War destroys capitalism. What could be worse than that?"[17] Kennedy, in later crises, went much further than Chamberlain in refusing to recognize war as the ultimate weapon in statecraft. Both men assumed a necessary relationship between peace, prosperity, and democracy. They dreaded the consequences of war and the radical changes in institutions which it unleashed. To conduct a successful war, capitalism would have to give way to some form of collectivism. And why fight to transform capitalism into socialism?

War would mean the destruction of European civilization, or at least Chamberlain's and Kennedy's conception of it. Civilization required the preservation of capitalism and the maintenance of the commercial ties between London and New York and the world centers of trade and business. Believing that he had to make an unhappy choice between two evils, Chamberlain preferred a noncommunist Germany to a communist Russia, an attitude shared by other foreign policy makers during this period. Out of distrust and distaste for Soviet Russia, he closed his eyes to much that he detested in the Third Reich and chose to develop a community of interests with Germany. Chamberlain hoped that this policy would help to remove the pressures for Germany's expansion. He and his fellow appeasers saw Germany as the key to Europe's situation and hoped to enable it to "settle down" by removing its genuine complaints and permitting it to establish its natural economic hegemony in central and southeastern Europe. In fact, Chamberlain opposed any course of action which would have prevented the satisfaction of what he regarded as Germany's legitimate grievances. To do so now, he reasoned, would merely prohibit Europe's political and economic recovery. He also believed that the fortunes of international communism would be greatly aided by a general war. As befitted a self-made millionaire, Kennedy shared his host's distrust of communist Russia and hoped that peace could be preserved by appeasing Germany, not an uncommon attitude among American diplomats and State Department officials in the twenties and thirties. Like his host, Kennedy interpreted Germany's expansion, as in the case of the Anschluss, as an attempt to alleviate its economic problems.[18]

Yet the views of these two businessmen, however complementary, were not identical. They gave a different emphasis to economic issues and held divergent opinions on the proper American diplomatic role. Before the outbreak of war, economics was the major factor in Kennedy's philosophy. Economics, he argued, "far overshadowed any political maneuverings." It, and not politics, would be "the determining factor in writing the fate of the world." To alleviate economic problems, he stated that America must assume the leadership since it had the manpower and resources.[19]

Like Hull, Kennedy believed that economic solutions could remedy political problems. He accepted the secretary of state's vision of economic internationalism and believed that measures like the Anglo-American Trade Agreement could be effective instruments for promoting cooperation and maintaining peace. He told Hull that wherever he went he constantly stressed the economic aspects of the situation. Kennedy even predicted that the United States would have an opportunity to develop an economic program more encompassing than trade agreements which would "save the world" and earn worldwide respect. He urged Roosevelt "to make a worldwide gesture [toward peace] and base it completely on an economic stand." Yet his advocacy of internationalism applied only to economic cooperation; it did not, in Kennedy's opinion, imply an acceptance of political commitments or any form of political interventionism.[20]

Politically, Kennedy was a staunch nationalist, an isolationist in the tradition of Senator William Borah, a Republican member of the powerful Foreign Relations Committee and an ally worth having. Borah considered Kennedy a very "sensible" spokesman. Like Borah, Kennedy believed that the United States should remain aloof from alliances or entanglements in European political affairs. Intervention in foreign affairs could threaten America's economic security and its own democratic institutions.[21] Thus, Kennedy was willing to endorse and sympathize with Chamberlain's policy, but only to the extent that it was pursued without the collaboration of the United States.

To Kennedy, economics was the central issue in diplomacy, to Chamberlain, it was equal to and inseparable from politics. At times Chamberlain indicated a preference for political solutions. And yet more often, like Kennedy, Chamberlain expressed the belief that economic appeasement in the form of increased Anglo-German trade, agreements in third markets, and colonial concessions would pave the way for political solutions. To Chamberlain, economic appeasement was as necessary as political appeasement.[22]

Chamberlain tried, throughout the spring and summer of 1938, to get American approval for his appeasement policy. At times he professed a desire to "go it alone," since he believed it was "always best and safest to count on nothing from the Americans but words." He pretended neither to want nor expect "America to pull our chestnuts out of the fire for us."[23] But at the same time, he continued to promote greater Anglo-American understanding and cooperation.

The new ambassador barely had time to become familiar with the embassy routine before Adolf Hitler carried out his long planned dream, "Operation Otto." Eleven days after Kennedy's arrival, Nazi troops rolled across the frontier into Austria on 12 March 1938. Although the invasion took Kennedy by surprise, his earlier prediction to Roosevelt regarding Britain's reaction proved to be accurate. "Nothing is likely to happen," he wrote, except that Austria will surrender.[24] Indeed, the British government protested and then resignedly accepted the fait accompli.

Kennedy was not alarmed by the crisis. Since he assumed that economic motives determined political actions, he interpreted Hitler's expansion into Austria as a move to secure markets and resources in order to alleviate Germany's economic problems. In fact he told former President Hoover that Hitler had "no idea of going to war." His expansion in Central Europe was motivated by a desire to attain natural resources which would enable Germany to become "a terrific factor in economic trade." Kennedy was neither frightened nor optimistic about Europe's problems; nor could he see how they had any significance for the United States.[25] Peace was still possible; war was not inevitable. His economic assumptions blinded him to the political results of the Anschluss. He was unconcerned about the transformation in the balance of power and the increased vulnerability of Czechoslovakia. Nor did he grasp the aggressive, expansionist nature of nazism or the demonic threat which Hitler posed.

Kennedy's initial fear, that the United States would abandon its tradition of nonintervention, proved groundless. Though Americans were angered by the Anschluss, Roosevelt as well as Hull made it clear that the government's policy would continue unchanged. The United States closed its embassy in Vienna and requested that Germany honor Austria's debts. It also granted de facto recognition of Austria's annexation by removing it from the most-favored-nation position under the Reciprocal Trade Agreements Act.[26]

Hitler's next victim was Czechoslovakia with whom the British had only a vague, casual commitment. The crisis, which unfolded during the spring and summer of 1938 and culminated in the Munich Agreement in September, tested the prime minister's appeasement policy toward Germany. Once again, the prim, Birmingham entrepreneur at 10 Downing Street could rely on the sympathy and endorsement of the self-made millionaire living at Grosvenor Square.

Kennedy saw the Czech crisis, like the Anschluss, largely through the eyes of his host. Like Chamberlain, Kennedy believed that, should Britain go to war, its military weakness spelled certain defeat. Years later, Kennedy told a friend that Chamberlain's position throughout 1938 was that Britain "had nothing with which to fight and that she should not risk going to war with Hitler." He was severely critical of Britain's jingoes and "war-mongers" like Churchill, whom he accused of urging war on an unprepared Britain. As always, he was determined from the outset to keep the United States out of any potential conflict.[27]

Recent historical research has tended to vindicate Kennedy's criticisms. In fact, as Watt argues, Britain's armed services were in a state of disarray and the armaments program was dominated by a concern for domestic economy and finance. If Britain had gone to war in 1938, the government could not have assumed the support of a united Commonwealth nor a unified British public.[28]

Throughout the Czech crisis, Kennedy faithfully stood by Chamberlain, serving as his loyal confidant and dutiful reporter to the American government. He was privy to Britain's secrets and had Halifax's promise that he would receive confidential information and be kept fully informed of "all British movements of importance." Halifax kept his word. Kennedy was thereby able to maintain an extremely effective channel of communication between the two capitals. In fact he did his job with such thoroughness that Sumner Welles later complimented him, "I can't tell you how admirably you have been keeping us informed. It couldn't be better."[29]

Increasingly troubled by the Sudeten issue, Kennedy decided to try his own form of personal diplomacy. Acting on his own authority, in late May and mid-June 1938, he initiated conversations with the German ambassador in London, Herbert von Dirksen. Kennedy told him that upon his return to the United States, he intended to urge Roosevelt to reduce tensions in Europe by establishing friendly relations with the German government. In a further conversation Kennedy, whom von Dirksen correctly regarded as "sincere" in his desire to strengthen German-American relations, told him that neither he, Roosevelt, nor the majority of Americans were anti-German. He blamed Germany's bad press on American Jews. In fact, Kennedy stated that "the present government has done great things for Germany." He further added "that in economic matters Germany had to have a free hand in the East as well as in the Southeast." Kennedy still believed that economic appeasement was the most effective way to preserve world peace.[30]

In late July, Kennedy renewed his conversations with von Dirksen and offered his services as mediator. The German ambassador confided to him that Hitler was willing to negotiate an Anglo-German rapprochement. Kennedy therefore told Chamberlain about his conversation with von Dirksen. Despite his desire for an Anglo-German agreement, Chamberlain informed Kennedy that he had no intention of acting until the Czech issue was settled. Influenced by the German ambassador's suggestions, Kennedy mentioned to Washington that Roosevelt might prod Chamberlain into taking the initiative.[31] His suggestion was ignored.

Throughout this episode, Kennedy did display a certain amount of professional diplomatic skill. He had been able to develop a personable, professional relationship with von Dirksen, who found Kennedy's motives and performance convincing. Kennedy was alarmed at the real possibility of war and obviously thought that an American-German rapprochement would greatly increase the chance of peace. If Kennedy's pro-German remarks were meant to flatter von Dirksen and Berlin officialdom, then Kennedy was acting like one more diplomat who masquerades his country's political advantage and willingly uses deceptive means to achieve his desired ends.

And yet Kennedy also made a number of potentially dangerous statements. His remark that he intended to strengthen German-American relations and to allow Germany to have freedom in the east and the southeast, if literally accepted, would hardly have discouraged Germany from expanding. He may also have undermined Chamberlain's position by telling von Dirksen that the prime minister wanted a settlement with Germany. This statement, if taken seriously, may have made Chamberlain's task of arranging a settlement more difficult. Perhaps Kennedy believed that his adventure into personal diplomacy was called for because he mistakenly assumed that Washington did not fully understand the seriousness of the European situation or appreciate the threat to peace. He incorrectly held the "career boys" in the State Department responsible for misinforming Roosevelt.[32] Actually, although Washington's foreign policy was vague to the point of shapelessness, Kennedy still need not have assumed the diplomatic initiative. His overtures to von Dirksen were really rather artless maneuvers which could have caused him and both governments far more embarrassment than they actually did.

By mid-July the crisis had subsided. Kennedy continued to keep Roosevelt informed and told him "that he [did] not regard the European situation as so critical." He now believed that if Germany did not go berserk in the fall, then "war is not likely to come until next spring at the earliest." One reason for Kennedy's favorable report was that the prime minister informed him of his decision to sponsor the Runciman mission to Czechoslovakia to try to mediate between the government and the Sudeten Germans. Chamberlain also intended to ask the American government to issue a public statement of approval. Kennedy argued that this "would have a favorable effect on world opinion and Lord Halifax would naturally be much gratified." Again, however, Washington ignored the request. Other than issuing a press statement reminding the public of the Kellogg Anti-War pact signed nearly ten years earlier and bemoaning the threat to peace, the American government preferred to remain aloof. Neither would it provide support for a strong stand against Germany, nor would it be drawn into approving British policy. It was determined to continue its "attitude of contemplation."[33]

The desire of Chamberlain and Halifax to wring a commitment from the United States led the wary president to believe that the British "would try to place the blame on the United States for fighting or not fighting . . . that if they went in it was on account of the support they would have gotten from us and if they did not it was because we held back." "This is an old game," complained one state department official, "but Joe Kennedy seems to have fallen for it."[34]

By mid-August, the Czech crisis was rapidly coming to a head. During an hour long conversation an anxious Chamberlain worried "out loud" to Kennedy and surprised him with the news that Hitler had become increasingly bellicose. In fact there was a 50—50 chance of war, since he intended to have Czechoslovakia one way or another. Given Britain's state of military unpreparedness, Chamberlain felt he dare not bluff. If France went to war, Chamberlain explained, then Britain "might be forced into it." Still, Chamberlain promised that "he definitely would not go until he was absolutely forced to." "It will be hell," said Kennedy. Upset by the war of nerves and worried about a general European war, the ambassador realized that the isolationist position of the United States would be extremely difficult to maintain. He asked the prime minister if there were anything the president might do. Chamberlain said no. Despite the prime minister's refusal, the excited ambassador, without consulting Washington, offered Chamberlain a "blank check." Giving him a sweeping assurance of Roosevelt's support, he said that the president had decided "to go in with Chamberlain" and that he would approve of "whatever course Chamberlain desires to adopt."[35] Kennedy conveyed a totally erroneous sense of approval and enthusiasm on Roosevelt's part, and apparently meant that the president would accept either a "sell out" of the Czechs, or war with Germany. Such a vague gesture, without implying any diplomatic or military commitment to Britain, was virtually meaningless and counter to Kennedy's desire to maintain America's isolation.

In the last days before Munich, Roosevelt remained extremely suspicious and critical of Chamberlain. He bitterly accused the prime minister of "playing the usual game of the British . . . peace at any price if he could get away with it and save his face." And far from being optimistic about Chamberlain's policy, as Kennedy thought, the president became increasingly discouraged. "I'll bet three-to-one," he told Henry Morgenthau, Jr., the secretary of the treasury, "that the Germans will be able to accomplish their objectives" without a war.[36]

In addition to his distrust of Chamberlain, Roosevelt was becoming increasingly incensed at Kennedy. Not only was the ambassador hinting in statements to British newspapers at American support of British appeasement policy, but he was also, according to the president, trying to force his hand in "the Chamberlain game." Hull, too, was dismayed. He accused Kennedy of pursuing his own private foreign policies and of starting the rumor of a London-Paris-Washington axis. The administration feared that because of Kennedy's misguided behavior the United States had become a party to the British game either way. The British "have us for the moment stymied," wrote Morgenthau, Roosevelt's confidant. "Kennedy is playing with the British Foreign Office and the prime minister. He has spilled the beans, and the President knows that."[37]

Certainly, throughout the Czech crisis Kennedy had been pursuing his own foreign policy in initiating conversations with von Dirksen and in his repeated attempts to gain Roosevelt's support for Chamberlain's appeasement policy. In both cases he was defining American foreign policy from Grosvenor Square, rather than accepting Washington's amorphous foreign policy views. His actions may be partially explained by his friendship with Chamberlain, his agreement with the prime minister's appeasement program, and his desire to maintain peace. They may also be explained by Kennedy's frustration at Washington's failure to seize the diplomatic initiative and to give direction to its ambassadors.

The crisis over Czechoslovakia continued to occupy Europe's attention. It was not until the night of 12 September, as many Europeans impatiently sat by their radios, that Hitler revealed his plans for Czechoslovakia in his broadcast from Nuremberg. As it was, he made his familiar demand for "justice" for the Sudeten Germans. Chamberlain responded to the demand by asking Hitler if he could meet with him to try "to find a peaceful solution."[38] Hitler replied by inviting him to confer with him at Berchtesgaden on 15 September and again at Godesberg on 22 September.

On the afternoon of 29 September, the prime minister received Hitler's invitation to attend a conference at Munich to which Italy's Mussolini and France's premier, Edouard Daladier, had also been invited. As Chamberlain left for Munich, Kennedy declared his faith in appeasement to Lord Halifax. He stated that "he himself was entirely in sympathy with, and a warm admirer of everything the Prime Minister had done." Although he fully recognized all the present difficulties, Kennedy said he was very hopeful about the outcome of the Munich Conference. The European situation required "a spirit of realism," he remarked, which meant doing anything necessary to preserve peace.[39]

Kennedy naturally defended the Munich Agreement of 30 September. Europe had faced two alternatives, one chaos and the other war. "And if there is any way of doing better than either of those, then it is worth trying. With me," the ambassador continued, "it is not a question of the strategy of the Munich Agreement. I am pro-peace. I pray, hope and work for peace."[40]

Kennedy's efforts for peace were at times confused and contradictory. On the one hand, he encouraged Roosevelt and Hull to make vague, nebulous statements about America's foreign policy. But he also tried to deter the Nazis by arranging for the dispatch of several American cruisers to British waters, and by unofficially aiding the government's censorship efforts. Yet he undermined his efforts by telling the councillor at the German embassy in London that "his main objective was to keep America out of conflict in Europe."[41]

Munich left a legacy of suspicion and distrust and had an unsettling impact on American foreign policy. Both Roosevelt and Hull viewed the post-Munich European situation with even greater alarm since once again Hitler had proved that Germany could expand without encountering anything other than verbal protests from the democracies.[42]

The president and his policymakers had become increasingly skeptical of America's policy of isolation and were no longer willing to accommodate Chamberlain's program. Soon after the conclusion of the Munich Agreement, Roosevelt and his advisers began to grope for some means of preventing war by aiding the European democracies. They began to urge "methods short of war."[43]

During the search for a definite, positive foreign policy, the differences between the foreign policy assumptions of Roosevelt and his now thoroughly pessimistic ambassador became all too glaring. Roosevelt now believed that war was likely; Kennedy insisted that it was inevitable, but somehow hoped that the United States could escape its consequences. Having become aware by the Munich crisis of the threat which Hitler posed, he did support the president's drive for rearmament and argued that the United States should become a bastion of peace and security in the Western Hemisphere. He even offered the same advice to Chamberlain. So long as his good friend lived at No. 10 Downing Street, Kennedy seemed to believe that Britain was worth saving, provided, of course, that the cost to the United States was minimal and did not involve American military action. But while Roosevelt began to urge "methods short of war," Kennedy tenaciously clung to Chamberlain's appeasement policy, recommending virtual pacifism, and at times, acquiescence to the totalitarian demands.[44] The ambassador's steadfast support of appeasement was motivated not just by loyalty to and sympathy for Chamberlain, but also by his own conception of America's self-interest. It was a policy designed to prevent a war which might involve the United States.

Hitler's next act of defiance lent credence to Kennedy's pessimistic conclusions and also jarred Chamberlain into a "right-about-turn" in Britain's foreign policy. In defiance of the Munich Agreement, international law, and his own principle of nationality, Hitler swallowed up the remnants of the tottering state of Czechoslovakia on 15 March 1939. A subdued Chamberlain calmly told the House of Commons that Czechoslovakia had "become disintegrated." His refusal to honor Britain's guarantee to the Czech state, as required by the Munich Agreement, aroused a barrage of criticism within his own party and within the press. Halifax tried to prod the surprised prime minister into unequivocally condemning the Nazis, broadening his cabinet to include leaders from all parties, and introducing a modified scheme of conscription. His arguments had their effect. At Birmingham on 17 March 1939, Chamberlain vigorously condemned Hitler's aggression. His speech marked if not the abandonment of Chamberlain's appeasement policy, then at least its abatement; it also ensured his continued political leadership. The reluctant prime minister subsequently informed the House of Commons that the British government would guarantee Poland's independence. This plan, which Kennedy considered "practical and expedient," now committed Britain to positive action in Eastern Europe.[45]

Regardless of his favorable attitude toward Britain's guarantee, Kennedy was still willing to play the appeaser. He encouraged Roosevelt to use his powers of persuasion to bring pressure on the Poles to make voluntary concessions to Hitler. This would permit Germany to pursue its objectives in the East, Kennedy reasoned. Adamant, Roosevelt rejected the request. By now thoroughly disillusioned with appeasement, the president argued that it looked as though Britain wanted the United States to assume responsibility for another Munich. Actually, he seemed to regard Britain's guarantee to Poland as a step forward since it committed Britain to positive action in Eastern Europe.[46]

Despite Roosevelt's delight, there was criticism in England of Chamberlain's new policy. Both Churchill and Lloyd George, the former Liberal prime minister during World War I, were worried about the exclusion of Russia from Poland's guarantee. "To halt with the guarantee to Poland would be to halt in No Man's Land under fire of both trench lines and without the shelter of either," said Churchill. And the wily Lloyd George shrewdly predicted that, "If we go in without the help of Russia, we shall be walking into a trap," since Russia was the only country which could quickly come to Poland's defense and whose air power could match Germany's. But Chamberlain was unable to overcome his aversion to the Kremlin and thus failed to cement an alliance with Russia.[47]

Kennedy fully sympathized with Chamberlain's attitude and told Roosevelt that he viewed Soviet Russia as "an imponderable in the situation." He saw absolutely no reason to assume that the two English speaking democracies could count on the Russians; all the more reason, he logically argued, to come to terms with Germany. Either Russia could come under Nazi domination, even without an invasion, or the Soviet "doctrinaires" would retire into "splendid isolation" behind the walls of the Kremlin until "the pickings in Europe or West China were ripe." Anticipating the worst, he concluded it would be "the height of optimism to expect Russia to come to the aid of the United States" after a totalitarian victory in Western Europe.[48] Events were soon to test Chamberlain's policy regarding Poland and Russia.

A little before three o'clock on the morning of 1 September 1939 Germany invaded Poland. Two days later, after a scene of utter pandemonium in the House of Commons over the delay, Chamberlain announced that Britain would honor its guarantee to Poland and that a state of war existed between Great Britain and Germany. Kennedy called Roosevelt, and in a state of complete despair, predicted that another Dark Age would descend over Europe. The half-choked voice kept repeating, "It's the end of the world, the end of everything." Roosevelt tried unsuccessfully to steady his emotional ambassador.[49]

The war touched everything in Britain including Kennedy's position and his relationship with Roosevelt. So long as Roosevelt remained indecisive about America's role in international affairs, Kennedy's advice may have had some impact on the president's thinking. But after the outbreak of war, when Roosevelt began to grope for a more active foreign policy and to urge American aid to Britain and France, decision making became increasingly centralized in Washington. Negotiations between the two great English speaking democracies were located more often in Washington than London, and once Churchill became prime minister in May 1940, negotiations were conducted personally between the two heads of state. Churchill's rise to power had a significant effect on Anglo-American relations. It represented the antithesis of appeasement. It meant the return of Britain's age old theory of the balance of power with its refusal to allow any single power to hold sway over Europe. It also hastened Kennedy's decline. The new prime minister simply ignored most of Kennedy's advice and enjoyed the privilege of confidential access to Roosevelt in his famous "Naval Person" communications.[50] Throughout much of this long and unique correspondence, Kennedy served as their messenger boy.

Thinking about Britain's chances and about the effects of war upon the United States, Kennedy became an understandably unrelieved prophet of gloom — defeatist and fatalistic. In many ways Kennedy's pessimism was justified. England was ill-prepared for war. Even in September 1939, Kennedy was predicting that the continuation of the war would devastate Britain and Europe economically, socially, and politically; nothing could be saved. But if, by chance, Britain did "win" its war, Kennedy still regarded it as a losing proposition, as an empty victory. Britain would be bankrupt, democracy would be crushed, civilization would be destroyed.[51]

Kennedy's greatest fear was that if it were a long war the United States would be dragged in. He could imagine a chivalrous but foolhardy America gallantly dashing to Britain's rescue. And inevitably, American boys would be sent to spill their blood on Europe's soil. Unquestionably, he explained, "the war will be conducted with British eyes constantly on the United States." Repeatedly, he urged Roosevelt to emphasize "that we don't want any part of this mess."[52]

With war just a week old, Kennedy told Roosevelt "that this situation may crystallize to a point where the president can be the savior of the world." The British government would probably not accept a proposal from Hitler, "but there may be a point when the president himself may work out the plans for world peace."[53]

Kennedy received a rather severe transatlantic slap across his knuckles for his suggestion. Roosevelt's rebuke illustrated not just his distrust of the talkative ambassador, but also a growing difference in attitudes. Kennedy regarded nazism as regrettable, but still tolerable and even preferable to the complete chaos which he predicted would result from total war. He believed that Hitler was at least a stabilizing force in Germany. Even if Hitler were destroyed, nazism would give way to communism. When Kennedy mentioned his fear to Roosevelt, the president politely dismissed it. "I do not think people in England should worry about Germany going Communist in the Russian manner," Roosevelt advised. Unlike his ambassador, Roosevelt almost ignored the consequences of war, so intent was he on eliminating an intolerable "regime of force and aggression."[54]

Despite his deep pessimism, Kennedy was not indifferent to Britain's plight. He had lived too long in Britain and liked the English too much not to be worried about their fortunes. He urged Roosevelt to be "considerate" of their friends; an attitude which came to mean the repeal of the Neutrality Act and limited intervention. After the British disasters at Dunkirk, arms, ammunition, and fifty destroyers were not too costly in aid for Britain. Kennedy also thought that principle could be shoved aside in favor of Lend-Lease.[55]

Regardless of his advocacy of "consideration," Kennedy's heart was not in the fight. His terror of the consequences of war all but led him to reject war as an instrument of national policy. And later he contemptuously repudiated the concept of "total war" and the self-righteous demand of "unconditional surrender," for which the Allies were clamoring. Kennedy's overriding goal was peace, even if it meant Nazi hegemony throughout Europe. American and British interests could both be served if Britain and Germany would agree to a compromise peace. One month after the outbreak of war he revived his "savior of the world" proposal, despite Roosevelt's chilly, initial reply, and hinted that the president should reconsider his refusal to mediate. "Some of my English friends," Kennedy told Roosevelt, "believe that only one man can save the world . . . and that man is yourself. . . . You are a combination of the Holy Ghost and Jack Dempsey." Roosevelt was obviously irked and sounded off to his Dutchess County neighbor Morgenthau. "Joe always has been an appeaser and always will be an appeaser. . . . He's just a pain in the neck to me," snapped the president.[56] Roosevelt refused to budge.

Ultimately, Roosevelt became increasingly hostile and wary of Kennedy. Originally friendly, the relationship between the two began to degenerate into one of barely concealed hostility. One source of tension was the fundamental emotional disparity between the two men. Kennedy's mercurial personality fluctuated between bearish pessimism and bullish optimism. Roosevelt, however, was seldom anything other than undaunted, serene, relentlessly cheerful. This innate temperamental difference became a source of considerable friction between them.

A brooding Kennedy remained in London for more than a year after the outbreak of war, temperamentally out of sorts with the administration and with the British.[57] Kennedy finally returned to the United States and submitted his resignation in November 1940. For the first time, the Kennedy name was associated with failure as the doors to government service were locked. Kennedy returned to private life and continued to amass a large fortune.

Years later, Kennedy looked back on his ambassadorship in the aftermath of World War II and during the Cold War. In particular, his attention focused on Munich which had had a profound effect on him. In his memoirs, which were written in the 1950s and not revealed until 1968, the ambassador staunchly defended the Munich Agreement. Although it had revived the vanishing hopes for peace, he wrote, it had also been "anti-climactic" since it only confirmed the unjust and inaccurate political assumptions of the interwar period. Beginning with the Versailles treaty, Europe's diplomatic retrogression continued, so much so that Chamberlain was left with no alternative but to accept the Fuehrer's demands at Munich. He could hardly do otherwise, Kennedy argued, because neither England nor France was in a position to fight. England's military production and armaments program were grossly inadequate, and many Britons arrogantly sneered at the prospect of going to war with Germany to save little Czechoslovakia.[58]

Kennedy also applauded Chamberlain for his realistic perception of Britain's total diplomatic isolation. French industry was riddled with internal dissension, and the country was on the verge of bankruptcy. France simply lacked the will to fight. The ambassador too regarded the Soviet Union as an unreliable ally whose army had been severely weakened by Stalin's recent purges. Nor did

Kennedy believe that Chamberlain could count on the United States to be even a minor arsenal of democracy. Prior to Munich, Americans were overwhelmingly pacifistic and doggedly maintained their isolationist tradition.[59]

Historians like Donald Watt offer evidence to show that Kennedy's defense of Munich and the appeasement policy were justified. Watt argues, like Kennedy, that Britain could not count on military support from any other power. This fact, plus Britain's own weakened military and armaments program, made appeasement the only realistic policy at that time. Hitler would not have been intimidated by diplomatic restraints, the threat of force, or attempts to create an international line-up to keep him in check. In fact, any restraints placed upon Hitler simply enraged him and goaded him into using more force and violence and into taking greater risks than he had planned. Nor would it have been politically possible for Chamberlain to argue for a more aggressive foreign policy. Had he done so, he could not have assumed the support of the Commonwealth, the British public, nor indeed, the majority of his own cabinet.[60] In the months following Munich, Britain's military strength improved and Chamberlain gained a more accurate assessment of Hitler's motives. This led to a reinterpretation of Britain's foreign policy and ultimately to the demise of appeasement.

Kennedy was also correct in his assessment of America's position. Up to the fall of 1939 the United States was swept up in a wave of isolation, and American foreign policy was vague and ill defined. The Neutrality Laws, if rigidly interpreted, could have denied Britain American goods. It was not until the outbreak of war that Americans were willing to accept even limited intervention. Thus, in many ways, Kennedy's perceptions of the practicality of appeasement throughout 1938 and of the realities of Anglo-American relations were accurate and sound. So too was his conduct as reporter and negotiator. He achieved considerable success and deserved the high praise he received from administration officials as a generally well informed reporter who furnished Washington with extensive and often reliable information and as an adept negotiator, particularly over the Anglo-American Trade Agreement.

Nevertheless, he was largely a diplomatic failure. He lacked the training and broad political knowledge necessary for an ambassador. Coming from the specialized world of business, he found it difficult to adapt his thinking to international political realities. His complete insistence upon the primacy of economic issues made him undervalue the political factors in international relations and blinded him to the interplay between political and economic issues. He also failed to grasp the consequences of Britain's military and political changes in the months following Munich and to see their significance to a reinterpretation of British foreign policy. Even after the government had rejected appeasement, he continued to argue tenaciously for it. His shallower notions of human motivations and his own rather unsuccessful attempts to devise American foreign policy also led to fundamental disagreements with

Roosevelt. After the outbreak of war, Kennedy found himself isolated and ignored. Like many diplomats of the 1930s, Kennedy did accept the views of his host country. But until the American government adopted a specific conception of foreign policy and devised practical means for implementing it, Kennedy, like other ambassadors, was left floundering. Thus, Kennedy's diplomacy was a reflection of the amorphous state of American foreign policy prior to the outbreak of war in Europe.

Notes

Abbreviations

AJ⁵   Délégation française à la Commission des Réparations des dommages de guerre, AJ⁵, Archives Nationales, Paris

BRM   Buero des Reichsministers

BSS   Buero des Staatssekretaers

DBFP   Great Britain, Foreign Office, *Documents on British Foreign Policy: 1919–1939*, ed. E. L. Woodward et al. (London: H.M.S.O., 1946–67)

DS   Department of State Decimal File [no.], General Records of the Department of State, Record Group 59, National Archives, Washington, D.C.

FDRL   Franklin D. Roosevelt Papers as President, Franklin D. Roosevelt Library, Hyde Park, N.Y.

FO   Records of the Foreign Office, General Correspondence after 1906, Political, FO [file and accession nos.], Public Record Office, Kew, Surrey, England

FRBNY   Federal Reserve Bank of New York, New York, N.Y.

FRUS, [year]   U.S. Department of State, *Papers Relating to the Foreign Relations of the United States*, [1921–1942] (Washington, D.C.: G.P.O., 1936–55)

FRUS, Japan   U.S. Department of State, *Japan: 1931–1941* (Washington, D.C.: G.P.O., 1943)

FRUS, Soviet Union   U.S. Department of State, *The Soviet Union, 1933–1939* (Washington, D.C.: G.P.O., 1952)

GPR   Prentiss Bailey Gilbert Papers, Rush Rhees Library, University of Rochester, Rochester, N.Y.

GPW   Mrs. Charlotte Gilbert Papers, Washington, D.C.

HHL   Herbert Hoover Papers, Herbert Hoover Presidential Library, West
             Branch, Iowa

PSF   President's Secretary's File

SF   Secretary's File, [box no.], General Records of the Department of
             the Treasury, Record Group 56, National Archives, Washington,
             D.C.

T-120   United States National Archives microfilm publication of the Rec-
             ords of the German Foreign Office received by the Department of
             State, Series T-120, [roll/serial/frame(s)]

Chapter 1

1. My discussion draws heavily upon the following works: William Appleman Williams, *The Contours of American History* (Chicago: Quadrangle Books, 1966); Grant
McConnell, *Private Power and American Democracy* (New York: Alfred A. Knopf,
1966); Robert H. Wiebe, *The Search for Order, 1877–1920* (New York: Hill and Wang,
1967); James Weinstein, *The Corporate Ideal in the Liberal State* (Boston: Beacon Press,
1968); Theodore J. Lowi, *The End of Liberalism: Ideology, Policy, and the Crisis of
Public Authority* (New York: W. W. Norton and Co., 1969); Ronald Radosh and Murray
N. Rothbard, eds., *A New History of Leviathan: Essays on the Rise of the American
Corporate State* (New York: E. P. Dutton and Co., 1972); Daniel Fusfeld, "Rise of the
Corporate State in America," *Journal of Economic Issues* 6 (1972): 1–22; Ellis W.
Hawley, "Techno-Corporatist Formulas in the Liberal State, 1920–1960: A Neglected
Aspect of America's Search for a New Order" (Paper delivered at the Conference on
Twentieth Century Capitalism, Harvard University, Cambridge, Mass., September
1974); Ellis W. Hawley, "The New Corporatism and the Liberal Democracies, 1918–
1925: The Case of the United States" (author's file); Hawley, "The Discovery and Study
of a 'Corporate Liberalism,' " *Business History Review* 52 (1978): 309–20; Richard
Hume Werking, "Bureaucrats, Businessmen, and Foreign Trade: The Origins of the
United States Chamber of Commerce," ibid., pp. 321–41; Kim McQuaid, "Corporate
Liberalism in the American Business Community, 1920–1940," ibid., pp. 342–68.

2. For different views on economic mobilization during the war see Murray N.
Rothbard, "War Collectivism in World War I," in Radosh and Rothbard, *New History of
Leviathan*, pp. 66–110; Robert D. Cuff, *The War Industries Board: Business-
Government Relations during World War I* (Baltimore: Johns Hopkins University Press,
1973).

3. Vincent P. Carosso, *Investment Banking in America: A History* (Cambridge:
Harvard University Press, 1970), pp. 193–200, 209, 211, 216, 222, 224–27, 230–32.

4. Ibid., pp. 197–99, 200, 204–7; Thomas W. Lamont, *Henry P. Davison: The
Record of a Useful Life* (New York: Harper and Bros., 1933), pp. 173–83, 186–230;
Lamont, *Across World Frontiers* (New York: Harcourt, Brace and Co., 1951), pp.
59–64, 67, 70; Harold Nicolson, *Dwight Morrow* (New York: Harcourt, Brace and Co.,
1935), pp. 167–78, 180–81, 186–87; U.S. Congress, Senate, Committee on Finance,
Sale of Foreign Bonds and Securities in the United States, 72d Cong., 1st sess., 1931,
p. 8.

5. The seven were J. P. Morgan, Henry P. Davison, Thomas W. Lamont, Edward R. Stettinius, Dwight W. Morrow, Russell C. Leffingwell, and S. Parker Gilbert.

6. Thomas W. Lamont, *My Boyhood in a Parsonage: Some Brief Sketches of American Life toward the Close of the Last Century* (New York: Harper and Bros., 1946); Lamont, *Across World Frontiers*, pp. 25–41, 67, 72, 75, 78–82; Carosso, *Investment Banking*, pp. 209 (n. 70), 227.

7. Lamont, *Across World Frontiers*, pp. 107, 122–24, 131–32; Lamont diary, 4 June 1919, box 164, folder 18 (hereafter box no./folder no.), Thomas W. Lamont Papers, Baker Library, Harvard University, Boston, Mass.; Michael J. Hogan, "The United States and the Problem of International Economic Control: American Attitudes toward European Reconstruction, 1918–1920," *Pacific Historical Review* 44 (1975): 97–98.

8. Vance McCormick diary, 10 June 1919, Herbert Hoover Presidential Library, West Branch, Iowa; Lamont memorandum (unsigned), 13 June 1919, 165/10, Lamont Papers; Hogan, "United States and International Economic Control," p. 96. Lamont's involvement in the struggle over reparations at the Paris Peace Conference can be followed in his diary notes, 164/18 and 20, Lamont Papers.

9. Lamont diary, 25 April 1919, 164/18, Lamont Papers; Hogan, "United States and International Economic Control," pp. 92–99.

10. Lamont, *Across World Frontiers*, pp. 136–37, 139–40, 163; Lamont diary, 1 and 3 April 1919, 164/18 and 20 respectively, Lamont Papers. For Lamont's judgment on Wilson's other failures at the peace conference see Lamont, *Across World Frontiers*, p. 159.

11. Lamont to Assistant Secretary of the Treasury Russell C. Leffingwell, 29 March 1919, 165/8, Lamont Papers.

12. Lamont diary, 25 April 1919, 164/18, Lamont Papers.

13. Lamont to Wilson, 15 May 1919, enclosing "Observations upon the European Situation: Possible Measures to be Taken," in Ray Stannard Baker, *Woodrow Wilson and World Settlement*, 3 vols. (Garden City, N.Y.: Doubleday, Page and Co., 1922–23), 3: 352–62. See also, Lamont and Davis to Leffingwell, 29 May 1919, SF 277. The major points in the Lamont-Davis memo were repeated in reconstruction proposals drafted individually by other members of the American peace delegation. See for example Bernard Baruch to Wilson, 7 May 1919, in Baker, *Wilson and World Settlement*, 3: 347–51; Herbert Hoover to Lamont, enclosing "Another Plan for the Financial Rehabilitation of Europe," 16 May 1919, 165/19, Lamont Papers; Hoover to Wilson, 27 June 1919, AG 15/15, U.S. Food Administration Documents, HHL.

14. Lamont to R. H. Brand, 10 June 1919, 165/10, Lamont Papers. For more on the Davison plan see Robert H. Van Meter, Jr., "The United States and European Recovery, 1918–1923: A Study of Public Policy and Private Finance" (Ph.D. diss., University of Wisconsin, 1971), pp. 115–20; Van Meter, "Herbert Hoover and the Economic Reconstruction of Europe, 1918–1921" (Paper delivered at the first Herbert Hoover Centennial Seminar, Herbert Hoover Presidential Library, West Branch, Iowa, February 1974).

15. The Treasury Department's position can be followed in Leffingwell to Davis, 6 May 1919, SF 83; Secretary of the Treasury Carter Glass to Davis, 24 June 1919, Letterbooks, vol. 31, Russell C. Leffingwell Papers, Library of Congress, Washington, D.C.; Glass to Wilson, 25 August and 11 September 1919, series 2, boxes 192 and 193 respectively, Woodrow Wilson Papers, Library of Congress, Washington, D.C. See also Hogan, "United States and International Economic Control," pp. 95, 98, 101–3.

16. For the details on banking legislation see Burton I. Kaufman, "The Organizational Dimension of United States Economic Foreign Policy, 1900–1920," *Business History Review* 46 (1972): 41–43; Cleona Lewis, *America's Stake in International Investments* (Washington: Brookings Institution, 1938), p. 195; Carl P. Parrini, *Heir to Empire: United States Economic Diplomacy, 1916–1923* (Pittsburgh: University of Pittsburgh Press, 1969), pp. 80–81.

17. Parrini, *Heir to Empire*, pp. 82–98; Van Meter, "United States and European Recovery," pp. 210–17.

18. Lamont, "The World Situation," *Atlantic Monthly*, September 1919, pp. 420–29. Lamont to H. deW. Fuller, 28 December 1921, 80/15; Lamont to Charles A. Kettle, 24 November 1922, 80/16; Lamont, "The Allied Debt to the United States Government," a confidential memorandum sent by Lamont to selected newspaper editors in November 1922, 80/17, all in Lamont Papers; Lamont, "Problems of the Incoming Administration: Taxation, the Tariff, and Foreign Trade Relations," *Harper's Monthly Magazine*, March 1921, pp. 432–43; Lamont, "World Debts, Some Comments and Opinions," *Pan American Magazine*, November 1922, pp. 234–37.

19. Lamont, "Problems of Incoming Administration," pp. 441–42; Lamont, *Across World Frontiers*, pp. 194, 216–18.

20. On the loan control system see Parrini, *Heir to Empire*, pp. 184–211; Joan Hoff Wilson, *American Business and Foreign Policy, 1920–1933* (Lexington: University of Kentucky Press, 1971), pp. 106–22; Herbert Feis, *The Diplomacy of the Dollar: First Era, 1919–1932* (Baltimore: Johns Hopkins University Press, 1950), pp. 18–38; Michael J. Hogan, *Informal Entente: The Private Structure of Cooperation in Anglo-American Economic Diplomacy, 1918–1928* (Columbia: University of Missouri Press, 1977), pp. 78–104. For Lamont's views see Lamont to Hughes, 31 March 1922, 94/18, Lamont Papers; Senate, *Sale of Foreign Bonds*, pp. 12–14.

21. Lamont, "The Chinese Consortium and American Trade Relations with China and the Far East," *Annals of the American Academy of Political and Social Science* 94 (1921): 87–93; Lamont, "Three Examples of International Cooperation," *Atlantic Monthly*, October 1923, pp. 542–45; Hogan, *Informal Entente*, pp. 84–89; Jerry Israel, *Progressivism and the Open Door: America and China, 1905–1921* (Pittsburgh: University of Pittsburgh Press, 1971), p. 148; Warren I. Cohen, *The Chinese Connection: Roger S. Green, Thomas W. Lamont, George E. Sokolsky and American-East Asian Relations* (New York: Columbia University Press, 1978), especially pp. 41–70.

22. Lamont, "Three Examples of International Cooperation," pp. 537–40; Senate, *Sale of Foreign Bonds*, p. 7; Hogan, *Informal Entente*, pp. 60–66; Van Meter, "United States and European Recovery," pp. 394–436.

23. Lamont, "Three Examples of International Cooperation," pp. 539–40.

24. Hogan, *Informal Entente*, p. 48; John M. Carroll, "The Paris Bankers' Conference of 1922 and America's Design for a Peaceful Europe," *International Review of History and Political Science* 10 (1973): 39–47.

25. Lamont to J. P. Morgan, 16 October 1922, 108/13, Lamont Papers.

26. Secretary of State Charles Evans Hughes's speech before the American Historical Association, 29 December 1922, 2: 199–202; Hughes to Ambassador (Paris) Myron T. Herrick, 17 October 1922, 2: 168–70; memos by Secretary Hughes of conversations with the French ambassador, 7 November and 14 December 1922, 2: 178–80, 187–92, all in *FRUS, 1922*; Hughes to Ambassador (Rome) Richard Washburn Child, 18 October

1922, DS 462.00R296/-.; [Beeritz memo], box 172, Charles Evans Hughes Papers, Library of Congress, Washington, D.C.

27. *FRUS, 1923*, 2: 85, 87; Frank Charles Costigliola, "The Politics of Financial Stabilization: American Reconstruction Policy in Europe, 1924– 30" (Ph.D. diss., Cornell University, 1972), p. 90; Melvyn P. Leffler, "The Struggle for Stability: American Policy toward France, 1921– 1933" (Ph.D. diss., Ohio State University, 1972), p. 102; Hogan, *Informal Entente*, p. 67. On France's financial weakness and its impact on French diplomacy see Stephen A. Schuker, *The End of French Predominance in Europe: The Financial Crisis of 1924 and the Adoption of the Dawes Plan* (Chapel Hill: University of North Carolina Press, 1976).

28. Harold G. Moulton, *The Reparation Plan* (New York: McGraw-Hill, 1924), pp. 149– 92.

29. Morgan and Co. to Morgan, Harjes and Co., 4 April 1924; Young to Gerard Swope (president of General Electric Co.), 27 February 1924; Swope to Young, 28 February 1924; George Whitney of Morgan and Co. to H. H. Harjes of Morgan, Harjes and Co., 29 February 1924; Swope to Young, 21 March 1924; Morgan and Co. to Morgan, Harjes and Co., 1 April 1924, all in 176/8, Lamont Papers.

30. Lamont to Morgan, Harjes and Co., 18 April 1924, 176/8, Lamont Papers.

31. Leffingwell to Lamont, 5 July 1924, 176/11, Lamont Papers.

32. For Lamont's views and those of Montagu Norman and the Morgan partners in New York see the documents of 9– 19 July 1924, 176/12, 15, and 16, Lamont Papers.

33. Lamont to Dwight Morrow, 11 July 1924; Lamont and E. C. Grenfell of Morgan, Grenfell and Co. to J. P. Morgan and Morrow, 10 July 1924; Lamont to Morgan and Co., 15 July 1924, all in 176/12, Lamont Papers; Schuker, *End of French Predominance*, pp. 295– 96, 308.

34. J. P. Morgan, Leffingwell, and Morrow to Lamont and Grenfell, 19 July 1924, 176/16; J. P. Morgan, W. H. Porter, E. R. Stettinius, Leffingwell, and Morrow to Grenfell and Lamont, 20 July 1924, 176/17, both in Lamont Papers.

35. Lamont to Morgan and Co., 20 July 1924, 176/17; Grenfell and Lamont to Morgan and Co., 21 July 1924, 176/17; Leffingwell to Lamont, 22 July 1924, 176/18, all in Lamont Papers.

36. J. P. Morgan, Porter, Stettinius, Leffingwell, and Morrow to Lamont, 20 July 1924, 176/17; Leffingwell to Lamont, 22 July 1924, 176/18, both in Lamont Papers.

37. Morgan, Grenfell and Co. to Morgan and Co., 25 July 1924 (enclosing Lamont to Prime Minister Ramsay MacDonald, 25 July 1924), 176/20; Lamont to Morrow, 28 July 1924, 176/20; Grenfell to Morgan and Co., 31 July and 1 August 1924, 176/21; Lamont to MacDonald, 6 August 1924, 176/22; Lamont to Premier Theunis, 9 August 1924, 176/24, all in Lamont Papers; Schuker, *End of French Predominance*, pp. 113, 143– 46.

38. Lamont, Grenfell, J. P. Morgan, and Charles Steele to Morgan and Co., 6 August 1924, 176/22; Lamont to Morgan and Co., 11 August 1924, 176/24, both in Lamont Papers.

39. Leffingwell to Lamont, 15 August 1924, 176/27; J. P. Morgan to Grenfell, 2 August 1924, 176/21; Morgan and Co. to Lamont and Grenfell, 3 August 1924 (two cables); J. P. Morgan to Morrow and Leffingwell, 6 August 1924, 176/22; Lamont, Grenfell, and J. P. Morgan to Morgan and Co., 11 August 1924, 176/24, all in Lamont Papers.

40. Lamont and Grenfell to Morgan and Co., 4 August 1924, 176/21; Lamont, Grenfell, J. P. Morgan, and Steele to Morgan and Co., 6 August 1924, 176/22; Lamont, Grenfell, and J. P. Morgan to Morgan and Co., 11 August 1924, 176/24, all in Lamont Papers.

41. Morgan and Co. to Lamont, 9 August 1924, 177/2, Lamont Papers. The position of agent general for reparations payments was especially important. Although bitterly disappointed when the administration of President Calvin Coolidge rejected Dwight Morrow, a Morgan partner, for that post, the firm was able to secure the appointment of S. Parker Gilbert. Gilbert was a former assistant secretary of the Treasury who would later become a Morgan partner himself. The story is well told in Schuker, *End of French Predominance*, pp. 284– 89; Kenneth Paul Jones, "Discord and Collaboration: Choosing an Agent General for Reparations," *Diplomatic History* 1 (Spring 1977): 119– 39.

42. See for example the scattered remarks in Lamont and Grenfell to J. P. Morgan, 26 July 1924, 176/20; Lamont to Morgan and Co., 12 August 1924, 176/25, and 18 August 1924, 177/1, all in Lamont Papers.

43. See for example Lamont to Morgan and Co., 22 August 1924, 177/4, Lamont Papers.

44. Morrow-Hughes correspondence, 18– 19 September 1924, DS 462.00R296/ 604 and 611; Lamont to Morgan and Co., 19 August 1924, 177/2; Kellogg to Lamont, 19 and 20 August 1924, 177/2; Morgan and Co. to Lamont and J. P. Morgan, 18 September 1924, 177/12; Morrow to Morgan, Grenfell and Co., 20 September 1924, 177/13; Morgan and Co. to Lamont and J. P. Morgan, 20 September 1924, 177/13, all in Lamont Papers.

45. Lamont to Leffingwell, 25 August 1924, 177/6; Lamont to Morgan and Co., 22 August 1924, 177/4; Lamont to Morgan and Co., 18 August 1924, 177/1; Lamont to J. P. Morgan, 25 August 1924, 177/6; Lamont to Kellogg, 25 August 1924, 177/6, all in Lamont Papers.

46. Stephen V. O. Clarke, *Central Bank Cooperation, 1924–1931* (New York: Federal Reserve Bank of New York, [1967]), p. 69.

47. Thomas W. Lamont, "What the International Bank Means," *Review of Reviews*, August 1929, pp. 81– 82; Lamont, "Taking Reparations out of Politics," *Review of Reviews*, July 1930, pp. 94, 96; Lamont, "The Final Reparations Settlement," *Foreign Affairs* 8 (1930): 336– 63. See also John M. Carroll's essay in this volume and Frank Costigliola, "The Other Side of Isolationism: The Establishment of the First World Bank, 1929– 1930," *Journal of American History* 59 (1972): 602– 20.

Chapter 2

1. Viscount Edgar Vincent D'Abernon, *The Diary of an Ambassador*, vol. 1, *Versailles to Rapallo, 1920–1922* (New York: Doubleday, Doran and Co., 1929), pp. 19– 20.

2. *Dictionary of American Biography: Supplement Three, 1941–1945* (New York: Charles Scribner's Sons, 1973), p. 365; "A Business Man as Ambassador to Germany," *Current Opinion* 73 (August 1922): 193– 95.

3. Castle to Attaché (Berlin) Ellis Loring Dresel, 31 January 1922, file 68, Ellis Loring Dresel Papers, Houghton Library, Harvard University, Cambridge, Mass.

4. Quote from John Dwight to Alanson B. Houghton, 12 February 1923, "Correspondence — Berlin," Alanson B. Houghton Papers, in family possession, Corning, N.Y.; Dwight to Houghton, 2 November 1923, ibid.; Harding to Ambassador

(London) George Harvey, 25 April 1922, microfilm roll 228, file 60, Warren G. Harding Papers, Ohio Historical Society, Columbus, Ohio; *New York Times*, 6 and 16 March 1926.

5. The most important studies are Dieter Bruno Gescher, *Die Vereinigten Staaten von Nordamerika und die Reparationen, 1920–1924: Eine Untersuchung der Reparationsfrage auf der Grundlage amerikanischer Akten* (Bonn: Ludwig Roehrscheid, 1956); Robert Gottwald, *Die deutsch-amerikanischen Beziehungen in der Aera Stresemann* (Berlin: Colloquium, 1965); Werner Link, *Die amerikanische Stabilisierungspolitik in Deutschland, 1921–32* (Duesseldorf: Droste, 1970); Frank Costigliola, "The United States and the Reconstruction of Germany in the 1920s," *Business History Review* 50 (Winter 1976): 477–502. Costigliola was the first to draw upon Houghton's private papers. Gescher, who saw neither Castle's nor Houghton's private correspondence, gives undue emphasis to the occasional criticism of Houghton found in Castle's diary. Gottwald is particularly good for Houghton's role in the Locarno negotiations of 1925—chap. 4. Two additional studies of Houghton's Berlin years have recently appeared: Sander A. Diamond, "Ein Amerikaner in Berlin: Aus den Papieren des Botschafters Alanson B. Houghton, 1922–1925," *Vierteljahrshefte fuer Zeitgeschichte* 27 (July 1979): 431–70; Hermann J. Rupieper, "Alanson B. Houghton: An American Ambassador in Germany, 1922–1925," *International History Review* 1 (October 1979): 490–508.

6. Gottwald, *Deutsch-amerikanischen Beziehungen*, p. 53.

7. "Business Man as Ambassador," pp. 194–95; *New York Times*, 22 February and 31 March 1922; speech to Metropolitan Club, 30 March 1922, "Germany," William R. Castle, Jr. Papers, Herbert Hoover Presidential Library, West Branch, Iowa. For an excellent discussion of Republican attitudes toward Europe see Melvyn P. Leffler, *The Elusive Quest: America's Pursuit of European Stability and French Security, 1919– 1933* (Chapel Hill: University of North Carolina Press, 1978).

8. See for example Federal Reserve Chairman Benjamin Strong to Governor of Bank of England Montagu Norman, 14 July 1922, file 1116.4, Benjamin Strong Papers, Federal Reserve Bank of New York, New York, N.Y.

9. Cf. Houghton to Castle, 8 July 1922, "Germany," Castle Papers; record of conversation by Joseph Grew with J. P. Morgan, Jr., 2 June 1922, vol. 20, Joseph P. Grew Papers, Houghton Library, Harvard University, Cambridge, Mass.

10. William McHenry Franklin, "The Origins of the Locarno Conference," (Ph.D. diss., Fletcher School of International Law and Diplomacy, 1941), p. 37—based on an interview with Alanson Houghton; Houghton to Castle, 19 June 1922, "Germany," Castle Papers.

11. For Wilson, see Arthur S. Link, *Wilson the Diplomatist* (Baltimore: Johns Hopkins Press, 1957), chap. 1. For Houghton, see his letter to Hughes, 23 October 1922, *FRUS, 1922*, 2: 171–75; Houghton to Coolidge, 19 August 1925, reel 53, file 66, Calvin Coolidge Papers, Manuscript Division, Library of Congress, Washington, D.C.

12. His diary is replete with a detailed listing of visits and dinners with the famous and not so famous in German life.

13. D'Abernon, *Diary of an Ambassador*, 1: 20; Houghton telegram to secretary of state, 25 June 1922, DS 862.00/1129.

14. Houghton to Castle, 6 June 1922; Houghton to Castle, 19 June and 13 July 1922, both in "Germany," Castle Papers.

15. Houghton to Castle, 26 August 1922; Houghton to Castle, 8 and 29 July 1922,

both in "Germany," Castle Papers; Houghton telegram to secretary of state, 24 August 1922, DS 862.00/1140.

16. Harding to Harvey, 3 May 1922, roll 228, file 60, Harding Papers; Castle to Houghton, 4 August 1922, "Germany," Castle Papers.

17. Harding to Under Secretary of State William Phillips, 26 August 1922, roll 186, frame 1673, Harding Papers; German chargé Thermann to secretary of state, 26 August 1922, *FRUS, 1922,* 2: 160.

18. For Houghton and Stinnes see Houghton telegrams to secretary of state, 15 and 23 September 1922, DS 462.00R29/2023 and 2031. For Houghton and Cuno see Houghton to Castle, 26 August 1922, "Germany," Castle Papers; Houghton to Hughes, 21 November 1922, box 4B, Charles Evans Hughes Papers, Manuscript Division, Library of Congress, Washington, D.C.

19. Castle diary entry, 21 November 1922, quoted in George Wolfgang Felix Hallgarten, *Hitler, Reichswehr und Industrie: Zur Geschichte der Jahre 1918–1933* (Frankfurt: Europaeische Verlagsanstalt, 1955), p. 59. Poincaré actually opposed Stinnes's diplomatic efforts—see Belgian Ambassador (Paris) Gaiffier d'Hestroy to Belgian Foreign Minister Henri Jaspar, 12213/5412– P.C.A., 3 October 1922, Henri Jaspar Papers, Archives Generales du Royaume, Brussels.

20. Houghton to Hughes, 23 October 1922, *FRUS, 1922,* 2: 171–75.

21. Ernest C. Bolt, Jr., *Ballots before Bullets: The War Referendum Approach to Peace in America, 1914–1941* (Charlottesville: University Press of Virginia, 1977), especially chap. 6 which notes Houghton's role but exaggerates Hughes's; Castle to Hughes, 24 October 1922, *FRUS, 1922,* 2: 176–77.

22. Hughes telegram to Houghton, 14 November 1922, 2: 181–82; on Hughes's negotiations with France, see the correspondence, 2: 165, both in *FRUS, 1922.*

23. Hughes and Wiedfeldt, 15 December 1922, box 174, Hughes Papers; Germany, Auswaertiges Amt, *Materialien zur Sicherheitsfrage* (Berlin: Reichsdruckerei, 1925), p. 10. For Houghton's role see Franklin, "Origins of Locarno," p. 43 (n. 22). Houghton also tried, unsuccessfully, to use Elihu Root as an intermediary with Hughes according to James T. Shotwell in *An Autobiography* (Indianapolis: Bobbs-Merrill, 1961), pp. 173–74.

24. See memos in *FRUS, 1922,* 2: 195–98, 204–9.

25. For Germany, Houghton telegram to secretary of state, 30 November 1922, DS 462.00R29/2213; for Britain, Hughes and British Ambassador Auckland Geddes, 18 December 1922, *FRUS, 1922,* 2: 192–95; for the Americans, Boyden telegram to secretary of state, 28 November 1922, DS 462.00R29/2209.

26. Charles Evans Hughes, *The Pathway of Peace: Representative Addresses Delivered during His Term as Secretary of State (1921–1925) by Charles E. Hughes* (New York: Harper and Bros., 1925), pp. 53–58. For an example of the domestic pressures see Castle to Houghton, 30 December 1922, "Correspondence—Berlin," Houghton Papers.

27. Karl-Heinz Harbeck, ed., *Das Kabinett Cuno, 22 November 1922 bis 12 August 1923,* Akten der Reichskanzlei, Weimarer Republik (Boppard am Rhein: H. Boldt, 1968), pp. 103–10; Houghton to Hughes, 3 January 1923, box 4B, Hughes Papers.

28. Hughes telegram to Herrick, 10 January 1923, 2: 192; Hughes and Geddes, 25 January 1923, 2: 52–55, both in *FRUS, 1923*; Hughes to Senator Henry Cabot Lodge, 1 February 1923, box 4B, Hughes Papers.

29. Notes of an interview with Houghton by a Mr. Mitchell, 6 March 1941,

Houghton Papers; memo of conversation between American unofficial delegate to Reparation Commission Roland Boyden and French Foreign Ministry official Jacques Seydoux, 5 December 1922, "Emprunts d'Allemagne. Informations," vol. 361, AJ[5]; Houghton to Castle, 17 January 1923, "Germany," Castle Papers.

30. Houghton to Castle, 12 and 20 February 1923, "Germany," Castle Papers; Houghton to Hughes, 27 February 1923, box 4B, Hughes Papers.

31. Houghton to Hughes, 6 March 1923; also see Houghton to Hughes, 27 February 1923, both in box 4B, Hughes Papers.

32. Hughes and Geddes, 25 January 1923, box 175; Hughes to Lodge, 1 February 1923, box 4B, both in Hughes Papers.

33. Castle to Houghton, 17 March and 19 April 1923, box 4B, Hughes Papers; Castle to Robbins, 15 June 1923, "Germany," Castle Papers. For Hughes's attitude also see memos of conversations with Ambassador Geddes: 11 and 25 January 1923, boxes 174– 75, Hughes Papers; 23 February 1923, *FRUS, 1923,* 2: 55– 56.

34. Castle to Robbins, 15 June 1923, "Germany," Castle Papers; Castle to Counselor Frederick Dolbeare, 12 March 1923, "England," Castle Papers. For Dolbeare's assurances that Houghton was not holding back information, see Dolbeare to Castle, 26 March 1923, "England," Castle Papers.

35. Castle to Houghton, 17 March 1923, "Correspondence — Berlin," Houghton Papers.

36. During the Ruhr crisis the ambassador shared his thoughts with his counselor, Warren Robbins. Although he knew Robbins's assessment of the situation differed, he encouraged him to communicate his views to Castle — letters by Robbins in "Germany," Castle Papers.

37. Hughes and Wiedfeldt, 3 May 1923, *FRUS, 1923,* 2: 57– 61; Houghton telegram to secretary of state, 24 January 1923, DS 862t.01/556.

38. Hughes telegram to Fletcher, 26 July 1923, DS 462.00R29/2961a; Hughes telegram to Fletcher, 17 August 1923, *FRUS, 1923,* 2: 66– 68. Concerning an autonomous Rhineland, Castle to Houghton, 25 July 1923, "Correspondence — Berlin," Houghton Papers; Gescher, *Vereinigten Staaten und Reparationen,* p. 186.

39. Houghton to Castle, 31 July 1923, "Germany," Castle Papers; Houghton telegram to secretary of state, 30 July 1923, DS 462.00R29/2930.

40. Houghton to Castle, 14 August 1923, "Germany," Castle Papers; Houghton telegrams to secretary of state, 13 and 22 August 1923, DS 862.00/1271 and 1274.

41. Castle to Houghton, 22 September 1923; Dwight to Houghton, 29 September 1923; Castle to Houghton, 2 November 1923, all in "Correspondence — Berlin," Houghton Papers.

42. Phillips to Coolidge, 24 September 1923, reel 92, file 198A, Coolidge Papers; William Phillips diary, 24 September 1923, box 1A, William Phillips Papers, Houghton Library, Harvard University, Cambridge, Mass.; Berlin Diary, 22– 23 September 1923, Houghton Papers.

43. See his Berlin Diary and correspondence for this period, Houghton Papers; Houghton telegrams for this period in DS 862.00 and 862t.00.

44. Phillips diary, 5 November 1923, box 1A, Phillips Papers; Hughes and Jusserand, 5 November 1923, box 174, Hughes Papers. Phillips to Ambassador (Paris) Henry P. Fletcher, 5 November 1923, box 10, Henry P. Fletcher Papers, Manuscript Division, Library of Congress, Washington, D.C.; Hughes telegram to Herrick, 9 November 1923, *FRUS, 1923,* 2: 94– 95.

45. Memo of conversation with Houghton by Carl von Schubert, 13 November 1923, T– 120, BRM, 1649/3243/D721768– 69.

46. Herrick telegram to secretary of state, 19 November 1923, DS 862.20/114.

47. For Logan's activities and creation of Dawes Committee, see Phillips diary, November– December 1923, box 1A, Phillips Papers; *FRUS, 1923,* 2: 98; unpublished memos, November– December 1923, box 175, Hughes Papers.

48. Phillips diary, 30 November 1923, box 1A, Phillips Papers. For the decline of the franc see Stephen A. Schuker, *The End of French Predominance in Europe: The Financial Crisis of 1924 and the Adoption of the Dawes Plan* (Chapel Hill: University of North Carolina Press, 1976), especially chaps. 2– 3. For evidence of Poincaré's attempts to limit the French delegates see the file "Documents signalés à l'attention des Experts," vol. 361, AJ[5].

49. Interview with Mr. and Mrs. Everett Case (son-in-law and daughter of Owen D. Young), 13 July 1974. Owen Young to Anson Burchard, 26 May 1923; Young radiogram to Houghton, 26 June 1923, both in Owen D. Young Papers, in family possession, Van Hornesville, N.Y. For Houghton's trip to Paris see Berlin Diary, 10– 17 January 1924, Houghton Papers. For Poincaré's pressure on the Germans see Houghton telegrams to secretary of state, 23 and 26 January 1924, DS 462.00R296/154 and R29/3308.

50. Berlin Diary, January– February 1924, Houghton Papers; Young's notes on his Berlin trip, box R– 6, Young Papers.

51. During Houghton's stay in Paris, he also used his influence on Young to bring about some important changes in the wording of the final text in order to make the plan more palatable to the German electorate. For the trip to Paris and its background see Berlin Diary, 26 March– 4 April 1924 (quote from 31 March entry), Houghton Papers; Journal of Leonard P. Ayres (technical adviser to American delegation), especially 24 March– 4 April 1924, box 4: Personal Papers, Leonard P. Ayres Papers, Manuscript Division, Library of Congress, Washington, D.C.

52. Schubert and Houghton, 29 February 1924, T– 120, BSS, 2228/4492/E098136– 37; State Secretary Ago von Maltzan and Houghton, 12 April 1924, ibid. /E098322– 23; Houghton to Castle, 24 April 1924, "Germany," Castle Papers; Houghton to Logan, 27 April 1924, "Correspondence — Berlin," Houghton Papers.

53. Houghton to Castle, 28 May 1924, "Germany," Castle Papers; Berlin Diary, 8 and 15 May 1924, Houghton Papers. For Houghton's activities see Stresemann and Houghton, 13 May 1924, 3117/7169/H155680– 81; Stresemann and Houghton, 19 May 1924, 3117/7169/H155739– 740; Schubert and Houghton, 30 May 1924, 3117/7169/H155810, all in T– 120, Nachlass Stresemann.

54. Berlin Diary, July 1924, Houghton Papers; Kellogg to Hughes, 18 June 1924, box 61, Hughes Papers.

55. German Ambassador (London) Friedrich Sthamer to Foreign Ministry, 19 July 1924, 1652/3243/D723925– 930; Sthamer to Berlin, 19 and 20 July 1924, 1936/3398/D740024 and D740043, all in T– 120, BRM.

56. Schubert and Houghton, 31 July 1924, T– 120, BSS, 2229/4492/E099637– 39; Kellogg to Hughes, 18 August 1924, box 8, Frank B. Kellogg Papers, Minnesota Historical Society, St. Paul, Minn.; Hughes telegram to Kellogg, 4 August 1924, DS 462.00R296/503.

57. Houghton telegram to secretary of state, 17 August 1924, DS 462.00R296/506.

58. For the meeting of 20 August 1924, see Berlin Diary for that date, Houghton Papers, and Houghton telegram to secretary of state, 20 August 1924, DS 462.00

R296/532. The long quote in the text appears only in his diary. Felix Hirsch has also described this meeting—"Stresemann, Ballin und die Vereinigten Staaten," *Viertel-jahrshefte fuer Zeitgeschichte* 3 (1955): 30– 31—but errs in dating it and in saying that Houghton had to delay his vacation plans.

59. In addition to the Berlin Diary, Houghton Papers, see Michael Stuermer, *Koalition und Opposition in der Weimarer Republik, 1924– 1928* (Duesseldorf: Droste, 1967), p. 65; Lewis Hertzmann, *DNVP: Right-Wing Opposition in the Weimar Republic (1918– 1924)* (Lincoln: University of Nebraska Press, 1963), pp. 219– 23. They describe the variety of pressures upon the DNVP.

60. On Houghton's campaign activities and London appointment see Houghton to Hughes, 18 October 1924, box 59, Hughes Papers; Chandler P. Anderson diary, 7 November 1924, Chandler P. Anderson Papers, Manuscript Division, Library of Congress, Washington, D.C. For his role in the Locarno Treaties see Franklin, "Origins of Locarno," p. 54; Houghton to Castle, 18 August 1925, "England," Castle Papers; Gottwald, *Deutsch-amerikanischen Beziehungen*, chap. 4.

61. Houghton to Coolidge, 26 June 1925; Houghton to Coolidge, 19 August 1925, both in reel 53, file 66, Coolidge Papers. Houghton to M. W. Alexander, 11 November 1923, "Correspondence— Berlin," Houghton Papers.

62. "To Put Wars to a Vote," *Literary Digest* 94 (16 July 1927): 8– 9; Robert H. Ferrell, *Peace in Their Time: The Origins of the Kellogg-Briand Pact* (New Haven: Yale University Press, 1952); Bolt, *Ballots before Bullets*, pp. 140– 42.

63. Houghton to Coolidge, 19 August 1925, reel 53, file 66, Coolidge Papers; *Dictionary of American Biography, Supplement Three*, p. 366; Bolt, *Ballots before Bullets*, pp. 142– 43.

64. On the London Conference see Berlin Diary, 5 August 1924, Houghton Papers. For his influence from London see for example the correspondence with Stresemann for 1925 in Gustav Stresemann, *Vermaechtnis: Der Nachlass in drei Baenden*, ed. Henry Bernhard, 3 vols. (Berlin: Ullstein, 1932– 33), vol. 2. Shortly before Houghton took up his duties as ambassador to Great Britain, State Secretary Maltzan expressed concern that the new American ambassador would not be able to play the same role that he had. According to Maltzan, Houghton very confidentially informed him that the direction of European and particularly German affairs would be handled through him in London— Gottwald, *Deutsch-amerikanischen Beziehungen*, p. 137 (n. 47).

65. Castle to Robbins, 12 September 1923, "Germany," Castle Papers.

66. Castle to Robbins, 11 September 1924, "Germany"; Castle to Percy Blair, 29 May 1925, "England," both in Castle Papers. For an example of Castle's temporary anger see Gescher, *Vereinigten Staaten und Reparationen*, p. 212 (quoting from Castle's diary).

67. Kenneth Paul Jones, "Discord and Collaboration: Choosing an Agent General for Reparations," *Diplomatic History* 1 (Spring 1977): especially 127– 28. For Hughes's reliance on Houghton's advice see Merlo J. Pusey, *Charles Evans Hughes*, 2 vols. (New York: Macmillan Co., 1951), 2: 580– 81.

Chapter 3

1. Thomas W. Lamont, "Reparations," in *What Really Happened at Paris: The Story of the Peace Conference, 1918– 1919*, ed. Edward M. House and Charles Seymour (New York: Charles Scribner's Sons, 1921), p. 272.

2. Young to Josiah Stamp, 3 March 1925, box marked Special Papers 1– 4, Owen D. Young Papers, in family possession, Van Hornesville, N.Y.

3. The capacity to pay formula, and the business approach to European diplomacy, reflected the American policymakers' belief that if complex problems such as reparations and war debts could be separated from their political context then scientific and objective analysis might lead to a reasonable solution. See Melvyn P. Leffler, "Political Isolationism, Economic Expansionism, or Diplomatic Realism: American Policy toward Western Europe, 1921–1933," in *Perspectives in American History*, ed. Donald Fleming and Bernard Bailyn (Cambridge: Harvard University Press, 1974), 8: 411–61.

4. Young speech to Foreign Policy Association of Cincinnati, 6 January 1926, O. D. Young Papers.

5. Ida M. Tarbell, *Owen D. Young: A New Type of Industrial Leader* (New York: Macmillan Co., 1932), pp. 9–11.

6. Brady A. Hughes, "Owen D. Young and American Foreign Policy, 1919–1929" (Ph.D. diss., University of Wisconsin, 1969), pp. 5, 8, 19.

7. Tarbell, *Young*, pp. 42–45.

8. Ibid., pp. 59–62.

9. Ibid., pp. 68–69.

10. Young speech at Queen's University, Kingston, Ontario, 28 October 1933, O. D. Young Papers.

11. Young speech at Bryn Mawr College, 7 June 1928, O. D. Young Papers.

12. For further discussion of this point see Michael J. Hogan, *Informal Entente: The Private Structure of Cooperation in Anglo-American Economic Diplomacy, 1918–1928* (Columbia: University of Missouri Press, 1977), pp. 209–12; also see Hogan's essay in this volume.

13. Young speech at Bryn Mawr, 7 June 1928, O. D. Young Papers.

14. Among the most outspoken critics of the reparations system was John M. Keynes, *The Economic Consequences of the Peace* (New York: Harcourt, Brace, and Howe, 1920). For a different view see Etienne Mantoux, *The Carthaginian Peace or the Economic Consequences of Mr. Keynes* (New York: Charles Scribner's Sons, 1952). On inflation see George P. Auld, *The Dawes Plan and the New Economics* (New York: Doubleday, Doran and Co., 1928), p. 28.

15. Hughes's New Haven speech is in Charles E. Hughes, *The Pathway of Peace: Representative Addresses...1921–1925* (New York: Harper and Bros., 1925), pp. 53–58. For a more careful survey of the reparations problem between 1921 and 1923 see Kenneth Paul Jones's essay in this volume.

16. On appointments see James A. Logan (reparations observer), telegram to Hughes, 20 December 1923, 2: 177–78; Ambassador Myron T. Herrick to Hughes, 21 December 1923, both in *FRUS, 1923*.

17. Young speech at Bryn Mawr, 7 June 1928, O. D. Young Papers.

18. Stuart M. Crocker, "Washington Trip," 27 December 1923; Fred I. Kent to Young, 4 February 1924, box 87, both in O. D. Young Papers.

19. Crocker, "Washington Trip," 27 December 1923, O. D. Young Papers.

20. Young speech at St. Lawrence University Club Dinner, 6 March 1925, O. D. Young Papers.

21. For a brief account of the previous conferences see Carl Bergmann, *The History of Reparations* (Boston: Houghton, Mifflin Co., 1927), pp. 67–167.

22. For an excellent account of the French financial difficulties and their impact see Stephen A. Schuker, *The End of French Predominance in Europe: The Financial Crisis of 1924 and the Adoption of the Dawes Plan* (Chapel Hill: University of North Carolina

Press, 1976), pp. 31–123. On Hughes's views see Raymond Robbins to William R. Castle (chief of Division of Western European Affairs), 12 March 1924, "Germany," William R. Castle, Jr. Papers, Herbert Hoover Presidential Library, West Branch, Iowa.

23. Young speeches at Waldorf Astoria, New York City, 11 December 1924, and St. Lawrence University Club, 6 March 1925, O. D. Young Papers.

24. On Austrian stabilization see Robert H. Van Meter, Jr., "The United States and European Recovery, 1918–1923: A Study of Public Policy and Private Finance" (Ph.D. diss., University of Wisconsin, 1971), pp. 394–436. For a survey of the Dawes Plan see Harold G. Moulton, *The Reparation Plan: An Interpretation of the Reports . . . 1923* (New York: McGraw-Hill, 1924).

25. Young speech at Waldorf Astoria, 11 December 1924, O. D. Young Papers.

26. For an analysis of the transfer provisions see Frank Charles Costigliola, "The Politics of Financial Stabilization: American Reconstruction Policy in Europe, 1924–30" (Ph.D. diss., Cornell University, 1972), pp. 105–9. The annuity was set at $250 million for the first year and gradually rose to $625 million for a standard year.

27. Goldsmith to Christian Herter (assistant to Hoover), 20 and 28 January and 19 February 1924, box 4, Leonard P. Ayres Papers, Manuscript Division, Library of Congress, Washington, D.C.

28. Charles G. Dawes. *A Journal of Reparations* (London: Macmillan and Co., 1939), p. 76; see also Kenneth Paul Jones's essay in this volume.

29. On the London Conference see Werner Link, *Die amerikanische Stabilisierungspolitik in Deutschland, 1921–32* (Duesseldorf: Droste, 1970), pp. 296–306; Schuker, *End of French Predominance*, pp. 295–382.

30. For a more in-depth treatment of the bankers' position see Schuker, *End of French Predominance*, pp. 300–18; Michael J. Hogan's essay in this volume.

31. Young speech before Harvard Alumni Association, 23 January 1925; Young to James Perkins, 6 January 1925, box 819, both in O. D. Young Papers.

32. Stephen V. O. Clarke, *Central Bank Cooperation: 1924–1931* (New York: Federal Reserve Bank of New York [1967]), pp. 68–69.

33. Young to James Perkins, 6 January 1925, box 819; Young to Crocker for A. C. Bedford, 18 October 1924, box R13, both in O. D. Young Papers; on the agent general controversy see Kenneth Paul Jones, "Discord and Collaboration: Choosing an Agent General for Reparations," *Diplomatic History* 1 (1977): 118–39.

34. Most surveys of American diplomacy adhere to this interpretation. See Thomas A. Bailey, *A Diplomatic History of the American People*, 8th ed. rev. (New York: Appleton-Century-Crofts, 1969), pp. 661–64; Alexander DeConde, *A History of American Foreign Policy*, 2nd ed. rev. (New York: Charles Scribner's Sons, 1971), pp. 557–59.

35. Young to Harold Johnson, 29 October 1925, box R15, O. D. Young Papers.

36. On the negative attitude toward the German bond market see Roland W. Boyden, "The Dawes Report," *Foreign Affairs* 2 (1924): 590.

37. Young to Tumulty, 6 October 1925, box 820, O. D. Young Papers.

38. Young to Hoover, 5 January 1926, box 9; Young speech to Foreign Policy Association of Cincinnati, 6 January 1926, both in O. D. Young Papers.

39. Other financial leaders concerned about a German default included Hjalmar Schacht (president of the Reichsbank) and Montagu Norman (governor of the Bank of England). See Frank Costigliola, "The United States and the Reconstruction of Germany in the 1920s," *Business History Review* 50 (1976): 498–99; Gilbert to Castle, 18

November 1927; Gilbert to Strong, 14 November 1927, both in "Germany," Castle
Papers.

40. Arthur N. Young memo, 12 March 1928, DS 462.00R296/2162. Elbridge Rand
(secretary, Paris embassy) telegram to Secretary of State Frank B. Kellogg, 18 September
1928, DS 462.00R296/2365; Dewitt Poole (chargé, Berlin) telegram to Kellogg, 19
October 1928, DS 462.00R296/24221/2; see also Jon Jacobson, *Locarno Diplomacy:
Germany and the West, 1925–1929* (Princeton: Princeton University Press, 1972), pp.
163, 193–94.

41. Gilbert telegrams to Young, 15 February and 22 November 1928, boxes 302 and
R30, O. D. Young Papers.

42. Herrick telegram to Kellogg, 19 January 1929, *FRUS, 1929*, 2: 1027–28.

43. Arthur N. Young memo, 12 October 1928, box 1, Arthur N. Young Papers,
Hoover Institution on War, Revolution, and Peace, Stanford, Calif.; Young speech
before Harvard Alumni Association, 23 January 1930, O. D. Young Papers.

44. Castle to Secretary of the Treasury Andrew W. Mellon, 11 February 1929, DS
462.00R296/2678; Young to Thomas Perkins, 23 January 1929, box R30, O. D. Young
Papers; excerpt from Department of State press notice, 5 February 1929, attached to
Kellogg to Hoover, 11 April 1929, "Foreign Affairs-Financial," Presidential Papers,
HHL.

45. Then Assistant Secretary of State William Castle blamed the confusion over
American reparations policy on Secretary Kellogg. He stated that Kellogg "is very tired
and is so much more interested in the fate of his treaty [the Kellogg-Briand Pact] than in
anything else that he dealt with this reparation matter in a more or less haphazard way."
Castle to unofficial American member of Reparation Commission Edwin Wilson, 15
February 1929, "France," Castle Papers.

46. Young to Thomas Perkins, 23 January 1929, box R30; Young to Coolidge, 11 July
1929, box 7, both in O. D. Young Papers.

47. Memo by Everett Case, 10 October 1929, box marked E. N. Case materials,
O. D. Young Papers.

48. Memo for Dwight Morrow by J. A. M. Sanchez, "The Bank for International
Settlements," n.d. (probably June 1929), box 108, folder 11 (hereafter box no./folder
no.), Thomas W. Lamont Papers, Baker Library, Harvard University, Boston, Mass.;
Crocker diary, 6 March 1929, O. D. Young Papers.

49. Crocker to Mrs. Owen Young, 1 March 1929, box 2, Stuart M. Crocker Papers,
Manuscript Division, Library of Congress, Washington, D.C.; Young to Henry Robin-
son, 22 July 1929, box R38, O. D. Young Papers; Young telegram to Kellogg, 19 March
1929, DS 462.00R296/2771; J. P. Morgan and Lamont telegram to Morgan and Co., 12
March 1929, 176/1, Lamont Papers; Frank Costigliola, "The Other Side of
Isolationism: The Establishment of the First World Bank, 1929–1930," *Journal of
American History* 59 (1972): 608.

50. Allied Powers, Reparation Commission, *Report of the Committee of Experts on
Reparations* (London: H.M.S.O., 1929); Shepard Morgan, "Conditions Precedent to
the Settlement," *Proceedings of the Academy of Political Science* 14 (1931): 5–16.

51. Young telegram to Kellogg, 3 and 28 March 1929, *FRUS, 1929*, 2: 1029–36.
One of the functions of the BIS would be to commercialize a part of the reparations
bonds which in turn might be used to pay off the war debt obligations in a lump sum
payment. See Henry Clay, *Lord Norman* (London: Macmillan and Co., 1957), p. 269.

52. "Statement Issued to the Press by the Secretary of State," 16 May 1929, 2:

1070– 71; Stimson telegram to Norman Armour (chargé, Paris), 25 May 1929, 2: 1081, both in *FRUS, 1929*. For Hoover's position on the debts see Hoover memo, 23 September 1925, "Personal-Debts, France," Commerce Papers, HHL.

53. Hoover to Coolidge, 8 April 1929, "Foreign Affairs-Financial," Presidential Papers, HHL; Coolidge to Hoover, 9 April 1929, DS 462.00R296/27751/2; Stimson telegram to Young, 8 April 1929, *FRUS, 1929*, 2: 1036– 38.

54. Crocker diary, 9– 10 April 1929, O. D. Young Papers; Lamont memo, 9 April 1929; Lamont to Root, 17 April 1929, both in 179/27, Lamont Papers.

55. Young telegram to Stimson, 11 April 1929, *FRUS, 1929*, 2: 1043– 45; Young to Mellon, 13 April 1929, box R35, O. D. Young Papers.

56. Armour telegram to Stimson, 10 and 17 May 1929, 2: 1067– 68, 1071– 72; Stimson telegram to Armour, 17, 21, and 25 May 1929, 2: 1072– 73, 1077, 1081, both in *FRUS, 1929*.

57. Tarbell, *Young*, pp. 192– 95. For published accounts of the conference see Link, *Amerikanische Stabilisierungspolitik*, pp. 463– 502; Jacobson, *Locarno Diplomacy*, pp. 239– 76.

58. Case memo, 16 October 1929, box marked Special E. N. Case materials, O. D. Young Papers; Lamont to Stimson, 25 June 1929, DS 462.00R296/30361/2; Lamont memo, 25 June 1929, contained in William Beck to George Akerson, 19 July 1929, "Foreign Affairs-Financial," Presidential Papers, HHL.

59. Young to Stamp, 26 August 1929 (not sent) and 6 February 1930, box 316, O. D. Young Papers; Jacobson, *Locarno Diplomacy*, pp. 310– 43.

60. Lamont to Snowden, 20 August 1929, 176/1; Lamont to Pierre Quesnay, 14 August 1929, 180/31, both in Lamont Papers; Young to Lamont, 29 July 1929, box R30, O. D. Young Papers. Instead of ratifying the Young Plan in May, Washington signed a separate agreement with Germany for the collection of Army costs and Mixed Claims on 23 June 1930. See Ogden L. Mills, "America's Separate Agreement with Germany," *Proceedings of the Academy of Political Science* 14 (1931): 54– 60.

61. In addition to Bailey and DeConde, cited in n. 34, see the following works critical of American reparations and war debts policy: Selig Adler, *The Uncertain Giant, 1921– 1941: American Foreign Policy between the Wars* (New York: Collier Books, 1974), pp. 74– 82; Foster R. Dulles, *America's Rise to World Power* (New York: Harper and Bros., 1963), pp. 129– 33; John D. Hicks, *Republican Ascendancy, 1921– 1933* (New York: Harper and Bros., 1963), pp. 135– 44.

62. Tarbell (*Young*) is Young's only biographer. She is very laudatory which is surprising in view of her muckraking reputation. Young is barely mentioned in most surveys of American diplomacy in the twentieth century.

63. For recent accounts of American diplomacy in the 1920s which have emphasized the positive side of America's European diplomacy and Young's contributions see Hogan, *Informal Entente*; Leffler, "Political Isolationism"; Costigliola, "The Other Side of Isolationism"; Joan Hoff Wilson, *American Business and Foreign Policy, 1920– 1933* (Lexington: University of Kentucky Press, 1971).

Chapter 4

1. Stetson to Secretary of State Frank B. Kellogg, 10 May 1926, DS 860c.51/567 (p. 10).

2. Kurt and Sarah Wimer, "The Harding Administration, the League of Nations, and the Separate Peace Treaty," *Review of Politics* 29 (January 1967): 15– 17; David J.

Danelski and Joseph S. Tulchin, eds., *The Autobiographical Notes of Charles Evans Hughes* (Cambridge: Harvard University Press, 1973), pp. 225– 26; Sally Marks-Denis Dulude, "German-American Relations, 1918– 1921," *Mid-America* 53 (October 1971): 221; David H. Jennings, "President Harding and International Organization," *Ohio History* 75 (Summer 1966): 155.

3. Hoover to Hughes, 6 April 1921, DS 711.62119/107. See also Hoover to Hughes, 9 April 1921, enclosing memorandum by John Foster Dulles, 7 April 1921, DS 711.62119/4; David Hunter Miller, *The Drafting of the Covenant*, 2 vols. (New York: G. P. Putnam's Sons, 1928), 1: 382– 84; Merlo J. Pusey, *Charles Evans Hughes* (New York: Macmillan Co., 1951), 1: 395– 99; Danelski and Tulchin, *Autobiographical Notes*, pp. 210– 12; Gary Dean Best, *The Politics of American Individualism: Herbert Hoover in Transition, 1918– 1921* (Westport, Connecticut: Greenwood Press, 1975), pp. 123, 138– 39.

4. Quoted in Betty Glad, *Charles Evans Hughes and the Illusions of Innocence* (Urbana: University of Illinois Press, 1966), p. 178.

5. For the separate peace, see Marks-Dulude, "German-American Relations," pp. 211– 26; Pusey, *Hughes*, 1: 441– 42; Danelski and Tulchin, *Autobiographical Notes*, pp. 225– 27; Werner Link, *Die amerikanische Stabilisierungspolitik in Deutschland* (Duesseldorf: Droste Verlag, 1970), 89– 100; *FRUS, 1921*, 1: 1– 24. For the Washington Conference, see Thomas H. Buckley, *The United States and the Washington Conference, 1921– 22* (Knoxville: University of Tennessee Press, 1970); John Chalmers Vinson, *The Parchment Peace* (Athens: University of Georgia Press, 1955); Roger Dingman, *Power in the Pacific* (Chicago: University of Chicago Press, 1976); C. Leonard Hoag, *Preface to Preparedness: The Washington Disarmament Conference and Public Opinion* (Washington: American Council on Public Affairs, 1941); James H. Mannock, "Anglo-American Relations, 1921– 28" (Ph.D. diss., Princeton University, 1962), pp. 1– 64; Robert H. Van Meter, Jr., "The United States and European Recovery, 1918– 1923: A Study of Public Policy and Private Finance" (Ph.D. diss., University of Wisconsin, 1971), pp. 296– 302; Melvyn P. Leffler, *The Elusive Quest: America's Pursuit of European Stability and French Security, 1919– 1933* (Chapel Hill: University of North Carolina Press, 1979), pp. 33– 40.

6. Herbert Hoover, *The Memoirs of Herbert Hoover*, 3 vols. (New York: Macmillan Co., 1942), 2: 11, 36; Best, *Politics of American Individualism*, pp. 166– 68; Joan Hoff Wilson, *Herbert Hoover: Forgotten Progressive* (Boston: Little, Brown and Co., 1975); Joseph H. Davis, "Herbert Hoover, 1874– 1964: Another Appraisal," *South Atlantic Quarterly* 68 (Summer 1969): 295– 318; David Burner, *Herbert Hoover: A Public Life* (New York: Alfred A. Knopf, 1979); Joseph Brandes, *Herbert Hoover and Economic Diplomacy: Department of Commerce Policy, 1921– 28* (Pittsburgh: University of Pittsburgh Press, 1962).

7. Benjamin M. Weissman, *Herbert Hoover and Famine Relief to Soviet Russia, 1921– 23* (Stanford: Hoover Institution Press, 1974); Harold H. Fisher, *The Famine in Soviet Russia, 1919– 23: The Operations of the American Relief Administration* (Freeport, New York: Books for Libraries Press, 1971).

8. Frank Costigliola, "The United States and the Reconstruction of Germany in the 1920s," *Business History Review* 50 (Winter 1976): 478– 502; Leffler, *Elusive Quest*, pp. 90– 112; John M. Carroll, "The Making of the Dawes Plan, 1919– 24" (Ph.D. diss., University of Kentucky, 1972).

9. For a general discussion of the peaceful change concept see Link, *Amerikanische Stabilisierungspolitik*, pp. 537– 41, 620– 30.

10. See for example F. Scott Fitzgerald to Edmund Wilson, in Andrew Turnbull, ed., *The Letters of F. Scott Fitzgerald* (New York: Charles Scribner's Sons, 1963), p. 326; Charles Pomaret, *L'Amerique à la conquête de l'Europe* (Paris: A. Colin, 1931); Julius Hirsch, *Das amerikanische Wirtschaftswunder* (Berlin: S. Fischer, 1926).

11. Theodor Lueddecke, "Amerikanismus als Schlagwort und als Tatsache," *Deutsche Rundschau* 221 (March 1930): 214– 21; Heinrich Mueller, "Die Amerikanisierung Europas," *Allgemeine Rundschau* 17 (October 1920): 510– 11; David Strauss, *Menace in the West: The Rise of French Anti-Americanism in Modern Times* (Westport, Connecticut: Greenwood Press, 1978), pp. 199– 204; Heinz K. Meier, *Friendship under Stress: U.S.-Swiss Relations, 1900– 1950* (Bern: Herbert Lang, 1970), pp. 126– 52.

12. Mitchell interview with Hughes, 4 and 11 November 1941, copy in Alanson B. Houghton Papers, in family possession, Corning, N.Y.

13. Alanson B. Houghton to Calvin Coolidge, 19 August 1925, Houghton Papers, chap. 2.

14. Houghton to Charles A. Coffin, 6 June 1925, Houghton Papers, chap. 2. For evidence of American prejudices about Poles, see for example Stetson to Kellogg, 26 March 1927, DS 860c.00/401; memo by Benjamin Strong of conversations with Stetson and Felix Mylnarski, 16 September 1926, Polish Stabilization file, FRBNY Archives.

15. William R. Castle, Jr. to H. Dorsey Newson, 23 December 1926, box 8, William R. Castle, Jr. Papers, Herbert Hoover Presidential Library, West Branch, Iowa.

16. Thomas W. Lamont to Russell Leffingwell, 24 March 1931, file 181/20, Thomas W. Lamont Papers, Baker Library, Harvard University, Cambridge, Mass. For Lamont's views, see chap. 2.

17. Edward W. Bennett, *Germany and the Diplomacy of the Financial Crisis, 1931* (Cambridge: Harvard University Press, 1962), pp. 269– 85.

18. Henry L. Stimson diary, 12 October 1931, Henry L. Stimson Papers, Sterling Library, Yale University, New Haven, Conn.

19. Ibid., 30 March 1931, Stimson Papers.

20. Cleona Lewis, *America's Stake in International Investments* (Washington: Brookings Institution, 1938), pp. 620, 622. See also Zbigniew Landau, "The Foreign Loans of the Polish State in the Years 1918– 1939," *Studia Historiae Oeconomicae* 9 (1974): 281– 97; Leopold Wellisz, *Foreign Capital in Poland* (London: G. Allen, 1938), pp. 131– 47, appendices A, C.

21. For the offer of the governorship of the FRBNY, see Owen D. Young to Gilbert, 12 November 1928; Young to Gilbert, 19 November 1928, both in Owen D. Young Papers, in family possession, Van Hornesville, N.Y. For Gilbert's role in communications between Secretary of the Treasury Andrew Mellon and Europeans see Emile Moreau, *Souvenirs d'un gouverneur de la Banque de France* (Paris: M. T. Géuin, 1954); Gilbert to Mellon, 22 June 1929, box 879, Presidential Papers, HHL. For his ties with State Department officials see for example Castle memo of conversation with Gilbert, 3 January 1928, DS 462.00R296/2189; Henry P. Fletcher to Kellogg, 12 April 1928, DS 462.00R296/2207; Gilbert to Castle ("Dear Bill"), 3 December 1927; Gilbert to Castle, 18 November 1927, both in Castle Papers. For the story of Gilbert's appointment as agent general, see Kenneth Paul Jones, "Discord and Collaboration: Choosing an Agent

General for Reparations," *Diplomatic History* 1 (Spring 1977): 119–39.

22. For Dewey's position in Poland and relations with Washington officials, see Stetson to Castle, 15 November 1928, box 8, Castle Papers; Dewey to Hoover, 13 July 1929, enclosed in Hoover to Stimson, 13 August 1929, DS 860c.51A/26; Charles S. Dewey, *As I Recall It* (Washington: Williams and Heintz Lithograph Corp., 1957), pp. 100–99.

23. The author has been unable to locate any John B. Stetson, Jr. Papers. This fragmentary description is based on *Who's Who in America, 1940–44* (Chicago: A. N. Marquis, 1940), p. 59; *New York Times*, 16 November 1952, p. 88.

24. Stetson to Kellogg, 7 December 1925, DS 860c.51/543.

25. Stetson to Kellogg, 7 December 1925, DS 860c.51/543, and 15 June 1926, DS 860c.51A/4.

26. Strauss, *Menace in the West*, p. 181; André Siegfried, *America Comes of Age* (New York: Harcourt, Brace and Co., 1927), pp. 166–89; Pomaret, *L'Amerique à la conquête*, pp. 220–48; Peter G. Filene, *Americans and the Soviet Experiment* (Cambridge: Harvard University Press, 1967), pp. 124–29; Charles S. Maier, "Between Taylorism and Technocracy: European Ideologies and the Vision of Industrial Productivity in the 1920s," *Journal of Contemporary History* 2 (1970): 27–61; Stetson to Kellogg, 7 December 1925, DS 860c.51/543.

27. Joseph Korbel, *Poland between East and West* (Princeton: Princeton University Press, 1963); Harold von Riekhoff, *German-Polish Relations, 1918–1933* (Baltimore: Johns Hopkins Press, 1971); Zygmunt J. Gasiorowski, "Stresemann and Poland after Locarno," *Journal of Central European Affairs* 18 (1958): 292–317; Gaines Post, Jr., "German Foreign Policy and Military Planning: The Polish Question, 1924–29" (Ph.D. diss., Stanford University, 1969). Stetson to Kellogg, 7 December 1925, DS 860c.51/543.

28. Stetson to Kellogg, 10 May 1926, DS 860c.51/567 (p. 7).

29. Ibid.

30. Stetson to Kellogg, 7 December 1925, DS 860c.51/543.

31. Stetson to Kellogg, 10 May 1926, DS 860c.51/567.

32. Leffler, *Elusive Quest*, pp. 127–30, 145–46; Costigliola, "U.S. and Germany," pp. 497–98.

33. Stetson to Kellogg, 10 May 1926, DS 860c.51/567. See also Stetson to Castle, 8 June 1926, box 8, Castle Papers.

34. Strong memo of conversation with Stetson and Felix Mylnarsk, 16 September 1926, Polish Stabilization File, FRBNY Archives.

35. John Ciechanowski to Strong, 7 March 1926, file C261.1 Poland; George Harrison memo of conversation with Hjalmar Schacht, 1 April 1927, Polish Stabilization File; Harrison to Strong, 29 March 1927, Polish Stabilization File, all in FRBNY Archives; Stetson to Kellogg, 23 April 1926, DS 860c.51/566; Norman to Arthur Salter, 1 February 1926; Seward Prosser to Norman, 29 January 1926, both in T176/23, Otto Niemeyer Papers, Public Record Office, Kew, Surrey, England.

36. Strong to Harrison, 3 August 1926, Benjamin Strong Papers; Strong to Harrison, 29 June 1926, Polish Stabilization File, both in FRBNY Archives; Neimeyer to Salter, 7 May 1926, T176/23, Niemeyer Papers.

37. Frank Costigliola, "American Foreign Policy in the 'Nutcracker': The United States and Poland in the 1920s," *Pacific Historical Review* 48 (February 1979): 98–105.

38. Benjamin Strong, Federal Reserve Bank of New York governor, acknowledged the tacit connection in a letter to George Harrison, 20 February 1927, Polish Stabilization File, FRBNY Archives.

39. Costigliola, "American Foreign Policy," pp. 104– 5.

40. On Stetson's role see H. Dorsey Newson to Kellogg, 29 January 1927, DS 860c.51/604.

41. Stetson to Kellogg, 6 July 1927, DS 860c.51/641.

42. Stetson to Kellogg, 22 June 1926, DS 860c.00/365; Stetson to Strong, 8 May 1926, Polish Stabilization File, FRBNY Archives.

43. Stetson to Kellogg, 20 April 1929, DS 860c.00/454.

44. Stetson to Castle, 29 November 1927, box 8, Castle Papers.

45. Alexander Skrzynski, "American and Polish Democracy," speech at Williamsburg Institute of Politics, July 1925, p. 20, Rockefeller Library, Brown University, Providence, R.I.

46. Sigismund Heryng to Stetson, transmitted in J. Webb Benton to Henry L. Stimson, 18 July 1929, DS 711.60c/9.

47. Stetson to Robert F. Kelley, 10 August 1929, DS 860c.6463 Harriman and Company/9; Stetson to Kelley, 13 August 1929, DS 860c.6463 Harriman and Company/10, for the quotations. See also J. Webb Benton to Stimson, 6 July 1929, DS 860c.6463 Harriman and Company/2; John C. Wiley to Stimson, 10 July 1920, DS 860c.6463 Harriman and Company/24.

48. Castle to Stetson, 24 June 1927, box 8, Castle Papers; Stetson to Kellogg, 26 November 1927, DS 860c.6373/23.

49. Zbigniew Landau, "Poland and America: The Economic Connection, 1918– 1939," *Polish American Studies* 32 (1975): 41.

50. Stetson to Kellogg, 19 November 1928, DS 811.503160c/6.

Chapter 5

1. For a brief, excellent summary of Republican policy on disarmament see Melvyn P. Leffler, "Political Isolationism, Economic Expansionism, or Diplomatic Realism: American Policy toward Western Europe, 1921– 1933," in *Perspectives in American History*, ed. Donald Fleming and Bernard Bailyn (Cambridge: Harvard University Press, 1974), 8: 433– 36.

2. Diary, 28 February 1905, carton M– 1, Hugh Gibson Papers, Hoover Institution on War, Revolution, and Peace, Stanford, Calif. For Gibson's entire diplomatic career see Ronald E. Swerczek, "The Diplomatic Career of Hugh Gibson, 1908– 1938" (Ph.D. diss., University of Iowa, 1972). On the development of the diplomatic service in the early twentieth century and Gibson's role in it, see Robert D. Schulzinger, *The Making of the Diplomatic Mind: The Training, Outlook, and Style of United States Foreign Service Officers, 1908 – 1931* (Middletown, Conn.: Wesleyan University Press, 1975); Martin Weil, *A Pretty Good Club: The Founding Fathers of the United States Foreign Service* (New York: W. W. Norton and Co., 1978).

3. Hugh Gibson, *Hugh Gibson, 1883 – 1954: Extracts from His Letters and Anecdotes from His Friends*, ed. Perrin C. Galpin (New York: Belgian American Educational Foundation, 1956), pp. 157– 58.

4. F. M. Huntington Wilson, *Memoirs of an Ex-Diplomat* (Boston: Bruce Humphries, 1945), p. 235; Grew to John Van A. MacMurray (second secretary of embassy at

St. Petersburg), 4 September 1910, in Joseph C. Grew, *Turbulent Era: A Diplomatic Record of Forty Years, 1904–1945*, ed. Walter Johnson, 2 vols. (Boston: Houghton Mifflin Co., 1952), 1: 76–77.

5. Gibson to his mother, 27 November 1922, Gibson Papers.

6. U.S. Congress, House, Committee on Foreign Affairs, *Hearings on H.R. 17 and H.R. 6357 (H.R. 6357 Reported Favorably) for the Reorganization and Improvement of the Foreign Service of the United States, and for Other Purposes, January 14–18, 1924*, 68th Cong., 1st sess., 1924, pp. 40, 85–89.

7. For a survey of American involvement in disarmament see Merze Tate, *The United States and Armaments* (Cambridge: Harvard University Press, 1948). On the Washington Conference see Thomas H. Buckley, *The United States and the Washington Conference, 1921–1922* (Knoxville: University of Tennessee Press, 1970).

8. Waldo H. Heinrichs, Jr., *American Ambassador: Joseph C. Grew and the Development of the United States Diplomatic Tradition* (Boston: Little, Brown and Co., 1966), pp. 52–53; Grew to Gibson, 1 October 1924, vol. 27, Joseph C. Grew Papers, Houghton Library, Harvard University, Cambridge, Mass.

9. See Coolidge's message to Congress, 4 January 1926, *FRUS, 1926*, 1: 40–42.

10. Kellogg to Gibson, 23 April 1926, *FRUS, 1926*, 1: 80–89.

11. Gibson to Kellogg, 3 October 1926, box 17, Gibson Papers; Gibson, *Extracts*, p. 57.

12. Gibson to Kellogg, 30 September 1926; Gibson to his mother, 11 February 1927, both in box 17, Gibson Papers. See also John W. Wheeler-Bennett, *Disarmament and Security since Locarno, 1925–1931: Being the Political and Technical Background of the General Disarmament Conference, 1932* (New York: Macmillan Co., 1932), pp. 103–6; David Carlton, "Great Britain and the Coolidge Naval Disarmament Conference of 1927," *Political Science Quarterly* 83 (1968): 573–75.

13. Wheeler-Bennett, *Disarmament and Security*, p. 108. See also Tate, *U.S. and Armaments*, p. 142.

14. Telegrams, Gibson to Kellogg, Acting Secretary of State Robert E. Olds to Gibson, 2 July 1927, *FRUS, 1927*, 1: 66–69; Gibson, *Extracts*, pp. 63–65.

15. Telegrams between Gibson and Kellogg, 23–28 July 1927, *FRUS, 1927*, 1: 131–33, 136–38. See also Wheeler-Bennett, *Disarmament and Security*, pp. 120–21.

16. Gibson to his mother, 4 August 1927, Gibson Papers.

17. Gibson to J. Theodore Marriner (chief of Division of Western European Affairs), 11 August 1927, box 26; Gibson to his mother, 30 August 1927, box 26; Gibson to Alan F. Winslow (first secretary of embassy at Mexico City), 14 November 1927, box 29, all in Gibson Papers.

18. Gibson telegram to Kellogg, 21 March 1928, *FRUS, 1928*, 1: 252. In supporting the Kellogg-Briand Pact, Gibson spoke not only for official consumption, but also from a sincere belief in the efficacy of the pact. Gibson to his mother, 18 July, 22 November, and 10 December 1928, Gibson Papers.

19. Gibson to Marriner, 29 March 1928, box 26, Gibson Papers.

20. See Robert H. Ferrell, *Peace in Their Time: The Origins of the Kellogg-Briand Pact* (New Haven: Yale University Press, 1952), pp. 203–5. Both the British and the French claimed to have undertaken the negotiations at Gibson's suggestion. Gibson, embarrassed, explained to Admiral Hilary P. Jones, the chief U.S. naval delegate to the Preparatory Commission, that he had done nothing more than make a statement at the

last session suggesting direct negotiations before the next meeting. Gibson to Jones, 26 October 1928, box 24, Gibson Papers.

21. Kellogg telegram to Gibson, 16 January 1929, DS 123.G35/402; Gibson to his mother, 22 February, 20 and 26 March 1929, Gibson Papers. See also Herbert Hoover, *The Memoirs of Herbert Hoover*, vol. 2, *The Cabinet and the Presidency, 1920–1933* (New York: Macmillan Co., 1952), p. 340; Marriner memo, 23 February 1929, DS 500.A15/854.

22. Gibson's speech is printed in *FRUS, 1929*, 1: 91–96. On the yardstick concept see Raymond G. O'Connor, "The 'Yardstick' and Naval Disarmament in the 1920s," *Mississippi Valley Historical Review* 45 (1958): 594–95.

23. Wheeler-Bennett, *Disarmament and Security*, p. 71; Tate, *U.S. and Armaments*, pp. 81, 87; Gibson's speech of 6 May 1929, 1: 102–4; Gibson telegram to Stimson, 6 May 1929, 104–5, both in *FRUS, 1929*.

24. Gibson to Castle, 3 July 1929, box 1, William R. Castle, Jr. Papers, Herbert Hoover Presidential Library, West Branch, Iowa; Raymond G. O'Connor, *Perilous Equilibrium: The United States and the London Naval Conference of 1930* (Lawrence: University of Kansas Press, 1962), p. 36.

25. Gibson to Castle, 30 September 1929, box 29, Gibson Papers; O'Connor, *Perilous Equilibrium*, pp. 45, 50–51; Robert H. Ferrell, *American Diplomacy in the Great Depression: Hoover-Stimson Foreign Policy, 1929–1933* (New Haven: Yale University Press, 1957), pp. 84–85.

26. Stimson to Hoover, 17 February 1930, vol. 13, Henry L. Stimson Papers, Yale University Library, New Haven, Conn.; Gibson to his mother, 19 January 1930, Gibson Papers; U.S. Department of State, *Proceedings of the London Naval Conference of 1930 and Supplementary Documents*, Conference Series, No. 6, Publication No. 187 (Washington, D.C.: G.P.O., 1931), pp. 66–70.

27. Gibson to Arthur Sweetser (assistant director of the information section of the League of Nations), 5 May 1930, box 28, Gibson Papers. In contrast, Admiral Jones disliked the treaty so much that he hoped the Senate would reject it: Jones to Gibson, 26 April 1930, box 24, Gibson Papers. For summaries of the treaty see O'Connor, *Perilous Equilibrium*, pp. 104–5; Tate, *U.S. and Armaments*, pp. 178–81; Ferrell, *American Diplomacy*, pp. 102–3.

28. Herbert Hoover and Hugh Gibson, *The Problems of Lasting Peace* (Garden City, N.Y.: Doubleday, Doran and Co., 1942), p. 181.

29. Copy of memo by Marriner and Winslow, 9 October 1930; memos prepared by Gibson for conversations with Tardieu and Grandi, 22 October 1930, both in box 20, Gibson Papers. See also Stimson memo of conversation with Italian Ambassador Nobile Giacomo de Martino, 9 October 1930, DS 500.A15A3/1138.

30. Norman Armour (counselor of embassy at Paris) telegrams to Stimson, 27 and 28 October 1930, 1: 153–55, 159–60; John W. Garrett (ambassador to Italy) telegram to Stimson, 30 October 1920, 1: 163–64, all in *FRUS, 1930*.

31. Gibson telegrams to Stimson, 11, 13, and 20 November 1930, *FRUS, 1930*, 1: 176–78, 180–81; Gibson to Castle, 25 February 1931, box 1, Castle Papers.

32. For Morrow's role see Harold Nicolson, *Dwight Morrow* (New York: Harcourt, Brace and Co., 1935), p. 393.

33. Telegrams to and from Gibson, 17–28 November 1930, *FRUS, 1930*, 1: 191, 195–96, 197–99, 200. See also Wheeler-Bennett, *Disarmament and Security*, pp.

96–97; Richard Dean Burns, "International Arms Inspection Policies between World Wars, 1919–1934," *Historian* 31 (1969): 594–95.

34. Gibson to Stimson, 6 December 1930, *FRUS, 1931*, 1: 471–76; Gibson to Stimson, 7 December 1930, box 18, Gibson Papers.

35. Memos by Gibson, 26 March 1931, box 41, Gibson Papers.

36. Stimson diary, 30 September 1931, vol. 18, Stimson Papers; Gibson to Wilson, 26 May 1931, box 30, Gibson Papers; Stimson diary, 4 November and 14 December 1931, vol. 19; Stimson diary, 5 and 18 January 1932, vol. 20, all in Stimson Papers.

37. Entry for 1 February 1932, Moffat Diplomatic Journals, Jay Pierrepont Moffat Papers, Houghton Library, Harvard University, Cambridge, Mass.

38. Memo of telephone conversation between Gibson and Stimson, 8 February 1932, *FRUS, 1932*, 1: 20–23; Stimson diary, 8 February 1932, vol. 20, Stimson Papers; entry for 8 February 1932, Moffat Diplomatic Journals, Moffat Papers; telegrams to and from Gibson, 26 March and 2 April 1932, *FRUS, 1932*, 1: 59–62, 70–71, 76; Jay Pierrepont Moffat, *The Moffat Papers: Selections from the Diplomatic Journals of Jay Pierrepont Moffat, 1919–1943*, ed. Nancy H. Hooker (Cambridge: Harvard University Press, 1956), p. 57; entry for 11 April 1932, Moffat Diplomatic Journals, Moffat Papers.

39. Gibson telegram to Castle, 22 April 1932, *FRUS, 1932*, 1: 102–3; Stimson diary, 15 April 1932, vol. 21, Stimson Papers.

40. Stimson telegram to Gibson, 7 June 1932, 1: 153–57; Gibson telegram to Stimson, 28 May 1932, 1: 145–50, both in *FRUS, 1932*.

41. Jeanette Marks, *Life and Letters of Mary Emma Woolley* (Washington: Public Affairs Press, 1955), p. 148; Hoover memo to Stimson, 24 May 1932, 1: 180–82; memos of telephone conversations among Gibson, Davis, Stimson, and Hoover, 21 June 1932, 1: 197–210, all in *FRUS, 1932*.

42. Telegrams exchanged between Stimson and Gibson, 29–30 June 1932, *FRUS, 1932*, 1: 244–49. See also Burns, "International Arms Inspection," pp. 597–98.

43. Gibson telegrams to Stimson, 2 and 5 July 1932, 1: 253–55, 266–67; Gibson telegram and copy of resolution to Stimson, 23 July 1932, 1: 316–22, all in *FRUS, 1932*. He concluded, because of the favorable response, that the plan had effectively saved the conference. A decade later, in *The Problems of Lasting Peace*, he and Hoover described it as the last chance for disarmament and for peace. Gibson to Castle, 24 June 1932, box 1, Castle Papers; Hoover and Gibson, *Problems of Peace*, p. 162.

44. Minutes of delegation meeting, 23 July 1932, box 40, Gibson Papers.

45. Gibson to Davis, 24 October 1932, box 22, Gibson Papers; Gibson to Castle, 28 November 1932, box 1, Castle Papers; telegrams exchanged between Stimson and Gibson, 2, 11, and 15 February and 2 March 1933, *FRUS, 1933*, 1: 8–9, 12–16, 21. See also John W. Wheeler-Bennett, *The Pipe Dream of Peace: The Story of the Collapse of Disarmament* (New York: William Morrow and Co., 1935), p. 94.

46. Gibson telegrams to Hull, 5, 13, and 18 March 1933, *FRUS, 1933*, 1: 22–25, 37–38, 63–64. See also Arnold A. Offner, *American Appeasement: United States Foreign Policy and Germany, 1933–1938* (Cambridge: Harvard University Press, Belknap Press, 1969), pp. 20–21.

47. Davis to Hull, 3 April 1933, DS 500.A15A4/1825.

Chapter 6

1. Biographical sketches of Prentiss Gilbert, *New York Times*, 26 February 1939; *American Foreign Service Journal* 16 (April 1939): 213–14, 269; data on other members of the family, GPR.

2. Interview with Ambassador James W. Riddleberger, Washington, D.C., 24 November 1967; "The Call Boy's Chat," *Philadelphia Inquirer*, 11 May 1930; [Prentiss Bailey Gilbert], "Religion? None," *Outlook and Independent* 151 (6 February 1929): 207–10, 237–40; letter to J. B. Donnelly from Professor Arthur J. May, University historian, University of Rochester, 9 January 1969.

3. Gilbert, "Positive Intelligence," undated (but pre-November 1918), typescript, GPR; Walter Lippmann, *Public Opinion* (New York: Harcourt, Brace and Co., 1922), chap. 26.

4. Joseph C. Grew, *Turbulent Era: A Diplomatic Record of Forty Years, 1904–1945*, 2 vols. (Boston: Little, Brown and Co., 1952), 2: 849; J. Rives Childs, *Foreign Service Farewell: My Years in the Near East* (Charlottesville: University Press of Virginia, 1969), pp. 69–70; letter to Donnelly from Denys P. Myers, retired executive secretary of the World Peace Foundation, Washington, D.C., 20 November 1967, and interview with Donnelly, Washington, D.C., 29 December 1967.

5. Interview with Myers; Donnelly's interview with Ambassador John Dewey Hickerson and Livingston Hartley, departmental associates of Gilbert in the twenties, Washington, D.C., 27 December 1967; diary entry, 28 March 1931; Moffat to Gilbert, 19 August 1931, both in Jay Pierrepont Moffat Papers, Houghton Library, Harvard University, Cambridge, Mass.; Robert A. Ferrell, *Peace in Their Time: The Origins of the Kellogg-Briand Pact* (New Haven, Connecticut: Yale University Press, 1952), p. 238.

6. Interview with Mrs. Charlotte Gilbert and Mrs. Henry Leverich, Washington, D.C., 24 November 1967. Gilbert to Assistant Secretary William R. Castle, Jr., 9 August 1929; Gilbert to Castle, 14 August 1929; Gilson G. Blake, Jr. (for Gilbert) to Secretary Henry Stimson, 22 October 1929, with covering letter by Castle, 5 December 1929, all in GPW.

7. *American Foreign Service Journal* 7 (July 1930): 247–48; *New York Times*, 24 August 1930; Gilbert to Stanley K. Hornbeck, 1 March 1933, Stanley K. Hornbeck Papers, Stanford University, Palo Alto, Calif.

8. Division of Western European Affairs, editorial clipping file, GPW; Edwin L. James, *New York Times*, 26 August 1930.

9. Interviews with Mrs. Gilbert and Mrs. Leverich, with Riddleberger, and with Hickerson and Hartley; George Abell, *Washington Daily News*, 17 October 1931; Lemuel F. Parton, *Baltimore Evening Sun*, 21 June 1934.

10. Interview with Riddleberger. Letters exchanged between Moffat and Gilbert, 1 and 4 August 1931; Gilbert to Moffat, 15 and 21 August 1931, all in the Moffat Papers.

11. For example Gilbert to Stimson, 20 February 1931, DS 125.3976/34; interview with Ralph Seward, Geneva graduate student and League aide in the early thirties, Washington, D.C., 27 December 1967; letter to Donnelly from Dr. Jacques LeClerq, one-time director of the Students International Union in Geneva, Switzerland, 5 December 1967; interview with Riddleberger; Hugh Wilson, Berne, to Castle, 31 May 1929, GPR; Wallace McClure, State Department official, to Gilbert, 9 March 1930, GPR; see comparison of Gilbert and Wilson, "Appendix: League of Nations," *Fortune* 12 (December 1935): 204–8.

12. William Hard, National Broadcasting Company correspondent, typescript, transatlantic broadcast from Geneva, 1 September 1931, GPR; telegrams exchanged between Gilbert and Stimson, 22 and 23 September 1931, DS 462.00R296/5123.

13. Moffat diary, 17 and 18 September 1931, Moffat Papers. The Manchurian crisis has been covered most recently in Christopher Thorne, *The Limits of Foreign Policy: The West, the League, and the Far Eastern Crisis* (New York: G. P. Putnam's Sons, 1973); Philip C. Jessup, *The Birth of Nations* (New York: Columbia University Press, 1974), chap. 8.

14. Stimson to Wilson, Geneva, 24 September 1931, 3: 60; Stimson to Gilbert, 5 October 1931, 3: 116–17, both in *FRUS, 1931*; exchange of letters between Stimson and Walter Lippmann of the Council on Foreign Relations, New York, 30 September and 1 October 1931, Henry Stimson Papers, Sterling Memorial Library, Yale University, New Haven, Conn.; see also Takehiko Yoshihashi, *Conspiracy at Mukden: The Rise of the Japanese Military* (New Haven, Connecticut: Yale University Press, 1963); Sadako N. Ogata, *Defiance in Manchuria: The Making of Japanese Foreign Policy, 1931–1932* (Berkeley and Los Angeles: University of California Press, 1964).

15. Stimson memo, 10 October 1931, *FRUS: Japan, 1931–1941*, 1: 19–20; Stimson to Elihu Root, former secretary of state, New York, 14 December 1931, Elihu Root Papers, Library of Congress, Washington, D.C.; diary entries, 9 and 10 October 1931, Stimson Papers; Herbert Hoover, *The Memoirs of Herbert Hoover*, vol. 2, *The Cabinet and the Presidency, 1920–1933* (New York: Macmillan Co., 1952), pp. 368–70; Gilbert to Moffat, 20 November 1931, Moffat Papers; J. B. Donnelly, "Prentiss Gilbert's Mission to the League of Nations Council, October 1931," *Diplomatic History* 2 (Fall 1978): 373–87.

16. Gilbert to Hornbeck, 1 March 1933, Hornbeck Papers; Stimson memo of transatlantic telephone conversation with Gilbert, 10 A.M., E.S.T., 12 October 1931, DS 793.94/2055½; cf. corresponding Geneva transcript of the call for mutual hearing errors, GPR; Stimson to Gilbert, 13 October 1931, *FRUS, 1931*, 3: 167–68.

17. Stimson memo of transatlantic telephone conversation with Gilbert, 1:10 P.M, E.S.T., 13 October 1931, *FRUS, 1931*, 3: 178–82; cf. corresponding Geneva transcript of call for errors, GPR; Stimson to Gilbert, 13 October 1931, *FRUS, 1931*, 3: 184–85.

18. Ogata, *Defiance in Manchuria*, pp. 88, 95; Gilbert to Stimson, 16 October 1931, *FRUS, 1931*, 3: 212–13; Ambassador Walter Edge, Paris, to Hoover and Stimson, 17 October 1931, DS 033.5111, Laval, Pierre/143; Walter Lippmann, *New York Herald-Tribune*, 13 October 1931.

19. State Department adviser Charles P. Howland memo, 1 October 1931, DS H/DP 033.5111, Laval, Pierre/256½; diary entries, 16 and 17 October 1931, Stimson Papers; C. Patteson (for Ambassador Sir Francis Lindley, Tokyo) to Sir Robert Vansittart, London, 12 and 19 October 1931, *DBFP*, 8: 624, 658; Yoshihashi, *Conspiracy at Mukden*, p. 199; *Baltimore Sun* and *New York Times*, 16 and 17 October 1931.

20. Gilbert to Stimson, 13 October 1931, *FRUS, 1931*, 3: 188; Ambassador Jacob D. Beam to Donnelly, Prague, 11 December 1967; diary entry, 16 October 1931, Arthur Sweetser Papers, Library of Congress, Washington, D.C.; Gilbert notes for Council appearance, GPW; exchange of telegrams between Gilbert and Stimson, 16 October 1931, *FRUS, 1931*, 3: 201, 203.

21. Interview with Arthur Sweetser, Washington, D.C., 29 December 1967; diary entry, 16 October 1931, Sweetser Papers; John T. Whitaker, *New York Herald-Tribune*,

17 October 1931; Joseph Green (Embassy, Rome) to Castle, 21 October 1931, DS 125.3973/142.

22. Stimson memo of transatlantic telephone conversation with Gilbert, 7:30 P.M. (Geneva time), 16 October 1931, *FRUS, 1931,* 3: 203–7; cf. corresponding Geneva transcript for errors, GPR; Patteson (for Lord Reading) to Vansittart, 17 October 1931, *DBFP,* 8: 647; Gilbert to Stimson, 17 October 1931, *FRUS, 1931,* 3: 224.

23. Hornbeck memo to Stimson, 19 October 1931, DS 793.94/2202; diary entries, 19, 20, and 23–25 October 1931, Stimson Papers; Stimson memo of transatlantic telephone conversation with Reading, 3:15 P.M., E.S.T., 19 October 1931, *FRUS, 1931,* 3: 248–58; cf. Patteson (for Reading) to Sir Ronald Lindsay, Washington, D.C., 19 October 1931, *DBFP,* 8: 660, for hearing errors; Yoshihashi, *Conspiracy at Mukden,* pp. 177, 189; Gilbert to Stimson, 21 October 1931, *FRUS, 1931,* 3: 283; reply, Stimson (Castle) to Gilbert, 21 October 1931, DS 793.94/2253.

24. For treatment of the Dawes mission, see Jessup, *Birth of Nations,* chap. 8; J. B. Donnelly, "An Empty Chair in Paris: Dawes, Sweetser, and the Manchurian Crisis, 1931," *Topic* 10 (Spring 1970): 37–49.

25. Sir Eric Drummond to Alexander Cadogan, 2 November 1931, FO 6355/1391/10; [Hugh Gibson] transcript, "Telephone Conversation between the Secretary and the Ambassador," Geneva, 1 A.M. (Geneva time), 1 February 1932, Hugh Gibson Papers, Hoover Institution on War, Revolution, and Peace, Stanford, Calif.; Stimson telegram to Wilson, 1 February 1932, DS 793.94/3902A; Stimson telegram to Gilbert, 1 February 1932, DS 793.94/3902B; letter to Donnelly from Ambassador Thanassis Aghnides, Geneva, 16 December 1967.

26. Wilson to Moffat, 6 May 1933, Moffat Papers; see rumors of a "feud" in, inter alia, *Washington Herald,* 19 October 1931; Drew Pearson and Robert S. Allen, *Rochester Times Union,* 12 August 1935. Wilson, Moffat, and other old boys are discussed sympathetically in Robert D. Schulzinger, *The Making of the Diplomatic Mind: The Training, Outlook, and Style of United States Foreign Service Officers, 1908–1931* (Middletown, Conn.: Wesleyan University Press, 1975); critically in Martin Weil, *A Pretty Good Club: The Founding Fathers of the U.S. Foreign Service* (New York: W. W. Norton and Co., 1978).

27. Gilbert to Hornbeck, 1 March and 26 December 1933, Hornbeck Papers; "pretty good club" is in Weil, *Pretty Good Club,* p. 47.

28. John T. Whitaker, *New York Herald* (Paris edition), 18 September 1933; Pearson and Allen, *Miles City Star* (Montana), 13 August 1934; Sweetser to Raymond B. Fosdick, 27 December 1939, Sweetser Papers; Gary B. Ostrower, "American Ambassador to the League of Nations—1933: A Proposal Postponed," *International Organization* 25 (1971): 46–58; Hornbeck to Gilbert, 8 January 1934, GPR; Gilbert to Hull, 30 September 1933, and Hull to Gilbert, 25 October 1933, DS 500.C/663; Moffat to Gilbert, 9 May 1935, GPR; Gilbert to Hull, 7 June 1933, DS 120.34 Cost of Living/161; Moffat to Gilbert, 30 July 1937, GPR; Gilbert to Hugh S. Cumming, Jr., Washington, D.C., 20 October 1936, DS 500.C111/1006½.

29. Gilbert to Hornbeck, 9 April 1934, Hornbeck Papers; Gilbert to Moffat, 1 September 1932, Moffat Papers; Gilbert to Hull, 21 December 1933, DS 500.C Covenant/117.

30. Gilbert to Hull, 18 April 1935, DS 862.20/930; Gilbert telegram to Hull, 9 September 1935, DS 765.84/1083; Gilbert to Hull, 4 November 1935, *FRUS, 1935,* 1:

681– 83; Wilbur Carr memo, 16 April 1934, DS 125.397/18.

31. A. J. Barker, *The Civilizing Mission: A History of the Italo-Ethiopian War of 1935–1936* (New York: Dial Press, 1968) is a good survey.

32. Gilbert to Hull, 15 October 1935, and Hull to Gilbert, 17 October 1935, *FRUS, 1935,* 1: 845– 48; Gilbert to Hull, 26 June 1936, *FRUS, 1936,* 3: 164– 66; Gilbert telegram to Hull, 13 October 1935, DS 125.3973/216; Gilbert to Wallace Murray, chief of Near Eastern Affairs, 1 June 1935, DS 765.84/501; letter to Donnelly from Ambassador Llewelyn Thompson, Moscow, 12 December 1967.

33. Gilbert to Hull, 29 January 1936, DS 765.84/3660; Gilbert telegram to Hull, 5 March 1936, DS 765.84/3887; Gilbert telegram to Hull, 15 May 1936, DS 765.84/ 4440; Gilbert to Hull, 15 October 1936, DS 500.C111/1003.

34. Letter to Donnelly from retired foreign correspondent Wallace R. Deuel, Washington, D.C., 26 December 1967; interview with Hickerson and Hartley; Gilbert memo to Hull, 22 June 1936, DS 765.84/4717. Gilbert's contemporary views often coincide with those of Brice Harris, Jr., *The United States and the Italo-Ethiopian Crisis* (Stanford: Stanford University Press, 1964).

35. Letter to Donnelly from Deuel, 19 December 1967; Wilbur Carr to Gilbert, 6 April 1935, GPW; Ambassador Breckinridge Long (Rome) to Gilbert, 12 February 1936, GPW.

36. Gilbert telegram to Hull, 9 September 1935, DS 765.84/1083; Emery Kelen, *Peace in Their Time: Men Who Led Us in and out of War, 1914– 1945* (New York: Alfred A. Knopf, 1963), pp. 346– 48: an unexcelled description of the League years.

37. Moffat to Gilbert, 30 July 1937, GPR; Gilbert to Moffat, 16 August 1937, Moffat Papers; interview with Riddleberger; letter to Donnelly from retired foreign correspondent Frederick Cable Oechsner, Washington, D.C., 11 December 1967; Moffat to Gilbert, 3 September 1937, GPR.

38. Robert Dallek, *Democrat and Diplomat: The Life of William E. Dodd* (New York: Oxford University Press, 1968), especially p. 310; Under Secretary Sumner Welles memo, 1 October 1937, *FRUS, 1937,* 2: 381– 83; Gilbert to Moffat, 21 September 1937, Moffat Papers; Gilbert telegram to Hull, 30 May 1933, DS 862.4016/1083; Gilbert to Moffat, 23 and 30 September 1937, Moffat Papers; Moffat to Gilbert, 30 August 1937, GPR; Arnold A. Offner, *American Appeasement: United States Foreign Policy and Germany, 1933– 1938* (New York: Cambridge University Press, 1969), pp. 206– 12. For Dodd's own conciliatory Berlin debut in 1933, see Offner, *American Appeasement*, pp. 69– 72; *New York Herald-Tribune,* 26 August 1937; "Jay Franklin," *Washington Evening Star,* 11 September 1937; Wallace R. Deuel, *Chicago Daily News,* 10 September 1937.

39. Diary entry, 7 September 1937, Moffat Papers; Gilbert to Moffat, 23 and 30 September 1937, Moffat Papers.

40. Gilbert to Moffat, 18 December 1937, Moffat Papers; Moffat to Gilbert, 1 February 1938, GPR; Gilbert telegram to Hull, 4 September 1937, DS 862.4016/1685; Gilbert to Hugh R. Wilson, London, 31 January 1938, GPR; interviews with Mrs. Gilbert and Mrs. Leverich, and with Riddleberger.

41. "Jay Franklin," *New York Post,* 5 March 1939; Wilson to Gilbert, 4 January 1939, GPW; Gilbert to Hull, 30 March 1938, DS 863.00/1698; Gilbert to Moffat, 25 August 1938, Moffat Papers; Moffat to Gilbert, 3 October 1938, GPR; diary entry, 14 November 1938, Moffat Papers; Gilbert telegram to Hull, 26 January 1939, DS 862.4016/2076.

42. Letters to Donnelly from retired foreign correspondents Oechsner and Deuel, 11 and 19 December 1967; Gilbert telegram to Hull, 6 February 1939, DS 124.623/449; Gilbert to Moffat, 7 and 8 December 1938 and 27 January 1939, Moffat Papers; Moffat to Gilbert, 28 December 1938, GPR; Howard K. Smith, *Last Train from Berlin* (New York: Alfred A. Knopf, 1943), p. 60.

43. Gilbert telegram to Hull, 22 December 1938, DS 842.48 Refugees/1170; Gilbert to Moffat, 27 and 29 January 1939, Moffat Papers.

44. Gilbert telegram to Hull, 21 January 1939, DS 849.48R/1323; Gilbert to Moffat, 10 December 1938 and 27 January 1939, Moffat Papers; Moffat to Gilbert, 13 February 1939, GPR.

45. Gilbert telegram to Hull, 1 January 1939, DS 362.115/379; Welles to Gilbert, 6 January 1939, DS 362.115/383; Ernst Woermann memo of interview with Gilbert, Germany, Auswaertiges Amt, *Documents on German Foreign Policy, 1918–1945: From the Archives of the German Foreign Ministry* (Washington, D.C.: G.P.O., 1951), Series D, 4: 522; letters to Donnelly from Deuel, 11 and 19 December 1967.

46. Gilbert to Hull, 5 December 1938, DS 862.00/3806; Gilbert to Moffat, 7 December 1938, Moffat Papers; Moffat to Gilbert, 28 December 1938, GPR; Gilbert to Moffat, 10 December 1938, Moffat Papers: "I do not wish the Department in any way to get the impression that I am a weak fellow who is sending soft notes or that I in any way whatever condone the dreadful things which are happening." Cf. Arthur D. Morse, *While Six Million Died: A Chronicle of American Apathy* (New York: Random House, 1968).

47. Gilbert to Moffat, 16 August 1937, Moffat Papers; Gilbert to Hull, 25 January 1939 (long quotation), DS 762.00/239; Gilbert to Hull, 24 February 1939, with covering letter from Jefferson Patterson, chargé, 27 February 1939, and two enclosures, DS 762.71/34; Mrs. Charlotte Gilbert to Moffat, 4 April 1939, Moffat Papers.

48. Interview with Riddleberger; John T. Whitaker, *We Cannot Escape History* (New York: Macmillan Co., 1943), p. 354; Otto Tolischus, *New York Times*, 26 February 1939.

49. Gilbert to Hornbeck, 26 December 1933, Hornbeck Papers; Gilbert to Alois Derso and Emery Kelen, New York, 6 February 1939, Emery Kelen Papers, Salisbury, Conn.

50. Reprinted Hull and Wilson tributes and editorials by the *New York Herald-Tribune* and the *Chicago Daily News*, *American Foreign Service Journal* 16 (April 1939): 213–14, 269.

Chapter 7

1. Phillips to Roosevelt, 16 October 1933, DS 862.00/3097½.

2. This argument is cautiously suggested by Lloyd C. Gardner, *Economic Aspects of New Deal Diplomacy* (Boston: Beacon Press, 1964, 1971), pp. 98–99.

3. Arnold A. Offner, *American Appeasement: United States Foreign Policy and Germany, 1933–1938* (Cambridge: Harvard University Press, Belknap Press, 1969), p. 279. Hans-Juergen Schroeder, *Deutschland und die Vereinigten Staaten, 1933–1939: Wirtschaft und Politik in der Entwicklung des deutsch-amerikanischen Gegensatzes* (Wiesbaden, Germany: Franz Steiner, 1970), pp. 171–99. The revisionist argument originates from the argument of William Appleman Williams, *The Tragedy of American Diplomacy* (New York: Delta Books, 1962), pp. 104–200. Messersmith's contributions

have been examined previously in Robert Dallek, "Beyond Tradition: The Diplomatic Careers of William E. Dodd and George S. Messersmith," *South Atlantic Quarterly* 66 (1967): 233– 44; Kenneth Moss, "George S. Messersmith: An American Diplomat and Nazi Germany," *Delaware History* 17 (Fall– Winter 1977): 236– 49.

4. Kenneth Moss, "The United States, the Open Door, and Nazi Germany: 1933– 1938," *South Atlantic Quarterly* 78 (Autumn 1979): 489– 506.

5. Messersmith, notes for memoir, item 1924, box 8, George S. Messersmith Papers, University of Delaware Library, Newark, Del.

6. Consul General Albert Halstead to Secretary of State Henry L. Stimson, 26 July 1939, DS 110.78 Coordination; Halstead to Stimson, 24 December 1930, DS 110.78 Coordination.

7. Roger R. Trask, "The Impact of the Cold War on United States-Latin American Relations, 1945– 1949," *Diplomatic History* 1 (Summer 1977): 276. See also Dodd to Phillips, 17 November 1933; note by Dodd attached to Messersmith to Hull, 14 November 1933, both in box 42, file M– R, William E. Dodd Papers, Library of Congress, Washington, D.C.

8. Carr memo, "The Foreign Services of the Department of State and the Department of Commerce and Suggestions for Their Improvement," 9 June 1933, DS F.W. 110.78 Coordination/11.

9. Messersmith to Stimson, 13 July 1932, DS 120.2/23.

10. Messersmith to Hull, 14 March 1933, item 118; Messersmith to Hull, 25 March 1933, item 125; Messersmith to Hull, 28 March 1933, item 128, all in box 1, Messersmith Papers.

11. Messersmith to Hull, 2 May 1933, 2: 426– 38; Messersmith to Hull, 12 May 1933, 2: 421– 26; Messersmith to Hull, 1 November 1933, 2: 361– 65, all in *FRUS, 1933*.

12. Messersmith to Hull, 10 April 1933, 2: 222– 27; for State Department caution on the Jewish issue see Hull to chargé d'affaires George Gordon, 24 March 1933, 2: 330– 31; Messersmith to Hull, 1 November 1933, 2: 361– 65, all in *FRUS, 1933*; diary of J. Pierrepont Moffat, 13 July 1933, J. Pierrepont Moffat Papers, Houghton Library, Harvard University, Cambridge, Mass.; Moffat memo, 9 June 1933, DS 862.4016/ 1142.

13. Messersmith to Phillips, 23 November 1933, item 312, box 2, Messersmith Papers.

14. Messersmith to Hull, 10 July 1933, item 211; Messersmith to Phillips, 26 June 1933, item 203, both in box 1, Messersmith Papers.

15. Robert Dallek, *Franklin D. Roosevelt and American Foreign Policy, 1932 – 1945* (New York: Oxford University Press, 1979), pp. 42– 44.

16. Offner, *American Appeasement*, pp. 99– 101.

17. Messersmith to Moffat, 14 April 1934, item 365, box 2, Messersmith Papers; Messersmith to Dodd, 3 April 1934, box 5, group 55, R. Walton Moore Papers, Franklin D. Roosevelt Library, Hyde Park, N.Y.

18. Hull memo, 2 March 1934, DS 611.5231/313; Herbert Feis (trade adviser to Secretary Hull) to Moffat, 6 March 1934, DS 611.6231/317.

19. Moffat to Messersmith, 4 May 1934, item 371, box 2, Messersmith Papers; Office of the Economic Adviser (Herbert Feis) memo, 4 June 1934, box 44, Germany 1933– 1938, PSF, FDRL; Dick Steward, *Trade and Hemisphere: The Good Neighbor Policy and Reciprocal Trade* (Columbia: University of Missouri Press, 1975), pp. 31– 61.

20. Messersmith to Hull, 18 October 1933, DS 611.623/66; Messersmith to Phillips, 19 October 1933, item 320, box 2, Messersmith Papers.

21. The spring of 1935 witnessed attempts to preserve a healthy trade relationship between Germany and the United States. See "Statement Issued to the Press, 1 April 1935, on the Policy of the United States concerning the Generalization of Tariff Concessions under Trade Agreements," enclosed with Hull to Diplomatic and Consular Officers, 6 June 1935, 1: 536– 39; Ambassador Hans Luther to Hull, 24 May 1935, 1: 448– 50, both in *FRUS, 1935*; Offner, *American Appeasement*, p. 99.

22. Messersmith to Dodd, 3 April 1934, box 5, group 55, Moore Papers.

23. Roosevelt to Joseph Guffey, 21 March 1934, box 1, Official File 166-B, FDRL. For the various endorsements of Messersmith's appointment see Oswald Villard to Phillips, 19 December 1933, file 2578, Oswald Garrison Villard Papers, Houghton Library, Harvard University, Cambridge, Mass.; Shlomo Shafir, "George S. Messersmith: An Anti-Nazi Diplomat's View of the German-Jewish Crisis," *Jewish Social Studies* 35 (January 1973): 35– 36; Dodd to Moore, 18 January 1934, box 5, group 55, Moore Papers; David K. Adams, "Messersmith's Appointment to Vienna in 1934: Presidential Patronage or Career Promotion?" *Delaware History* 18 (Summer 1978): 24; Frankfurter to Bullitt, 18 March 1934; Bullitt to Frankfurter, 22 May 1934, both in box 115, Felix Frankfurter Papers, Library of Congress, Washington, D.C.

24. For Hitler and Austria see Juergen Gehl, *Austria, Germany, and the Anschluss, 1931–1938* (New York: Oxford University Press, 1963); Telford Taylor, *Munich: The Price of Peace* (Garden City, N.Y.: Doubleday, 1979), pp. 332– 33.

25. Messersmith memo, 5 July 1934, item 385, box 2, Messersmith Papers.

26. The debate over Nazi foreign policy seems endless, as historians dispute Hitler's ultimate aims. The English historian A. J. P. Taylor has attempted to connect Hitler with earlier German statesmen in *The Origins of the Second World War* (New York: Atheneum, 1961, 1964). Most scholarship has stressed Hitler's expansionist objectives in Europe. Gerhard L. Weinberg, *The Foreign Policy of Hitler's Germany: Diplomatic Revolution in Europe, 1933–1936* (Chicago: University of Chicago Press, 1970) is particularly good in relating German trade policy and domestic conditions to Nazi foreign policy. See also Karl Dietrich Bracher, *The German Dictatorship: The Origins, Structure, and Effects of National Socialism* (New York: Praeger, 1970). Other important works include Alan Bullock, *Hitler: A Study in Tyranny* (New York: Harper and Row, 1964); Klaus Hildebrand, *The Foreign Policy of the Third Reich* (Berkeley and Los Angeles: University of California Press, 1973); Joachim Fest, *Hitler* (New York: Harcourt Brace Jovanovich, 1974); Norman Rich, *Hitler's War Aims: Ideology, the Nazi State, and the Course of Expansion* (New York: W. W. Norton and Co., 1973).

27. Messersmith to Moffat, 1 August 1934, item 395, box 2; the Crowe memo, 1 January 1907, item 1, box 1, both in Messersmith Papers. See also Messersmith to Phillips, 1 August 1934, DS 863.00/1077; Messersmith, "A Resume of Some of the Major Factors in the Economic, Financial, and Political Situation Facing Europe Today," undated essay, vol. 6, Moffat Papers.

28. Messersmith telegram to Hull, 28 July 1934, *FRUS, 1934*, 2: 33– 34.

29. Messersmith to Hull, 9 February 1937, roll 14, series 40– 41, microfilm edition, Cordell Hull Papers, Library of Congress, Washington, D.C.

30. Dallek, *Franklin D. Roosevelt*, pp. 91– 168. For similarities between Roosevelt's conduct and his predecessors see the essays in the first part of this volume as well as Melvyn P. Leffler, *The Elusive Quest: America's Pursuit of European Stability and*

French Security (Chapel Hill: University of North Carolina Press, 1979).

31. Messersmith to Moore, 5 December 1936, item 790, box 3, Messersmith Papers.

32. Messersmith to Phillips, 17 August 1934, item 403, box 2, Messersmith Papers.

33. Messersmith to Moffat, 21 August 1934, item 405; Moffat to Messersmith, 22 August 1934, item 406, both in box 2, Messersmith Papers; Messersmith to Phillips, 21 August 1934, DS 863.00/1082; Messersmith to Phillips, 28 September 1934, item 423, box 2, Messersmith Papers; Weinberg, *Foreign Policy of Hitler's Germany,* pp. 110– 18, 268; Cedric J. Lowe and F. Marzari, *Italian Foreign Policy, 1870 – 1940* (London: Routledge and Kegan Paul, 1975), pp. 237– 39.

34. Messersmith to Moffat, 21 August 1934, item 405; Messersmith to Phillips, 7 September 1934, item 411; Messersmith to Dodd, 1 July 1935, item 513, all in box 2, Messersmith Papers.

35. Telford Taylor, *Munich,* p. 159.

36. Dallek, *Franklin D. Roosevelt,* pp. 116– 17. Messersmith to James Clement Dunn, 13 December 1935, item 629; Messersmith to Dunn, 20 December 1935, item 634, both in box 3, Messersmith Papers.

37. See Douglas Little's essay in this volume on Claude Bowers who also urged a relaxation of American trade policy in order to strengthen the anti-fascist government in Spain.

38. Messersmith to Hull, 6 November 1934, DS 611.6331/141.

39. Moffat memo, 19 March 1935, DS 611.6331/132.

40. Hull to Messersmith, 17 June 1936, 1: 488; Stewart telegram to Hull, 20 June 1936, 1: 488– 89; Sterling to Hull, 20 June 1936, 1: 491– 92, all in *FRUS, 1936.*

41. Messersmith to Hull, 8 July 1936, item 691; Messersmith to Hull, 20 July 1936, item 699, both in box 3, Messersmith Papers; Messersmith to Hull, 12 July 1936, DS 863.00/1296.

42. Messersmith to Phillips, 13 March 1936, item 670, box 3, Messersmith Papers; Dallek, *Franklin D. Roosevelt,* p. 124.

43. Messersmith to Phillips, 7 September 1934, item 411, box 3, Messersmith Papers.

44. The anti-Soviet opinion of most of the professionals in the State Department is explained in Weil, *A Pretty Good Club,* pp. 50– 63, 92; Long to Hull, 1 April 1935, *FRUS, 1935,* 1: 212– 16.

45. Bullitt to Moore, 7 April 1935, in *For the President, Personal and Secret: Correspondence between Franklin D. Roosevelt and William C. Bullitt,* ed. Orville H. Bullitt (Boston: Houghton Mifflin Co., 1972), pp. 106– 8; Bullitt to Roosevelt, 8 April 1935, ibid., pp. 109– 10; Beatrice Farnsworth, *William C. Bullitt and the Soviet Union* (Bloomington: Indiana University Press, 1967), pp. 149– 50. For Loy Henderson and other foreign service professionals in Moscow, see Thomas Maddux's essay in this volume and "Watching Stalin Maneuver between Hitler and the West: American Diplomats and Soviet Diplomacy, 1934– 1939," *Diplomatic History* 1 (Spring 1977): 140– 54.

46. Messersmith to John Flournoy Montgomery, 24 November 1936, box 2, vol. 3, John Flournoy Montgomery Papers, Sterling Library, Yale University, New Haven, Conn.; Messersmith to Moore, 5 December 1936, item 790, box 3, Messersmith Papers.

47. See Messersmith to Roosevelt, 12 March 1945, item 1684, box 6, Messersmith Papers.

48. Messersmith, notes for memoir, item 2013, box 9, Messersmith Papers.

49. Messersmith wanted American economic and military aid extended to France and Britain. See Messersmith to Hull, 26 March 1940, roll 19, microfilm edition, Hull Papers; *New York Times*, 24 November 1939, p. 13.

50. Moffat diary, 5 and 6 November and 15 and 16 October 1938, Moffat Papers.

51. Irwin F. Gellman, *Roosevelt and Batista: Good Neighbor Diplomacy in Cuba, 1933–1945* (Albuquerque: University of New Mexico Press, 1973), pp. 177–78.

52. Kenneth Moss is completing a biography of Messersmith, which will include his years in Latin America.

53. Messersmith, notes for memoir, item 2012, box 9, Messersmith Papers.

54. The best works in this vein are Waldo H. Heinrichs, *American Ambassador: Joseph C. Grew and the Development of the United States Diplomatic Tradition* (Boston: Little, Brown and Co., 1966); Richard Hume Werking, *The Master Architects: Building the United States Foreign Service, 1890–1913* (Lexington: University of Kentucky Press, 1977); Martin Weil, *A Pretty Good Club: The Founding Fathers of the U.S. Foreign Service* (New York: W. W. Norton and Co., 1978); Robert D. Schulzinger, *The Making of the Diplomatic Mind: The Training, Outlook, and Style of United States Foreign Service Officers, 1908–1931* (Middletown, Conn.: Wesleyan University Press, 1975). Of these studies, Werking and Schulzinger have done the best job of analyzing the relationship between the consular and diplomatic branches.

55. Schulzinger, *Making of the Diplomatic Mind*, pp. 9–10.

Chapter 8

1. Claude Bowers, *My Mission to Spain: Watching the Rehearsal for World War II* (New York: Simon and Schuster, 1954), p. 418.

2. F. Jay Taylor, *The United States and the Spanish Civil War* (New York: Bookman Associates, 1956), pp. 39–48; Richard Traina, *American Diplomacy and the Spanish Civil War* (Bloomington: Indiana University Press, 1968), pp. 46–75; Robert Dallek, *Franklin D. Roosevelt and American Foreign Policy* (New York: Oxford University Press, 1979), pp. 126–32.

3. Bowers, *My Mission to Spain*, pp. 411–14.

4. Claude Bowers, *My Life: The Memoirs of Claude Bowers* (New York: Simon and Schuster, 1962), chaps. 1–6; Merrill Peterson, *The Jefferson Image in the American Mind* (New York: Oxford University Press, 1960), pp. 347–54; Claude Bowers, *Jefferson and Hamilton: The Struggle for Democracy in America* (Boston: Houghton Mifflin Co., 1925).

5. Bowers, *My Life*, pp. 177–78, 227–28, 260; Peterson, *Jefferson Image*, pp. 351–52; Raymond Moley, *After Seven Years* (New York: Harper Bros., 1939), p. 132; Claude Bowers diary, 23 February 1933, Claude Bowers Papers, Lilly Library, Indiana University, Bloomington, Ind.

6. Moley, *After Seven Years*, pp. 131–32; Martin Weil, *A Pretty Good Club: The Founding Fathers of the U.S. Foreign Service* (New York: W. W. Norton and Co., 1978), pp. 67–71; Frank Freidel, *Franklin D. Roosevelt: Launching the New Deal* (Boston: Little, Brown and Co., 1973), pp. 359–64.

7. Weil, *Pretty Good Club*, pp. 21, 46–63; Robert D. Schulzinger, *The Making of the Diplomatic Mind: The Training, Outlook, and Style of United States Foreign Service Officers, 1908–1931* (Middletown, Conn.: Wesleyan University Press, 1975), pp. 81–141; Richard H. Werking, *The Master Architects: Building the United States Foreign*

Service, 1890–1913 (Lexington: University of Kentucky Press, 1977), pp. 121–42.

8. Dallek, *Franklin D. Roosevelt*, p. 33; Weil, *Pretty Good Club*, pp. 71–74; Moley, *After Seven Years*, pp. 131–32.

9. Bowers diary, 11 April 1933, Bowers Papers. On Wiley, see U.S. Department of State, *Register of the Department of State, 1934* (Washington, D.C.: G.P.O., 1934), p. 275.

10. Bowers diary, 27 and 28 April, and 2 May, 1933, Bowers Papers; Bowers, *My Life*, pp. 263–65.

11. Bowers to Daniels, 3 July 1933, box 67, Josephus Daniels Papers, Library of Congress, Washington, D.C.; Laughlin to Pierrepont Moffat, 3 January 193[3], box 13; Laughlin to Hugh Gibson, 5 January 1933, box 7, both in Irwin B. Laughlin Papers, Herbert Hoover Presidential Library, West Branch, Iowa.

12. Bowers diary, 31 May 1933, Bowers Papers; Bowers to Daniels, 3 July 1933, box 67, Daniels Papers; Hallett Johnson, *Diplomatic Memoirs: Serious and Frivolous* (New York: Vantage Press, 1963), pp. 106–7; Ambassador (Madrid) George Grahame to Foreign Secretary John Simon, 1 January 1934, FO 371, W324/324/41.

13. Bowers to Roosevelt, 28 June 1933, in *Franklin D. Roosevelt and Foreign Affairs*, 3 vols., ed. Edgar Nixon (Cambridge: Harvard University Press, 1969), 1: 259–61 (hereafter cited as *FDR and Foreign Affairs* with appropriate volume); Bowers to Assistant Secretary of State R. Walton Moore, 27 June 1934, box 3, R. Walton Moore Papers, Franklin D. Roosevelt Presidential Library, Hyde Park, N.Y.

14. Bowers to Roosevelt, 28 June 1933; Roosevelt to Bowers, 11 July 1933, both in Official File 303, FDRL.

15. Hull memos, 6 and 20 April 1933, microfilm edition, reel 32 ("Spain"), Cordell Hull Papers, Library of Congress, Washington, D.C.; Phillips memo, 27 June 1933, DS 611.5231/761.

16. Bowers to Hull, 19 July 1933, DS 611.5231/776; Bowers to Daniels, 26 July 1933, box 67, Daniels Papers; Hull to Bowers, 6 September 1933, DS 652.113/77.

17. Bowers telegram to Phillips, 21 December 1933, *FRUS, 1933,* 2: 697–98; Bowers telegram to Hull, 10 January 1934, DS 652.116/34; Bowers to Roosevelt, 10 January 1934, *FDR and Foreign Affairs,* 1: 586–87.

18. Jay Pierrepont Moffat diary, 21 December 1933 and 12 January 1934, vols. 34 and 35, Jay Pierrepont Moffat Papers, Houghton Library, Harvard University, Cambridge, Mass.; Phillips telegram to Bowers, 13 January 1934, DS 652.116/34.

19. Bowers diary, 14 January 1934, Bowers Papers.

20. Moffat diary, 12 January 1934, vol. 35, Moffat Papers.

21. Roosevelt memo to Phillips, 24 January 1934, 1: 609; Phillips to Roosevelt, 29 January 1934, 1: 616–17, both in *FDR and Foreign Affairs*; Agreement between the S. B. Smith Company and the Second Export-Import Bank, Credit File 11, Record Group 275, Records of the Export-Import Bank, National Archives, Washington, D.C.; William Phillips diary, 18 August 1934, vol. 5, William Phillips Papers, Houghton Library, Harvard University, Cambridge, Mass.

22. Bowers to Daniels, 11 December 1934, box 67, Daniels Papers.

23. Hull telegram to Bowers, 17 May 1935, 2: 705–6; Henry Grady memo, 17 May 1935, 2: 706–8; Bowers telegram to Hull, 18 July 1935, 2: 715–16, all in *FRUS, 1935*; Bowers to Assistant Secretary of State Francis Sayre, 27 June 1935, DS 611.5231/987.

24. Economic Adviser Herbert Feis memo to Hull, 28 October 1935, DS 611.5231/

1051; Bowers telegram to Hull, 28 December 1935, DS 651.5231/167; Hull telegram to Bowers and reply, 4 and 8 January 1936, *FRUS, 1936*, 2: 787– 88.

25. Bowers telegram to Hull, 20 February 1936, DS 611.5231/135; Bowers telegram to Hull, 5 March 1936, DS 852.51/325.

26. Dallek, *Franklin D. Roosevelt*, pp. 124– 25; Hull memos, 25 March and 11 May 1936, *FRUS, 1936*, 2: 791– 95.

27. Laughlin telegram to Stimson, 16 April 1931, *FRUS, 1931*, 2: 985– 86; Robert E. Bowers, "Hull, Russian Subversion in Cuba, and the Recognition of the U.S.S.R.," *Journal of American History* 53 (December 1966): 542– 54; Augustin Ferrin to John Wiley, 17 May 1933, box 1, John C. Wiley Papers, Franklin D. Roosevelt Library, Hyde Park, N.Y.

28. Bowers to Roosevelt, 28 June 1933, *FDR and Foreign Affairs*, 1: 259– 61; Bowers to Daniels, 3 July 1933, box 67, Daniels Papers.

Historical accounts supporting Bowers's contemporary interpretation of the Spanish Republic include Gabriel Jackson, "The Azaña Regime in Historical Perspective," *American Historical Review* 64 (January 1959): 282– 300; Frank Sedwick, *The Tragedy of Manuel Azaña and the Fate of the Spanish Republic* (Columbus: Ohio State University Press, 1963), pp. 89– 99; Raymond Carr, *Spain, 1808 – 1939* (Oxford: Oxford University Press, 1966), pp. 605–15.

29. Bowers to Roosevelt, 13 December 1933, *FDR and Foreign Affairs*, 1: 528– 29; Bowers diary, 12 and 22 April 1934, Bowers Papers.

30. Bowers to Hull, 30 April 1934, DS 852.00/1998; Bowers to Roosevelt, 19 September 1934, *FDR and Foreign Affairs*, 2: 218.

31. Bowers diary, 4 and 8 October 1934, Bowers Papers; Gabriel Jackson, *The Spanish Republic and the Civil War, 1931– 1939* (Princeton: Princeton University Press, 1965), pp. 148– 68.

32. Hull to Bowers, 6 September 1933, DS 652.113 Auto/77; Moffat diary, 27 April and 6, 7, and 17 October 1934, vols. 35 and 36, Moffat Papers; Bowers to Hull, 26 March 1935, DS 852.00/2095.

33. Bowers to Daniels, 27 November 1935, box 67, Daniels Papers; Bowers diary, 23 December 1935, Bowers Papers; Bowers to Hull, 23 December 1935, DS 852.00/2127; Bowers telegram to Hull, 17 February 1936, DS 852.00/2133; Bowers telegram to Hull, 24 February 1936, DS 852.00/2136.

34. For examples of the State Department's reactions to the Soviet united front strategy, see William Bullitt to Hull, 21 August 1935, pp. 244– 47, and E. L. Packer memo, 9 October 1935, pp. 260– 61, both in *FRUS: The Soviet Union, 1933 –1939*.

35. Phillips diary, 20 February 1936, vol. 10, Phillips Papers; Johnson to Hull, 11 March 1936, DS 852.00/2145.

36. Stephen Fuqua to G– 2, 7 April 1936, Military Intelligence File 2657 S.168/1, Records of the War Department General Staff, Military Intelligence Division, 1917– 1941, Record Group 165, National Archives, Washington, D.C.; Naval Attaché A. T. Beauregard to ONI, 2 April 1936, Naval Intelligence File C– 10– J 20792D ("Political Conditions— Spain"), Naval Attaché Reports, 1886– 1939, Record Group 38, National Archives, Washington, D.C.

37. Bullitt to Hull, 20 April 1936, DS 861.01/2120. Roosevelt's copy is located in "Russia," box 67, PSF, FDRL.

38. Bowers telegram to Hull, 14 March 1936, DS 852.00/2143; Bowers to Hull, 20

May 1936, DS 852.00/2166; Bowers to Hull, 27 May 1936, DS 852.00/2169.

39. Phillips diary, 2 June 1936, vol. 10, Phillips Papers.

40. Bowers to Roosevelt, 29 August 1936, *FDR and Foreign Affairs*, 3: 395–400; Phillips diary, 4 August 1936, vol. 11, Phillips Papers.

41. Bowers to Roosevelt, 26 August 1936, *FDR and Foreign Affairs*, 3: 395–400.

42. Johnson, *Diplomatic Memoirs*, p. 106; Hull draft memoirs, 31 July 1946, microfilm edition, reel 40, Hull Papers.

43. Traina, *American Diplomacy*, pp. 46–47; Dallek, *Franklin D. Roosevelt*, p. 127.

44. Hull memo to Roosevelt, 20 July 1936, Official File 422–C, FDRL; Bowers, *My Mission to Spain*, pp. 257–71.

45. Ambassador (Paris) Jesse Straus telegram to Hull, 26 July 1936, *FRUS, 1936*, 2: 645–46; Bowers, *My Mission to Spain*, p. 288.

46. Dante Puzzo, *Spain and the Great Powers, 1936–1941* (New York: Columbia University Press, 1962), pp. 53–110; David Cattell, *Communism and the Spanish Civil War* (Berkeley and Los Angeles: University of California Press, 1955), pp. 69–75; John Coverdale, *Italian Intervention in the Spanish Civil War* (Princeton: Princeton University Press, 1975), pp. 78–80, 102–7.

47. Straus telegram to Hull, 22 July 1936, DS 852.00/2196; Johnson to Hull, 24 July 1936, DS 852.00/2407.

48. Wendelin telegram to Hull, 1 August 1936, DS 852.00/2349; *Washington Post*, 2 August 1936, 1: 5; Hull telegram to Wendelin, 3 August 1936, *FRUS, 1936*, 2: 657–58. John H. Morgan, the department's Spanish desk officer, estimated total American investment in Spain later that year at $80 million, most of which lay in the republican zone. Morgan to Moore, 10 November 1936, *FDR and Foreign Affairs*, 3: 478–81.

49. John Hickerson telegram to Bowers, 27 August 1936, DS 852.00/2867A.

50. Cochran telegram to Hull, 7 August 1936, DS 852.00/2463.

51. Fuqua to G–2, 10 August 1936, enclosed in Wendelin to Hull, 12 August 1936, DS 852.00/2980.

52. Chapman telegram to Hull, 28 September 1936, DS 352.115/1806.

53. Bowers telegram to Hull, 8 August 1936, *FRUS, 1936*, 2: 472; Bowers to Roosevelt, 26 August 1936, *FDR and Foreign Affairs*, 3: 395–400.

54. Bowers to Hull, 11 August 1936, microfilm edition, reel 13, Hull Papers; Bowers to Roosevelt, 26 August 1936, *FDR and Foreign Affairs*, 3: 395–400.

55. Bowers to Hull, 23 September 1936, *FDR and Foreign Affairs*, 3: 435–37.

56. Bowers to Hull, 20 November 1936, *FRUS, 1936*, 2: 564.

57. Bowers to Roosevelt, 16 December 1936, "Spain," box 69, PSF, FDRL.

58. Ibid.

59. Bowers to Roosevelt, 26 August 1936, *FDR and Foreign Affairs*, 3: 395–400.

60. Bowers to Hull, 23 September 1936, *FDR and Foreign Affairs*, 3: 435–37; Bowers to Hull, 10 December 1936, *FRUS, 1936*, 2: 600–605.

61. Bowers telegram to Hull, 30 December 1936, DS 852.00/4230; Bowers to Hull, 12 January 1937, DS 852.00/4478.

62. Bowers to Hull and Phillips, 30 October 1936, *FDR and Foreign Affairs*, 3: 465–69; Bowers to Hull, 10 December 1936, *FRUS, 1936*, 2: 600. On the decisive nature of Italian and German intervention, see Jackson, *Spanish Republic*, pp. 329–32; Coverdale, *Italian Intervention*, pp. 391–98; and Hugh Thomas, *The Spanish Civil War*, rev. and enl. (New York: Harper and Row, 1977), pp. 939–42.

63. Bowers to Hull, 12 April 1937, *FRUS, 1937*, 1: 278–80.

64. Bowers diary, 24 June 1937, Bowers Papers.

65. Bowers to Hull, 20 July 1937, *FRUS, 1937*, 1: 362– 64.

66. Bowers to Hull, 20 March 1938, DS 852.00/7645; Bowers to Hull, 10 June 1938, DS 852.00/8133.

67. Traina, *American Diplomacy*, pp. 118– 43; Dallek, *Franklin D. Roosevelt*, pp. 158– 61.

68. Hickerson to Moffat, 25 August and 14 October 1936, vol. 10, Moffat Papers.

69. Herbert Feis, "Some Notes on Historical Record-Keeping, the Role of Historians, and the Influence of Historical Memories during the Era of the Second World War," in *The Historian and the Diplomat: The Role of History and Historians in American Foreign Policy*, ed. Francis L. Loewenheim (New York: Harper and Row, 1967), p. 105.

70. Moffat diary, 12 and 14 March 1938, vol. 40, Moffat Papers.

71. Moffat diary, 4, 5, and 27 February, and 1 March 1939, vol. 42, Moffat Papers.

72. Moffat diary, 8, 9, 13, and 29 March, and 1 and 2 April 1939, vol. 42, Moffat Papers; Bowers, *My Mission to Spain*, pp. 411– 22.

73. Bowers diary, 18 February 1938, Bowers Papers.

74. Robert Dallek, *Democrat and Diplomat: The Life of William E. Dodd* (New York: Oxford University Press, 1968), pp. 305– 15.

75. Bowers to Roosevelt, 20 February 1938, "Spain," box 69, PSF, FDRL.

Chapter 9

1. George F. Kennan, *Memoirs, 1925 – 1950* (Boston: Little, Brown and Co., 1967), p. 84; Kelley memo to Secretary Cordell Hull, 27 October 1933, DS 800.00B/27. Interviews with Loy W. Henderson, 29 June and 17 November 1967.

2. Loy W. Henderson, "Memoirs of Loy W. Henderson," 8 vols., Hoover Institution on War, Revolution and Peace, Stanford, Calif., 2: 231– 326, 3: 436– 59. Permission of the author is required to review the "Memoirs" which cover Henderson's career through 1940.

3. Martin Weil, *A Pretty Good Club: The Founding Fathers of the U.S. Foreign Service* (New York: W. W. Norton and Co., 1978), pp. 52– 53; Kennan, *Memoirs*, pp. 24– 37, 74; Charles E. Bohlen, *Witness to History, 1929– 1969* (New York: W. W. Norton and Co., 1973), pp. 3– 11, 53, 57– 58.

4. For the evaluation of Henderson, see Betty Crump Hanson, "American Diplomatic Reporting from the Soviet Union, 1934– 1941" (Ph.D. diss., Columbia University, 1966), pp. 14– 15. See also Natalie Grant, "The Russian Section: A Window on the Soviet Union," *Diplomatic History* 2 (Winter 1978): 107– 15; Henderson, "Memoirs," 2: 329– 427.

5. Kennan, *Memoirs*, pp. 29– 30; Henderson to Thomas R. Maddux, 24 April 1979; Henderson, "Memoirs," 1: 80– 147.

6. Weil, *Pretty Good Club*, pp. 50– 56; Daniel Yergin, *Shattered Peace: The Origins of the Cold War and the National Security State* (Boston: Houghton Mifflin Co., 1977), pp. 10– 11, 17– 41; Daniel F. Harrington, "Kennan, Bohlen, and the Riga Axioms," *Diplomatic History* 2 (Fall 1978): 423– 37. Although Harrington focuses on their post– 1945 observations, his criticism can be supported for the thirties. See Hanson, "American Diplomatic Reporting," pp. 161– 98; Thomas R. Maddux, "Watching Stalin Maneuver between Hitler and the West: American Diplomats and Soviet Diplomacy, 1934– 1939," *Diplomatic History* 1 (Spring 1977): 144– 45.

7. Henderson, "Memoirs," 3: 457– 95, 555– 56.

8. Henderson despatch to Hull, 16 November 1936, DS 711.61/611.

9. Henderson despatch to Hull, 19 November 1936, DS 852.00/3939; Henderson telegram to Hull, 17 October 1936, *FRUS, 1936*, 2: 540.

10. Henderson despatches to Hull, 26 January and 18 February 1938, DS 761.00/ 292– 93; Henderson memo to Hull, 22 July 1939, *FRUS: Soviet Union, 1933 – 1939*, pp. 773– 75; Henderson, "Memoirs," 7: 1216– 66.

11. Henderson to Samuel Harper, 24 August 1939, Letters 1949, Samuel Harper Papers, University of Chicago Library, Chicago, Ill.

12. Henderson, "Memoirs," 7: 1267– 84.

13. Robert Paul Browder, *The Origins of Soviet-American Diplomacy* (Princeton: Princeton University Press, 1953), pp. 176– 213; Edward M. Bennett, *Recognition of Russia: An American Foreign Policy Dilemma* (Waltham, Mass.: Ginn and Co., 1970), pp. 189– 218; Donald G. Bishop, *The Roosevelt-Litvinov Agreements: The American View* (Syracuse: Syracuse University Press, 1965), pp. 41– 60, 152– 78; Thomas R. Maddux, *Years of Estrangement: American Relations with the Soviet Union, 1933 – 1941* (Tallahassee: University Presses of Florida, 1980).

14. For this interpretation of Soviet policy see the detailed analysis by Max Beloff, *The Foreign Policy of Soviet Russia*, 2 vols. (New York and London: Oxford University Press, 1947– 1949); and the incisive analysis by Adam B. Ulam, *Expansion and Coexistence: The History of Soviet Foreign Policy, 1917 – 1967* (New York: Praeger, 1968), pp. 203– 8. See also James E. McSherry, *Stalin, Hitler, and Europe*, 2 vols. (Cleveland: World Publishing Co., 1968– 1970), 1: 41– 56, for a conflicting evaluation; B. Ponomaryov et al., *History of Soviet Foreign Policy, 1917 – 1945* (Moscow: Progress Publishers, 1969), pp. 327– 42, for an unconvincing Soviet-Marxist assessment.

15. Henderson despatch to Hull, 18 January 1936, DS 761.00/265; Maddux, "Watching Stalin Maneuver," pp. 146– 48; Henderson, "Memoirs," 5: 965– 79.

16. Henderson to Kelley, 27 April 1937, DS 761.00/264. See also Henderson to Arthur Bliss Lane, 19 May and 7 and 18 June 1937, Arthur Bliss Lane Papers, Sterling Library, Yale University, New Haven, Conn.

17. Maddux, *Years of Estrangement*, pp. 89– 91.

18. Davies diary, 2 January 1937, Joseph E. Davies, *Mission to Moscow* (New York: Simon and Schuster, 1941), p. 6; Davies despatches to Hull, 26 March 1937 and 6 June 1938, DS 852.00/5091 and 861.00/11786; Faymonville memo to Davies, 6 June 1938, box 7, Joseph E. Davies Papers, Library of Congress, Washington, D.C.; James S. Herndon and Joseph O. Baylen, "Col. Philip R. Faymonville and the Red Army, 1934– 1943," *Slavic Review* 34 (September 1975): 483– 505.

19. Maddux, *Years of Estrangement*, pp. 91– 98.

20. Henderson telegram to Hull, 16 January 1936, *FRUS: Soviet Union, 1933 – 1939*, p. 286. See also Henderson telegrams to Hull, 30 December 1935, 8 January, 31 July, and 4 August 1936, DS 765.84/3286, 852.00/2338 and 2395.

21. Henderson telegram to Hull, 9 June 1937, DS 852.00/5686; Henderson despatch to Hull, 20 September 1937, *FRUS: Soviet Union, 1933 – 1939*, pp. 391– 94; Henderson to Kelley, 27 April 1937, DS 761.00/264; Henderson, "Memoirs," 5: 984– 91.

22. Henderson despatches to Hull, 2 and 18 February 1938, DS 751.61/210 and 76100/293.

23. For a full analysis of the Moscow embassy's assessments, see Thomas R. Maddux, "American Diplomats and the Soviet Experiment: The View from the Moscow Embassy, 1934– 1939," *The South Atlantic Quarterly* 74 (Autumn 1975): 468– 87.

24. See Henderson despatches to Hull, 20 April, 30 July, and 2 December 1936, DS 761.50/868 and 871– 72.

25. Henderson despatch to Hull, 1 September 1936, DS 861.00/11636. See also Henderson telegrams and despatch to Hull, 18 and 27 August and 31 December 1936, DS 861.00/11629– 30 and 11652; Henderson to Samuel Harper, 27 December 1934, Letters 1934, Harper Papers. For Stalin's purge see Robert Conquest, *The Great Terror: Stalin's Purge of the Thirties* (New York: Macmillan Co., 1968); Roy A. Medvedev, *Let History Judge: The Origins and Consequences of Stalinism*, trans. Colleen Taylor, ed. David Joravsky and George Haupt (New York: Alfred A. Knopf, 1971); Aleksandr I. Solzhenitsyn, *The Gulag Archipelago, 1918–1956: An Experiment in Literary Investigation*, trans. Thomas P. Whitney, 3 vols. (New York: Harper and Row, 1973– 78).

26. Henderson to Kelley, 30 April 1937, Lane Papers; Henderson to Harper, 6 May 1937, Letters 1937, Harper Papers.

27. Henderson telegram to Hull, 8 June 1937, *FRUS: Soviet Union, 1933–1939*, p. 378. See also Henderson telegrams and despatches to Hull, 9 and 13 June and 2 October 1937 and 18 February 1938, *FRUS: Soviet Union, 1933–1939*, pp. 383– 85, 519– 20 and DS 861.00/11692 and 11734; Henderson, "Memoirs," 5: 909– 39.

28. Henderson despatch to Hull, 2 October 1937, DS 861.00/11734; Henderson, "Memoirs," 4: 662– 66, 5: 921– 23, 941– 50.

29. Henderson memo, 2 June 1939, DS 741.6111/57 1/2; Henderson memo, 22 July 1939, *FRUS: Soviet Union, 1933–1939*, pp. 773– 75; Henderson, "Memoirs," 7: 1175, 1216– 66.

30. Henderson memo, 2 September 1939, DS 761.62211/194; Henderson to Harper, 24 August 1939, Letters 1939, Harper Papers; Henderson, "Memoirs," 8: 1447– 52. For the Nazi-Soviet pact see Gerhard L. Weinberg, *Germany and the Soviet Union* (Leiden, Netherlands: E. J. Brill, 1954), pp. 5– 48.

31. Henderson to Harper, 9 December 1939, Letters 1939, Harper Papers; Henderson, "Memoirs," 8: 1447– 52.

32. Henderson to John Wiley, 19 December 1939, box 7, John Cooper Wiley Papers, Franklin D. Roosevelt Library, Hyde Park, N.Y.; Henderson to Steinhardt, box 29, Laurence A. Steinhardt Papers, Library of Congress, Washington, D.C.

33. Memo by Henderson, 15 July 1940, *FRUS, 1940*, 1: 389– 92. See also Henderson to Harper, 20 July 1940, Letters 1940, Harper Papers; Henderson, "Memoirs," 8: 1378– 88.

34. Henderson to Steinhardt, 13 December 1940, box 29, Steinhardt Papers.

35. Henderson to Harper, 17 January 1941, 1941 Data-Post Confidential, Harper Papers. See also Steinhardt to Henderson, n.d., and memo by Ray Atherton, 26 November 1940, and memo by the Division of European Affairs, 26 November 1940, *FRUS, 1940*, 3: 406– 8, 413– 14; Henderson memo to Welles, 27 November 1940, DS 711.61/800.

36. Hull telegram to Steinhardt, 14 June 1941; Steinhardt telegram to Hull, 17 June 1941, *FRUS, 1941*, 1: 757– 58, 764– 66.

37. Memo by Atherton and Henderson to Welles, 21 June 1941, *FRUS, 1941*, 1: 766– 67. See Kennan, *Memoirs*, pp. 133– 34, for his agreement with these guidelines.

For the extension of Lend-Lease aid to the Soviet Union, see Raymond H. Dawson, *The Decision to Aid Russia, 1941* (Chapel Hill: University of North Carolina Press, 1959).

38. See Henderson memo to Welles, 9 April 1942, *FRUS, 1942,* 3: 435– 36; Henderson memo to Ray Atherton, 11 June 1943, *FRUS, 1943,* 3: 543– 44.

39. Weil, *Pretty Good Club,* pp. 131– 40; interviews with Loy W. Henderson, 29 June and 17 November 1967.

40. Kennan, *Memoirs,* p. 61; Bohlen, *Witness,* p. 125; Lane to Stuart E. Grummon, 18 October 1937, Correspondence 1937, Lane Papers; Davies to Kelley, 10 February 1937, box 3, Davies Papers.

Chapter 10

1. Minute by J. V. Perowne, 3 September 1940, FO 371/24251/A1945/605/45, pp. 6– 7; diary entry, 7 November 1940, Harold Ickes, *The Secret Diary of Harold Ickes,* 3 vols. (New York: Simon and Schuster, 1954), 3: 370.

2. Donald C. Watt, "The Rise of a Revisionist School," *Appeasement of the Dictators,* ed. W. Laird Kleine-Ahlbrandt (New York: Holt, Rinehart and Winston, 1970), pp. 122– 34; Watt, "Appeasement Reconsidered," *Round Table,* September 1963, p. 358. Two biographies on Kennedy are Richard Whalen, *The Founding Father* (New York: Signet Books, 1964) and David E. Koskoff, *Joseph P. Kennedy: A Life and Times* (New Jersey: Prentice Hall, 1974). The most important analysis of Kennedy's ambassadorship is William W. Kaufmann, "Two American Ambassadors: Bullitt and Kennedy," in *The Diplomats: 1919– 1939,* ed. Gordon A. Craig and Felix Gilbert (Princeton: Princeton University Press, 1953), pp. 649– 81. Michael R. Beschloss has just published a study of the Kennedy-Roosevelt relationship based upon their private papers: *Kennedy and Roosevelt: The Uneasy Alliance* (New York: W. W. Norton and Co., 1980).

3. Watt, "Rise of a Revisionist School," pp. 128– 34; Watt, "Appeasement Reconsidered," pp. 358– 71; Watt, "Some Aspects of A. J. P. Taylor's Work as Diplomatic Historian," *Journal of Modern History* 49 (March 1977): 19– 33; Watt, "Sir Lewis Namier and Contemporary European History," *Cambridge Journal* 7 (July 1954): 479– 600. See A. J. P. Taylor, *Origins of the Second World War* (London: Hamilton, 1961) and Simon Newman, *March 1939: The British Guarantee to Poland* (Oxford: Clarendon Press, 1976) for examples of the revisionist view. See also Keith Feiling, *The Life of Neville Chamberlain* (London: Macmillan and Co., 1946) and Viscount Templewood, *Nine Troubled Years* (London: Collins, 1954) for a defense of Chamberlain's diplomacy.

4. William L. Langer and S. Everett Gleason, *The Challenge to Isolation,* 2 vols. (New York: Harper and Row, 1952), vol. 1; Manfred Jonas, *Isolationism in America, 1935– 1941* (Ithaca: Cornell University Press, 1966), p. 23; Leroy N. Rieselbach, *The Roots of Isolationism* (New York: Bobbs Merrill, 1966); Robert A. Divine, *The Illusion of Neutrality* (Chicago: University of Chicago Press, 1962).

5. James MacGregor Burns, *Roosevelt: The Lion and the Fox* (New York: Harcourt Brace Jovanovich, 1970), pp. 247– 63; William Leuchtenberg, *Franklin D. Roosevelt and the New Deal* (New London: Harper and Row, 1963), pp. 197– 230; Robert Dallek, *Franklin D. Roosevelt and American Foreign Policy, 1932– 1945* (New York: Oxford University Press, 1979), pp. 122– 44. Franklin D. Roosevelt, *The Public Papers and Addresses of Franklin D. Roosevelt, 1935,* ed. Samuel Rosenman, 13 vols. (New York: Random House, 1938), 4: 410; Franklin D. Roosevelt, *F. D. R.: His Personal Letters,*

1928–1945, ed. Elliott Roosevelt, 4 vols. (New York: Duell Sloan Pearce, 1950), 1: 472.

6. Brief sections of this essay have been published in Jane Karoline Vieth, "The Donkey and the Lion: The Ambassadorship of Joseph P. Kennedy at the Court of St. James's, 1938–1940," *Michigan Academician* 10 (Winter 1978): 274. Roosevelt, *F. D. R.*, 2: 913–14.

7. James A. Farley, *Jim Farley's Story* (New York: Whittlesey House, 1948), p. 126. See also C. L. Sulzberger, *A Long Row of Candles* (New York: Macmillan Co., 1969), p. 22. See Ernest K. Lindley, "Will Kennedy Run for President?" *Liberty Magazine* reprint, Fall 1971, originally published in *Liberty Magazine*, 21 May 1938; also in "The Look Years," *Look Magazine*, 1972, p. 5.

8. Henry M. Morgenthau, Jr. diary, 22 January 1938, vol. 108, pp. 114–19, Henry M. Morgenthau, Jr. Papers, Franklin D. Roosevelt Library, Hyde Park, N.Y. Koskoff, *Joseph P. Kennedy*, pp. 114–19. "Story of a Week," *Literary Digest*, 25 December 1937, p. 6.

9. Whalen, *Founding Father*, p. 209.

10. Ibid.

11. Lindley, "Will Kennedy Run for President?" p. 27.

12. Whalen, *Founding Father*, p. 226.

13. Freda Kirchwey, "Watch Joe Kennedy!" *Nation*, 14 December 1940, p. 593.

14. Ickes, *Secret Diary*, 2: 377. This same charge was noted in a summary, "General Observations on 23 April 1938," Annual Report for 1938, FO 371/288/32/2099, pp. 8–38.

15. Kaufmann, "Two American Ambassadors," p. 678. Morgenthau diary, 1 September 1938, vol. 138, p. 34, Morgenthau Papers.

16. Langer and Gleason, *Challenge to Isolation*, 1: 26–35. Louis Fischer, *Men and Politics* (New York: Harper and Row, 1941), p. 625. Feiling, *Neville Chamberlain*, p. 124. Donald Lammers, *Explaining Munich: The Search for Motive in British Policy* (Stanford: Hoover Institution on War, Revolution, and Peace, 1966), p. 29. Feiling, *Neville Chamberlain*, p. 320.

17. *New York Post*, 11 January 1961, as cited in Whalen, *Founding Father*, p. 228.

18. Lammers, *Explaining Munich*, pp. 24–25. Kennedy to Hull, 22 March 1938, file 104, Cordell Hull Papers, Manuscript Division, Library of Congress, Washington, D.C. For a similar appraisal of Nazi foreign policy, see the essay in this volume by Kenneth Moss.

19. Kennedy to Roosevelt, 11 March 1938, box 10, PSF, FDRL; Kennedy to Jimmy Roosevelt, 3 March 1938, file 104, Hull Papers.

20. Despite some difference of opinion between Hull and Kennedy, the secretary of state acknowledged that he had been "influenced" by the ambassador's "excellent" reports and that Kennedy's assistance as a negotiator during the treaty deliberations had been "of great value." Hull to Kennedy, 3 November 1938, *FRUS, 1938*, 2: 69–70; Kennedy to Hull, 22 March 1938, file 104, Hull Papers; Kennedy to Roosevelt, 11 March 1938, box 10, PSF, FDRL.

21. See Marian C. McKenna, *Borah* (Ann Arbor: University of Michigan Press, 1961), p. 354, for correspondence between Kennedy and Borah.

22. C. A. MacDonald, "Economic Appeasement and the German 'Moderates,' 1937–1939," *Past and Present* 56 (August 1972): 105–35.

23. Feiling, *Neville Chamberlain*, pp. 323, 325.

24. Kennedy to Roosevelt, 11 March 1938, box 10, PSF, FDRL.

25. Kennedy to Hull, 22 March 1938, file 104, Hull Papers. Kennedy to Bernard Baruch, 21 March 1938, as cited in Koskoff, *Joseph P. Kennedy*, p. 130.

26. Arnold A. Offner, *American Appeasement: United States Foreign Policy and Germany, 1933–1938* (New York: W. W. Norton and Co., 1969), pp. 238–39; Langer and Gleason, *Challenge to Isolation*, 1: 29–32.

27. James Forrestal, *The Forrestal Diaries*, ed. Water Millis (New York: Viking Press, 1951), pp. 121–22. Arthur Krock, *Memoirs: Sixty Years on the Firing Line* (New York: Funk and Wagnalls, 1968), p. 334.

28. Watt, "Appeasement Reconsidered," pp. 365–67.

29. Kennedy to Hull, 23 March 1938, 1: 40; Welles to Kennedy, 26 September 1938, 1: 661, both in *FRUS, 1938*.

30. Dirksen to Weizsaecker, 13 June 1938, Germany, Auswaertiges Amt, *Documents on German Foreign Policy, 1918–1945: From the Archives of the German Foreign Ministry*, ser. D. (London: H.M.S.O., 1949), 1: 718, 136–38; see also *Newsweek*, 12 September 1960, p. 29; Offner, *American Appeasement*, pp. 251–53.

31. Kennedy to Hull, 20 and 21 July 1938, DS 741.62/280 and 282.

32. Koskoff, *Joseph P. Kennedy*, p. 137. Ickes, *Secret Diary*, 2: 405.

33. Ickes, *Secret Diary*, 2: 420. Kennedy to Hull, 29 July 1938, *FRUS, 1938*, 1: 539, 520–21; Langer and Gleason, *Challenge to Isolation*, 1: 32.

34. Morgenthau diary, 1 September 1938, vol. 138, p. 34, Morgenthau Papers. J. P. Moffat, *The Moffat Papers*, ed. Nancy H. Hooker (Cambridge: Harvard University Press, 1956), p. 203.

35. Kennedy to Hull, 29 August 1938, *FRUS, 1938*, 1: 560–61. Viscount Halifax to Sir Ronald Lindsay, 2 September 1938, *DBFP*, 2: 213; Annual Report for 1938, FO 371/228/32/2099 (pp. 8–38).

36. Morgenthau diary, 1 September 1938, vol. 138, p. 34, Morgenthau Papers.

37. Ibid., pp. 34–35. Cordell Hull, *The Memoirs of Cordell Hull*, 2 vols. (New York: Macmillan Co., 1948), 1: 588. Morgenthau diary, 1 September 1938, vol. 138, p. 35, Morgenthau Papers.

38. Chamberlain to Fuehrer, 13 September 1938, *DBFP*, 2: 314.

39. Chamberlain to Fuehrer, 29 September 1938, *DBFP*, 2: 625.

40. *New York Times*, 16 December 1938, p. 13.

41. Viscount Halifax to Sir R. Lindsay, 11 September 1938, *DBFP*, 2: 295; *New York Times*, 24 November and 8 December 1938, pp. 1, 23. Ribbentrop memo, 10 June 1938, *DBFP*, 1: 713.

42. Langer and Gleason, *Challenge to Isolation*, 1: 35–40.

43. Ibid., pp. 45–47.

44. *New York Times*, 11 January 1939, p. 1; *Times* (London), 12 January 1939, p. 10. Kennedy to Roosevelt, 19 December 1938, "Great Britain," PSF, FDRL; see also Kaufmann, "Two American Ambassadors," p. 667.

45. Great Britain, *Parliamentary Debates* (Commons), 5th ser., 15 March 1939, 345: 439. Christopher Thorne, "Continuing Appeasement," in Kleine-Ahlbrandt, *Appeasement of the Dictators*, pp. 91–97. Kennedy to Hull, 22 March 1939, *FRUS, 1939*, 2: 93.

46. Moffat, *Moffat Papers*, pp. 253, 233–35, 237–38; Hull, *Memoirs*, 1: 662; Langer and Gleason, *Challenge to Isolation*, 1: 77.

47. Langer and Gleason, *Challenge to Isolation*, 1: 75. See Feiling, *Neville Chamberlain*, pp. 403– 6, for evidence of Chamberlain's opinion.

48. Kennedy to Roosevelt, 3 March 1939, "Great Britain," PSF, FDRL.

49. Whalen, *Founding Father*, p. 263.

50. See Francis L. Loewenheim et al., *Roosevelt and Churchill: Their Secret Wartime Correspondence* (New York: E. P. Dutton and Co., 1975) for a detailed review of their correspondence.

51. A. J. P. Taylor, *English History, 1914 – 1945* (New York: Oxford University Press, 1965), pp. 463– 66. Kennedy to Roosevelt, 30 September 1939, 6 pages, box 10, PSF, FDRL.

52. Kennedy to Roosevelt, 10 September 1939; Kennedy to Roosevelt, 30 September 1939, 7 pages, both in box 10, PSF, FDRL.

53. Kennedy to Hull, 11 September 1939, *FRUS, 1939*, 1: 421– 24; Joseph P. Kennedy, "Joseph P. Kennedy," chap. 37, pp. 483– 85, James M. Landis Papers, Manuscript Division, Library of Congress, Washington, D.C.

54. Kennedy to Roosevelt, 30 September 1939, 7 pages, box 10, PSF, FDRL. Roosevelt, *Public Papers and Addresses*, 2: 949. Hull to Kennedy, 11 September 1939, *FRUS, 1939*, 1: 421– 24.

55. Kennedy to Roosevelt, 30 September 1939, 7 pages, box 10, PSF, FDRL. Kaufmann, "Two American Ambassadors," pp. 669– 70.

56. Kennedy to Roosevelt, 3 November 1939, box 44, PSF, FDRL. Morgenthau diary, 3 October 1939, 2: 317, Morgenthau Papers.

57. See examples of the British hostility to Kennedy in the Foreign Office minutes, 18 January, 14 February, and 2 and 6 March 1940, FO 371/24251/A605/A138(p. 6)/A1945(p. 86)/A1723(p. 45)/605/45.

58. Kennedy, "Joseph P. Kennedy," chap. 18, Landis Papers.

59. Ibid.

60. Watt, "Appeasement Reconsidered," pp. 358– 71.

Selected Bibliography

I. 1919–1941

A. General Studies

Adler, Selig. *The Isolationist Impulse: Its Twentieth Century Reaction.* New York: Abelard-Schuman, 1957.

_____. *The Uncertain Giant, 1921–1941: American Foreign Policy between the Wars.* New York: Collier Books, 1974.

Craig, Gordon A., and Gilbert, Felix, eds. *The Diplomats, 1919–1939.* Princeton: Princeton University Press, 1953.

Dulles, Foster R. *America's Rise to World Power.* New York: Harper and Bros., 1955.

Duroselle, Jean-Baptiste. *From Wilson to Roosevelt: Foreign Policy of the United States, 1913–1945.* Cambridge: Harvard University Press, 1963.

Graebner, Norman Arthur. *An Uncertain Tradition: American Secretaries of State in the Twentieth Century.* New York: McGraw-Hill Book Co., 1961.

Kennan, George F. *American Diplomacy, 1900–1950.* Chicago: University of Chicago Press, 1951.

Offner, Arnold A. *The Origins of the Second World War: American Foreign Policy and World Politics, 1917–1941.* New York: Praeger, 1975.

Osgood, Robert E. *Ideals and Self-Interest in America's Foreign Relations.* Chicago: University of Chicago Press, 1953.

Tate, Merze. *The United States and Armaments.* Cambridge: Harvard University Press, 1948.

Weil, Martin. *A Pretty Good Club: The Founding Fathers of the United States Foreign Service.* New York: W. W. Norton and Co., 1978.

Williams, William A. *The Tragedy of American Diplomacy.* 2nd rev. ed. New York: Dell, 1972.

B. Printed Documents

Documents on American Foreign Relations. New York: Harper and Row, 1953– .

Germany. Auswaertiges Amt. *Documents on German Foreign Policy, 1918–1945.* Washington, D.C.: G.P.O., 1949– .

Great Britain. Foreign Office. *Documents on British Foreign Policy, 1919–1939.* London: H.M.S.O., 1946– .

225

United States. Department of State. *Papers Relating to the Foreign Relations of the United States*. Washington, D.C.: G.P.O., 1939– .

C. Diaries, Letters, and Memoirs

Biddle, Anthony Joseph Drexel, Jr. *Poland and the Coming of the Second World War: The Diplomatic Papers of A. J. Drexel Biddle, Jr., United States Ambassador to Poland, 1937–1939*. Columbus: Ohio State University Press, 1976.

Bohlen, Charles E. *Witness to History, 1929–1969*. New York: W. W. Norton and Co., 1973.

Bowers, Claude. *My Life: The Memoirs of Claude Bowers*. New York: Simon and Schuster, 1962.

––––––– . *My Mission to Spain: Watching the Rehearsal for World War II*. New York: Simon and Schuster, 1954.

Davies, Joseph E. *Mission to Moscow*. New York: Simon and Schuster, 1941.

Dawes, Charles G. *A Journal of Reparations*. London: Macmillan and Co., 1939.

Dodd, William Edward. *Ambassador Dodd's Diary, 1933–1938*. New York: Harcourt, Brace and Co., 1941.

Einstein, Lewis. *A Diplomat Looks Back*. New Haven: Yale University Press, 1968.

Gibson, Hugh. *Hugh Gibson, 1880s–1954: Extracts from His Papers and Anecdotes from His Friends*. New York: Belgian American Educational Foundation, 1956.

Grew, Joseph C. *Turbulent Era: A Diplomatic Record of Forty Years, 1904–1945*. Boston: Houghton Mifflin Co., 1952.

Hull, Cordell. *The Memoirs of Cordell Hull*. 2 vols. New York: Macmillan Co., 1948.

Kennan, George F. *From Prague after Munich: Diplomatic Papers, 1938–1940*. Princeton: Princeton University Press, 1968.

––––––– . *Memoirs, 1925–1950*. Boston: Little, Brown and Co., 1967.

Lamont, Thomas W. *Across World Frontiers*. New York: Harcourt, Brace and Co., 1951.

Lee, Raymond E. *The London Journal of General Raymond E. Lee, 1940–1941*. Boston: Little, Brown and Co., 1971.

Moffat, Jay Pierrepont. *The Moffat Papers: Selections from the Diplomatic Journals of Jay Pierrepont Moffat, 1919–1943*. Cambridge: Harvard University Press, 1956.

Murphy, Robert. *Diplomat among Warriors*. Garden City, N.Y.: Doubleday, 1964.

Phillips, William. *Ventures in Diplomacy*. Boston: Beacon Press, 1952.

Roosevelt, Franklin D. *For the President, Personal and Secret: Correspondence between Franklin D. Roosevelt and William C. Bullitt*. Boston: Houghton Mifflin Co., 1972.

––––––– . *Franklin D. Roosevelt and Foreign Affairs: January 1933–January 1937*. 3 vols. Cambridge: Harvard University Press, Belknap Press, 1969.

Seymour, Charles. *The Intimate Papers of Colonel House*. 4 vols. Reprint. London: Scholarly Press, 1971.

Wilson, Hugh Robert. *Diplomat between Wars*. New York: Longmans, Green, and Co., 1941.

II. 1919–1933

A. General Studies

Fleming, Denna Frank. *The United States and World Organization, 1920–1933*. New York: Columbia University Press, 1938.

Hicks, John. *Republican Ascendancy, 1921 – 1933*. New York: Harper and Bros., 1960.

Leffler, Melvyn P. *The Elusive Quest: America's Pursuit of European Stability and French Security, 1919 – 1933*. Chapel Hill: University of North Carolina Press, 1978.

Marks, Sally. *The Illusion of Peace: International Relations in Europe, 1918 – 1933*. New York: St. Martins Press, 1976.

Schulzinger, Robert D. *The Making of the Diplomatic Mind: The Training, Outlook, and Style of United States Foreign Service Officers, 1908 – 1931*. Middletown, Conn.: Wesleyan University Press, 1975.

Wilson, Joan Hoff. *American Business and Foreign Policy, 1920 – 1933*. Lexington: University of Kentucky Press, 1971.

B. Special Studies

Bailey, Thomas A. *Woodrow Wilson and the Peacemakers*. New York: Macmillan Co., 1947.

Baker, Ray Stannard. *Woodrow Wilson and World Settlement*. 3 vols. Garden City, N.Y.: Doubleday, Page and Co., 1922.

Baruch, Bernard. *The Making of the Reparation and Economic Sections of the Treaty*. New York: Harper and Bros., 1920.

Bennett, Edward W. *Germany and the Diplomacy of the Financial Crisis, 1931*. Cambridge: Harvard University Press, 1962.

Birdsall, Paul. *Versailles Twenty Years After*. New York: Reynal and Hitchcock, 1941.

Brandes, Joseph. *Herbert Hoover and Economic Diplomacy: Department of Commerce Policy, 1921 – 28*. Pittsburgh: University of Pittsburgh Press, 1962.

Bryn-Jones, David. *Frank B. Kellogg: A Biography*. New York: G. P. Putnam's Sons, 1937.

Buckley, Thomas H. *The United States and the Washington Conference, 1921 – 22*. Knoxville: University of Tennessee Press, 1970.

Burnett, Philip. M. *Reparations at the Paris Peace Conference from the Standpoint of the American Delegation*. 2 vols. New York: Columbia University Press, 1940.

Clarke, Stephen V. O. *Central Bank Cooperation, 1924 – 1931*. New York: Federal Reserve Bank of New York, 1967.

Current, Richard N. *Secretary Stimson: A Study in Statecraft*. New Brunswick, N.J.: Rutgers University Press, 1954.

Ellis, Lewis Ethan. *Frank B. Kellogg and American Foreign Relations, 1925 – 1929*. New Brunswick, N.J.: Rutgers University Press, 1961.

Feis, Herbert. *The Diplomacy of the Dollar: First Era, 1919 – 1932*. Baltimore: Johns Hopkins University Press, 1950.

Ferrell, Robert H. *American Diplomacy in the Great Depression: Hoover-Stimson Foreign Policy, 1929 – 1933*. New Haven: Yale University Press, 1957.

_____ . *Frank B. Kellogg. Henry L. Stimson*. The American Secretaries of State and Their Diplomacy, 1776 – 1925, edited by Samuel F. Bemis, vol. 11. New York: Cooper Square Pubs., 1963.

_____ . *Peace in Their Time: The Origins of the Kellogg-Briand Pact*. New Haven: Yale University Press, 1952.

Filene, Peter G. *Americans and the Soviet Experiment, 1917 – 1933*. Cambridge: Harvard University Press, 1967.

Fleming, Denna Frank. *The United States and the League of Nations, 1918 – 1920*. New York: G. P. Putnam's Sons, 1932.

Fry, Michael G. *Illusions of Security: North Atlantic Diplomacy, 1918–1922.* Toronto: University of Toronto Press, 1972.

Glad, Betty. *Charles Evans Hughes and the Illusions of Innocence: A Study in American Diplomacy.* Urbana: University of Illinois Press, 1966.

Hogan, Michael J. *Informal Entente: The Private Structure of Cooperation in Anglo-American Economic Diplomacy, 1918–1928.* Columbia: University of Missouri Press, 1977.

Jacobson, Jon. *Locarno Diplomacy: Germany and the West, 1925–1929.* Princeton: Princeton University Press, 1972.

Kennan, George F. *Soviet-American Relations, 1917–1920.* 2 vols. Princeton: Princeton University Press, 1956–58.

Levin, N. Gordon, Jr. *Woodrow Wilson and World Politics.* New York: Oxford University Press, 1968.

Link, Arthur S. *Wilson the Diplomatist.* Baltimore: Johns Hopkins University Press, 1957.

Mayer, Arno J. *The Politics and Diplomacy of Peacemaking: Containment and Counterrevolution at Versailles, 1918–1919.* New York: Alfred A. Knopf, 1967.

Meyer, Richard H. *Banker's Diplomacy.* New York: Columbia University Press, 1970.

Nelson, Keith L. *Victors Divided: America and the Allies in Germany, 1918–1923.* Berkeley and Los Angeles: University of California Press, 1975.

O'Connor, Raymond G. *Perilous Equilibrium: The United States and the London Naval Conference of 1930.* Lawrence: University of Kansas Press, 1962.

Parrini, Carl P. *Heir to Empire: United States Economic Diplomacy, 1916–1923.* Pittsburgh: University of Pittsburgh Press, 1969.

Pusey, Merlo John. *Charles Evans Hughes.* 2 vols. New York: Macmillan Co., 1951.

Schuker, Stephen A. *The End of French Predominance: The Financial Crisis of 1924 and the Adoption of the Dawes Plan.* Chapel Hill: University of North Carolina Press, 1976.

Stone, Ralph A. *The Irreconcilables: The Fight against the League of Nations.* Lexington: University of Kentucky Press, 1970.

Yates, Louis A. *United States and French Security, 1917–1921: A Study in American Diplomatic History.* New York: Twayne Pubs., 1957.

III. 1933–1941

A. General Studies

Dallek, Robert. *Franklin D. Roosevelt and American Foreign Policy.* New York: Oxford University Press, 1979.

Divine, Robert A. *The Illusion of Neutrality.* Chicago: University of Chicago Press, 1969.

Gardner, Lloyd C. *Economic Aspects of New Deal Diplomacy.* Madison: University of Wisconsin Press, 1964.

Maddux, Thomas R. *Years of Estrangement: American Relations with the Soviet Union, 1933–1941.* Tallahassee: University Presses of Florida, 1980.

Offner, Arnold A. *American Appeasement: United States Foreign Policy and Germany, 1933–1938.* Cambridge: Harvard University Press, 1969.

Tansill, Charles C. *Back Door to War: The Roosevelt Foreign Policy, 1933–1941.* Chicago: H. Regnery Co., 1952.

B. Special Studies

Adams, Frederick C. *Economic Diplomacy: The Export-Import Bank and American Foreign Policy, 1934–1939.* Columbia: University of Missouri Press, 1976.

Bennett, Edward W. *German Rearmament and the West, 1932–1933.* Princeton: Princeton University Press, 1979.

Beschloss, Michael R. *Kennedy and Roosevelt: The Uneasy Alliance.* New York: W. W. Norton and Co., 1980.

Browder, Robert P. *The Origins of Soviet-American Diplomacy.* Princeton: Princeton University Press, 1953.

Compton, James V. *The Swastika and the Eagle: Hitler, the United States and the Origins of World War II.* Boston: Houghton Mifflin Co., 1967.

Dallek, Robert. *Democrat and Diplomat: The Life of William E. Dodd.* New York: Oxford University Press, 1968.

Divine, Robert A. *The Reluctant Belligerent: American Entry into World War II.* New York: John Wiley and Sons, 1965.

Friedlander, Saul. *Prelude to Downfall: Hitler and the United States, 1939–1941.* New York: Alfred A. Knopf, 1967.

Haight, John M., Jr. *American Aid to France, 1938–1940.* New York: Atheneum, 1970.

Harris, Brice, Jr. *The United States and the Italo-Ethiopian Crisis.* Stanford: Stanford University Press, 1964.

Jonas, Manfred. *Isolationism in America, 1935–1941.* Ithaca, N.Y.: Cornell University Press, 1969.

Langer, William L., and Gleason, S. Everett. *The Challenge to Isolation, 1937–1940.* New York: Peter Smith, 1964.

———. *The Undeclared War, 1940–1941.* New York: Peter Smith, 1953.

Morison, Elting E. *Turmoil and Tradition: A Study of the Life and Times of Henry L. Stimson.* Boston: Houghton Mifflin Co., 1960.

Nicolson, Harold. *Dwight Morrow.* New York: Harcourt, Brace and Co., 1935.

Pratt, Julius W. *Cordell Hull.* 2 vols. The American Secretaries of State and Their Diplomacy, 1776–1925, edited by Samuel F. Bemis, vols. 12–13. New York: Cooper Square Pubs., 1964.

Sherwood, Robert Emmet. *Roosevelt and Hopkins.* New York: Harper and Bros., 1950.

Taylor, F. Jay. *The United States and the Spanish Civil War.* New York: Bookman Associates, 1956.

Traina, Richard P. *American Diplomacy and the Spanish Civil War.* Bloomington: Indiana University Press, 1968.

Contributors

JOHN M. CARROLL is an associate professor of history at Lamar University. He received his Ph.D. from the University of Kentucky with a dissertation on "The Making of the Dawes Plan, 1919–1923." He is the editor of two books of original essays concerning twentieth century American diplomacy and is preparing a book tentatively titled "Five Faces of Diplomacy in the 1920s."

FRANK COSTIGLIOLA is an associate professor of history at the University of Rhode Island where he has been teaching since he received his Ph.D. from Cornell University. He has written several articles concerning American diplomacy during the 1920s and has completed a book on U.S. political, economic, and cultural relations with Europe from 1919 to 1933.

J. B. DONNELLY entered the world of American diplomatic history after spending several years in the armed forces. He is a professor of history at Washington and Jefferson College and has a Ph.D. from the University of Virginia. After writing several essays on Prentiss Gilbert's activities in the 1930s, he has turned his attention to the Paris Peace Conference.

MICHAEL J. HOGAN, an associate professor of history at Miami University in Oxford, Ohio, is at present serving as a Woodrow Wilson fellow at the Woodrow Wilson International Center for Scholars. His doctoral dissertation for the University of Iowa was published as *Informal Entente: The Private Structure of Cooperation in Anglo-American Economic Diplomacy, 1918–1928.* He was the 1979–80 Tom L. Evans fellow at the Truman Library Institute and is preparing a history of the Marshall Plan.

KENNETH PAUL JONES is a professor of history at the University of Tennessee at Martin. He has written two articles concerning the Ruhr crisis of 1923–24 and served as Fulbright junior lecturer at Mainz University in Germany during

1974–75. He is preparing a book on "The Diplomacy of the Ruhr Crisis" which will be an expanded version of his doctoral dissertation for the University of Wisconsin–Madison.

DOUGLAS LITTLE received his Ph.D. from Cornell University in 1978 with a dissertation on Anglo-American policies toward Spain, 1931–36. Since then he has been an assistant professor of history at Clark University. He has published an article in *Business History Review* concerning "Twenty Years of Turmoil: ITT, the State Department and Spain, 1924–44."

THOMAS R. MADDUX, a professor of history at California State University, Northridge, has published several articles concerning American diplomats and Soviet diplomacy. The University Presses of Florida recently published his revised doctoral dissertation as *Years of Estrangement: American Relations with the Soviet Union, 1933–1941.*

KENNETH MOSS is a staff associate with the House Subcommittee on Europe and the Middle East of the House Foreign Affairs Committee. His essay is the by-product of his 1978 doctoral dissertation, "Bureaucrat as Diplomat: George S. Messersmith and the State Department's Approach to War, 1933–1941," for the University of Minnesota at Minneapolis. He has published two articles concerning American relations with Nazi Germany and is preparing a book-length biography of Messersmith.

RONALD E. SWERCZEK is assistant chief for diplomatic records in the Legislative and Diplomatic Branch, National Archives and Records Service. His essay is based on his extensive research for a doctoral dissertation at the University of Iowa on "The Diplomatic Career of Hugh Gibson, 1908–1938."

JANE KAROLINE VIETH received her Ph.D. from Ohio State University with a dissertation on "Joseph P. Kennedy: Ambassador to the Court of St. James's, 1938–1940." The *Michigan Academician* published an earlier article on Kennedy. She is now revising and expanding her dissertation into a book. She is an associate professor of humanities at Michigan State University.

Subject Index